11.17.95
12.1.95

HISTORY
OF THE SS

HISTORY OF THE SS

G. S. Graber

David McKay Company, Inc.
New York

To my wife Phyl, in love and gratitude

CONTENTS

At the time of the capitulation of Germany there were half a million men, the greater part of them foreigners, wearing the insignia of the SS on their German uniforms. In addition to the Armed SS there were tens of thousands of office employees who belonged to the General SS and there were hundreds of high-placed German officials who belonged to the Honorary SS. . . . Among the activities of the SS there were offices whose concern was Germanic archaeology and ancestral research, other offices devoted to forging foreign banknotes, collecting information on alchemy and astrology, institutes for the cultivation of medicinal herbs and wild rubber roots. The SS also controlled a mineral water and a porcelain factory, numerous nightclubs in foreign capitals and a publishing firm.

Gerald Reitlinger,
The SS: Alibi of a Nation.

HISTORY
OF THE SS

1
THE MAN ON
THE MOTORCYCLE

On February 25, 1924, a man in his early twenties heavily muffled against the cold, was to be seen roaring on a secondhand Swedish motorcycle from one village to another in Lower Bavaria. He had a slightly receding chin, wore spectacles, was of medium height, and, apart from a slightly mongoloid quality about his features, was indistinguishable from thousands of lower-middle-class officials you might have come across in any German town of the time. He could have been standing behind a bank counter, he might have studied your income tax returns, or he could have been a teacher at the local school.

His name was Heinrich Himmler, and he was to become the most notorious mass murderer of all time. Presently he was doing his bit for his country and taking himself very seriously indeed in the process. He was against a large number of institutions and people. He abhorred the Jews, he could not abide Freemasons, he conveyed a profound hatred for capitalism, almost matched by his intense aversion to Bolshevism. What he was *for* was not so easy to discern. One group which almost certainly captured his enthusiasm was the peasantry. He never really understood town life, and what he knew of it repelled him. By contrast, the picture of the noble peasant at his timeless, simple work was irresistibly attractive to Himmler. He knew, from his agricultural studies, something about herbs, and learned things from their cultivation which were to influence him in his later theories on human breeding.

When he got home at the end of the day, he wrote in his diary: "23 February, speeches in Eggmuhl, Lanwaid, and Birnbach. 24 February, discussions in Kelheim and Saal followed by individual enlightenment. 25 February, lecture in Rohr, one and a half hours."

Himmler was born in Munich in an apartment on the second floor of 2 Hildegardstrasse on October 7, 1900. His father, Gebhard Himmler, made his living as a private tutor and numbered among his students Prince Heinrich of Wittelsbach of the reigning Bavarian royal family. In a pedantic, self-effacing letter to the prince, the elder Himmler announced among other things that his new son weighed seven pounds, three ounces. The prince responded politely, gave permission for the baby to be named after him, and accepted the role of godfather. However trivial such a gesture may appear in retrospect, at the time there is no doubt that the young Heinrich had the Establishment very firmly on his side.

There were three Himmler sons. Gebhard junior preceded Heinrich by two years while, Ernst, the youngest, was born in 1905.

A great deal of speculation has occurred about the nature of Himmler's family life. In an age replete with investigation of the subconscious, it is not surprising that any attempt to explain Heinrich Himmler should be larded with psychological conjecture. Unfortunately, amateur psychologists have been given very little to go on. There is nothing in Heinrich Himmler's background to explain why he should have developed into a monster. Almost out of pique, one biographer, Gerald Reitlinger, has described Himmler's family life as "depressingly normal." It was certainly normal, but why this should be depressing throws more light on the biographer than it does on Himmler.

In fact, such reports of Himmler's father that have been gathered show that he was a relatively genial man, something of a pedant who, like most teachers of his time, spent considerable energy in relating to his students the benefits of hard work. He sported a small goatee beard, and surviving photographs display a definite twinkle in his eyes. His library contained a great number of works on German history—evidently a subject which absorbed him. No doubt he passed this interest on to his sons. Himmler's mother was a shadowy figure, devoutly Catholic and firmly entrenched in middle-class values.

If you do not know that you are going to become famous or infamous, there is no reason to maintain a family record to lighten the work of future historians. Thus the only source material on the young Heinrich Himmler are the diaries he kept, and these do not create a continuous record. He started a diary on August 23, 1914, about six weeks before his fourteenth birthday. But intervals between entries became longer and longer. He would start again, usually announcing that it was typical of his inherent laziness and self-indulgence that he had permitted such long gaps to occur.

It was only by accident that these diaries ever came to light. In the heyday of souvenir hunting which appears to have constituted the main activity of the American GI's at the cessation of hostilities in 1945, one soldier found them in Himmler's villa at Gmund on the

Tegernsee, a lake in Bavaria. Their existence came to the attention of an American intelligence officer. He sent them home together with other mementos of his war career. There they sat until 1957, possibly occasionally shown with some pride to house guests after dinner. Then, in 1957, the ex-intelligence officer came into contact with an American historian who, not surprisingly, pounced on this "find" and persuaded the owner to deposit the diaries at the Hoover Institute. The historian has described the diaries in the following way: "They consist of six cheap, soft-covered notebooks of varying size. The first covers 23 August 1914 to 26 September 1915 and has some isolated shorthand notes for 1916. The second covers 1 August 1919 to 2 February 1920. It contains, in a rear pocket, a number of keepsakes: snapshots of unidentified girls, an ice-rink ticket, a guitar ribbon inscribed with a date, and an unused theater ticket. The third notebook covers 1 November 1921 to 12 December 1921. Other periods are 12 January 1922 to 6 July 1922 and 11 to 25 February 1925."

The documents reveal some clues to Himmler's formative years. By the time the First World War broke out, the Himmler family had moved to Landshut, a town to the northeast of Munich. Heinrich's diary of the period is understandably full of references to the progress of the war. Sometimes he would simply copy down information garnered from the official Army bulletins or the fuller reports in the newspaper to which the family subscribed, the *Münchner Neueste Nachrichten*. Such personal asides as he would interpose consisted of passages condemning the local citizenry of Landshut for not showing sufficient enthusiasm for the war. He also repeatedly expressed profound regret that he was too young to join the Army. When his brother Gebhard, the elder by two years, enlisted in the Landsturm in 1915, Himmler wrote, "Oh, if only I were as old as that and could go to the front." He nagged at his father. Surely he could pull some strings at Court to expedite Heinrich's entry into the Army. The father succumbed to his son's entreaties, and in late 1917 Heinrich Himmler entered the Second Bavarian Infantry Regiment, the Von der Tann. Meanwhile Prince Heinrich had been killed in action and Himmler's father received a letter from the Court which informed him that "The J. N. Oberndorffer Bank, 18 Salvatorstrasse, Munich, has been instructed to send you 1000 5% German War Loan Bonds. Please accept this sum as a gift for your son Heinrich from his late godfather, Weiland, His Royal Highness Prince Heinrich."

If Heinrich Himmler had dreams of leading his troops to victory at the front, they were never to be realized. He was discharged at the end of 1918 as a Fahnenjunker—an officer candidate—without ever having obtained a commission. The war simply ended too soon for him. He had six months' basic infantry training at Regensburg, and between June and September 1918 he participated in a cadets' course at Freising. He spent a couple of weeks in late September of that year with No. 17 Machine Gun Company at Bayreuth and two months later he was discharged. This did not prevent him from indulging in fantasies about his wartime record. Shortly before his death he told Count Bernadotte that he had gone to war with his men, and elsewhere there are references to his participation in battles on the western front. This reflects Himmler's capacity for daydreaming. Yet before we overinterpret this tendency, we should remember that it is by no means an exceptional form of behavior. In times of peace many boys want to drive locomotives. In times of war they see themselves as dashing, highly decorated young officers. The "Walter Mitty" syndrome lives on in all of us, and Heinrich Himmler's youthful yearnings are by no means unique.

One of the more exasperating gaps in the Himmler diaries is the period June 1916 to August 1919, because we cannot tell how he responded to that series of crises which beset social life in Germany at the time. What did he feel about the Revolution of November 1918 and the rise and fall of the Bavarian Soviet Republic in 1919? We know, because of his later statements, how they appeared in retrospect, but what of his reactions at the time? It has been claimed that he joined the Lauterbacher Freikorps and that in May 1919 he participated in the so-called Liberation of Munich. This claim has not been substantiated, though from time to time in 1919 he refers to his membership in an unidentified military reserve unit. What this unit was remains an open question. He apparently paid dues to the Freikorps Oberland in the autumn of 1919, but a receipt exists for equipment he drew from a Bavarian Einwohnerweher (civil guard unit) in May 1920. Did he belong, possibly not concurrently, to several units?

In the end it probably does not matter to which Freikorps he belonged. What is significant is what membership in a Freikorps implied. This knowledge is essential not only for the light it throws on an important chapter in German social history, but also for a true understanding of Heinrich Himmler and the SS he fashioned. In his late teens and early twenties, the Freikorps shaped him, as well as many thousands of other young Germans of the time. It is no accident that as the fortunes of national socialism progressed, the ranks of the SA and SS should have been swollen by former Freikorps members. Through his association with these war veterans, the young Heinrich

Himmler became enmeshed in specious social theory and political debate. Because of his character, Himmler took everything literally. It is not an overstatement to suggest that millions of people were to meet their death as a result of this quality.

Some prominent Nazis were simply career politicians jumping on what appeared to be the most suitable bandwagon. One such was Albert Krebs, senior Nazi party official in Hamburg. He had the misfortune in the Spring of 1929 to sit opposite Himmler on a train traveling from Elberfeld to Hamburg. Himmler regaled his colleague with a summary of his political views. Politics, said Himmler, was simply a matter of people's private affairs. How, for example, had an SA commander called Conn come by his name? Did it not sound as though it had been conveniently changed from Cohen? And what about Gauleiter (District Leader) Lohse—had he not been a bank official and did this not imply that he must, by definition, have come under the influence of Jewish capital? In his memoirs, Krebs remembers Himmler's diatribe as "a remarkable mixture of martial bombast, lower-middle-class beer-hall gossip, and the impassioned forecasts of a nonconformist preacher."

These thoughts did not represent gossip to Himmler. He had worked them all out diligently and slowly, as his father had taught him to do. In fact he had become, at an early age, a self-appointed teacher. To his brother Ernst, who was only five years his junior, he wrote in November 1920, "I am very pleased with your school report, but don't rest on your laurels. What is more, I expect a better result in History. Don't become unbalanced. Be a good boy and don't give any trouble to Daddy and Mummy." One wonders why Ernst did not punch his brother in the nose. Gebhard, who was after all two years older than Heinrich, had an even more difficult time. After courting a certain Fräulein Paula Stolzle, Gebhard announced his engagement to her. His younger brother Heinrich, having pursued his own investigations in the matter, decided that Paula had been leading a somewhat fast life. He even engaged a private detective to watch her, and diligent as he was, put his thoughts on paper in a letter written to Paula dated April 18, 1923: "If your union is to be a happy one for the two of you and salutary for our people, the very foundation of which must be healthy, clean-living families, you will have to be ridden on a tight rein and with the utmost severity. Since your own code of behavior is not a strict one and your future husband is too kind-hearted, someone else must perform this function. I feel it my duty to do so." Strangely enough, Gebhard did not box his younger brother's ears for this effrontery, and behind the actions of

Heinrich Himmler must have loomed the early influence of Himmler père, the genial but authoritative schoolmaster on whom Heinrich was quite evidently modeling himself.

The excerpt from the above letter can be contrasted with the following entry in Himmler's diary dated February 5, 1922: "I have experienced, as one lay so closely together, in couples, body to body, hot, human by human, that one gets all fired up and must summon all one's rational faculties. The girls are then so far gone, they no longer know what they are doing. It is the hot, unconscious longing of the whole individual for the satisfaction of an extremely powerful natural drive. . . . Deprived as they are of their will power, one could do anything with these girls and at the same time one has enough to do to struggle with oneself. I am certainly sorry for the girls. . . ."

It is not unusual for repressed sexuality to express itself in these terms, but it is certainly significant in Himmler's case that he felt he had fought the good battle with his own lusts and that life had given him the mission to explain the nature of the struggle to others. He managed to induce his elder brother to give up his relationship with Paula Stolzle; moreover he felt it necessary to put his thoughts and injunctions on paper rather than arrange a face-to-face confrontation. Letters are useful because they can be placed in files. Files are of paramount importance. You can study them at your leisure, they can be used as evidence against people, and they endorse your feelings of self-importance. The warped and inhuman side of Heinrich Himmler was beginning to show itself.

The Himmler diaries contain important entries during the period of his student life. Those which he may have written between September 1915 and August 1919 have disappeared, but entries do exist for the period from August 1, 1919, to February 2, 1920. The August 1919 entries show that he was working on a farm near Ingolstadt, to the north of Munich, presumably as part of his agricultural studies. On September 4 he suddenly collapsed and was admitted to a hospital with what was diagnosed as paratyphoid fever. During his stay at this hospital his family moved to Ingolstadt, where his father had been granted a teaching position at a local high school. After a convalescence, the family must have decided that Heinrich's constitution, at least for the time being, was too suspect to permit him to pursue a career in agriculture. If he were to continue with his study of agriculture, therefore, it must take a more academic form, and on October 20, 1919, he enrolled in the Technische Hochschule of Munich University. Of his final medical checkup on September 24, Himmler wrote: "At 3:00 P.M. to Dr. Grünstadt. Dilation of the heart not significant, but must interrupt [farmwork] for a year and study."

So began Himmler's career as a student in Munich. Life in that city had only recently stabilized itself. Since the end of the war, those with the conservative background of the Himmlers viewed with horror the events which took place. With the collapse of the German armies on the western front, a Socialist Republic was proclaimed on November 8, 1918, by Kurt Eisner. Eisner's sin in initiating this move in Catholic Bavaria was compounded by one further inexcusable fact: he was a Jew. Right-wing historians of the period have often labeled their chapters on Bavaria after World War I: "When Israel Ruled Bavaria." Eisner had a certain probity which compelled him to announce publicly that the finger of guilt for the outbreak of the war pointed directly at Germany. He set about collecting documents to prove this fact, another action which enraged all patriots and caused one historian of the Freikorps movement to label him "A hated Jewish ideologue" (Schmidt-Pauli). In fact Eisner was a scholarly, relatively gentle figure but unfortunately somewhat lacking in organizational skills. Paul Gentizon, a French journalist who visited him shortly after his appointment as Minister-President, describes his meeting with Eisner: "Diplomatic acts, parchments, revolutionary proclamations, even telegrams, cover tables and armchairs in a confusion suggestive of the backroom of a shop, and he hardly tries to conceal the most compromising documents from the indiscretion of journalists who besiege him. . . . No method and no organization seems to prevail in the functioning of this odd ministry."

In any event, Eisner's regime lasted for only three months. In the elections of January 1919 his party returned only three members to the Bavarian Diet, but so keen was Eisner to stay in office that he continued to attempt to deal with the Majority Socialists and Communists, all to no avail. On the morning of February 21, 1919, he strolled through Munich to hand in his resignation to Auer, the leader of the Majority Socialists. En route he was shot by Count Arco auf Valley, a member of the pro-Nazi Thule Society. The very same morning Auer himself was assassinated in the diet by a young Communist, a butcher's apprentice, who walked into the building, murdered Auer, and then calmly walked out.

On March 20, 1919, Bela Kuhn installed his Communist dictatorship in Hungary—an event that gave left-wing radicals throughout Europe a shot in the arm. A group of intellectuals whose spokesman was Ernst Toller announced a Republic of Soviets in Bavaria on the evening of April 6. The coalition government headed by the Majority

Socialists fled to Bamberg. It is difficult to understand why they did not stay and give fight, for Toller's circle, while basically anarchistic, was composed of gentle idealists. Munich was starving, but one of Toller's first acts as President of the Executive Council was to issue a decree directing the people to a form of free artistic expression, for only in this way, he asserted could they rediscover their souls. Gustav Landauer, the new Commissar for Public Instruction, announced that the University of Munich was henceforth open to all Bavarians of eighteen and over. Once there, everybody would be educated according to his own ideas. Furthermore, "History, that enemy of civilization, is herewith suppressed." The Commissar for Foreign Affairs, a certain Franz Lipp, had a field day. He wrote to the pope announcing that Hoffmann (leader of the Majority Socialists, now cowering in Bamberg) had stolen the key to his toilet. In a Minute to the Minister of Transport he said: "My dear colleague—I have just declared war on Württemberg and Switzerland because these dogs did not send me sixty locomotives immediately. I am certain of victory." All houses in Bavaria were requisitioned by the Commissar for Public Housing; that department also decreed that no home should henceforth contain more than three rooms and the living room should always be placed above the kitchen and bedroom.

The Communists had no time for the haphazard but somewhat intriguing theorizing of Toller and his circle. On Palm Sunday in April 1919 they seized power in Bavaria. Their leaders, Leviné, Axelrod, and Levien, were all men of Russian background. Then followed that period in Bavarian history described, with some justification, as the "Red Terror." The "Red Army," believed to have been the best-paid army in history, existed in a state of almost continuous drunkenness and ran through the streets looting and plundering. Schools, newspaper offices, banks, and the theaters were closed, prisoners were removed from jails, and police files were burned.

Hoffmann and his government in exile at Bamberg were finally compelled to approach the hated central government in Berlin for assistance, and once again detachments of the Freikorps were used to restore order. By May 2, 1919, Munich was relieved of the Red Terror. It is believed that Heinrich Himmler participated in this act, known as the "Liberation of Munich."

Yet if the citizens of Munich had welcomed the troops of the Freikorps as their deliverers, they were in for some nasty shocks. The correspondent of the London *Times* cabled home on May 16, 1919: "The White Terror of Prussian military rule is far worse than the Red Terror of Communism. All suspected of extreme views are shot without trial. Numerous notables suspected of even moderate socialist views disappear without trace. The Press is completely muzzled. . . ." One Freikorps leader, Major Schultz of the Lutzow Freikorps, announced to his men: "It is a lot better to kill a few innocent people than to let one guilty person escape. . . . You know how to handle it . . . shoot them and report that they attacked you or tried to escape." Members of the Freikorps patrolled the streets of Munich at will. The numbers of bodies in the streets created a problem for the city health department. Improvised prisons were established by the Freikorps units, forerunners of those which were to be set up in Berlin in later years, in which summary justice was dispensed. Nonetheless by May 6, 1919, Berlin was informed that Munich was now under control and the government could return. The uneasy government of the Majority Socialists lasted until March 1920 and was therefore still in power when Himmler started his student life in Munich.

He lived in a rented room and took his meals in the apartment of a certain Frau Loritz. It was a busy household. In addition to Frau Loritz there were her two daughters Maja and Käthe, her little son Willi, and several other students and young office workers who also ate there. It was a warm and active place. Himmler fell in love with Maja, but his diary indicates that she did not respond to his overtures. A life of dancing and parties now held sway. Himmler was compelled to take dancing lessons. On November 25, 1919, his diary states: "From 8:00 to 10:00 P.M. dancing lesson. Every beginning is hard, but we shall manage it somehow. I'll be glad once I can; the dancing course itself leaves me absolutely cold and only takes up my time." By late January of the following year his diary faithfully records that he had mastered the "Boston." Himmler was not exactly what one might call a "natural mover." Later on, in parades, with his overlong SS greatcoat flapping around his legs, he summoned, in the words of one biographer, "all the grace of a ridiculous gander." In fact, however persistently he tried, he was unable to bring off any convincing show of physical prowess. Schellenberg, who was later to become chief of the Foreign Intelligence Service of the SD (Sicherheitsdienst, or Security Service), has described Himmler attempting physical exercise in his back garden with conspicuous lack of grace. Schellenberg also could not repress a giggle when during the course of the war, Himmler, dressed in full regalia, was summoned to the Führer's special train. In a mad dash to be on time for the conference to which he had been invited, he climbed up two steps into the carriage, lost his balance, and fell flat on his face on the railway tracks.

Himmler joined a student fraternity on November 19, 1919, one which practiced dueling. He longed to have that special scar on his face which was the distinguishing mark of manhood and virility in those days. The trouble was, he just could not find anybody within the fraternity who considered him a worthy opponent in a *Paukpartie* —a fencing match. He had to wait until his final semester at the agricultural school before his dream was realized. On June 17, 1922, somebody was persuaded to cut his face in the approved tradition. This event was recorded by Himmler with considerable satisfaction.

Himmler also had trouble in digesting beer. Nothing in Munich is more likely to make one feel an outsider. Initiation into a student fraternity normally took the form of inviting the applicant to stand on a table and down liter after liter of beer. But Himmler had a weak stomach and could not manage it. His comrades gave him a special dispensation which absolved him from meeting this particular requirement.

It is clear that physically Himmler represented exactly the opposite of that breed he was so anxious to develop: the blond, strong *Ubermensch,* or superman. It is possible that if he had possessed a body more suited to physical exercise and had had more physical dexterity, a few million people more might be alive today.

There is ample evidence in his diaries that Himmler most earnestly wanted to be a "good boy." He would turn with alacrity to the performance of good works, visiting the sick, doing favors for people. There is little doubt that he also enjoyed being patted on the head as a result. During the Christmas vacation of 1919 he made repeated visits to a Herr Lang, who was blind. Himmler tried to ease Herr Lang's lot by reading to him. In 1921 his diary states: "Visit to Frau Kernberger. The poor old woman. This is real misery. She is nearly too weak from hunger and exhaustion to walk. . . . She eats watersoups and drinks a lot of tea. . . . How hard and pitiless people can be. . . . I fetched rolls for her and added a small cake, which I put down without her noticing it. If only I could do more, but we are ourselves poor devils." On December 5, 1921, Himmler visited the famous Platzl restaurant in Munich with some of his fraternity comrades and had this to say about the waitress: "I felt sorry for her. Every waitress inevitably gets dragged in the mire [*wird versumpft*]. If I were rich I would give enough to her to get married instead of being forced to come down in the world." When any of Himmler's fellow students fell ill, they found in him a diligent and sympathetic visitor. He would run errands for them and their families. Just causes found his ever-ready support. He also acted in a benefit play for underprivileged Viennese children.

Another notable characteristic revealed in the diaries is a capacity for self-criticism. Himmler writes most scathingly about his own deficiencies. "I am much too warm-hearted and always talk too much" (November 4, 1921). "I cracked a lot of jokes and mocked a lot. Why can't I stop it?" (November 13, 1921). "I still lack the gentlemanly certainty of manners. . . . When shall I stop talking too much?" (November 18, 1921). When his mother visited him in Munich in January 1922 Himmler piously recorded his impressions in his diary: "The result of these past days: I am a phrasemonger and chatterbox, without energy, and I achieve nothing. . . . They think of me as a jolly fellow who is amusing and takes care of everything" (January 29, 1922).

The diaries also show that from an early age one of Himmler's main activities was to pry into the affairs of others. He evaluates other people's character and behavior and records tidbits of gossip in pretentious prose, totally without humor but conveying one aspect of himself about which apparently he had complete certainty: his ability to make sound judgments about others.

Himmler's mind during his late teens and early twenties was a confused melting pot of wild ambition and pedestrian social comment. When Maja Loritz failed to respond to his attentions, he toyed with the idea of pursuing a military career ("Perhaps I shall take part in fighting and war within a few years. I am looking forward to this war of liberation. I shall take part if I can still move a limb"—November 14, 1919) or of emigrating somewhere in order to farm. "If there is another campaign in the East," he wrote on November 22, 1921, "I'll go along. The East is most important for us. The West will die easily. In the East we must fight and colonize." There is no doubt that Himmler suffered from fits of depression from time to time as he reviewed the futility of his existence. By contrast, the life of a soldier in wartime seemed to offer an exciting escape. "If only there would be fighting again, war, departing troops . . ." (February 19, 1922).

Himmler's Catholicism was very important to him. He attended church regularly, took Communion, confessed, and prayed. He listened patiently to all the Sunday sermons and often commented on them in his diary. On learning that a girl for whom he had feelings of affection went to Communion daily, he wrote: "This was the greatest joy I have experienced this past eight days" (October 20, 1919). But the nihilistic tendencies within the Freikorps did not leave him unmoved. The Freikorps was anticlerical and wanted to remove all Christian trappings from society. Christianity preached pity, remorse, help to the weak and needy—and these were all attitudes which ran counter to the antibourgeois nature of corps members. Even within his student fraternity Himmler was to experience religious conflict, for its practice of dueling violated the official views of his church. On December 15, 1919, he wrote, "I believe I had come into conflict with my religion. Come what may, I shall always love God, shall pray to Him, shall remain faithful to the Catholic Church, and shall defend it even if I should be expelled from it."

Himmler's most earnest wish was to be a good boy and earn the praise of his father and mother. He knew he must be a good Catholic, but then, what should he do about dueling? He was exposed, as a member of a nationalistic student fraternity and of one or other of the Freikorps, to some very radical influences, all of which challenged the basic precepts of his orderly conservative background. How could he nod his head when these men of fiery temperament spoke and yet continue to enjoy the favor of his parents? His was a plodding, meticulous, and very literal mind. If he was told that certain elements within society must be eliminated, he knew exactly what this meant: they must be wiped out. Despite all his dreams of military glory, he did not want to see the blood flow. Seated at a desk with some official papers before him, he would gladly consign these undesirable social elements to oblivion with a stroke of his pen. But he could not be expected to pull a trigger or directly inflict pain on his victims, because this would induce soul-searching, not to mention stomach cramps. His later behavior on one of his rare visits to an extermination camp confirms this.

At some point during the early 1920s Himmler cast his lot with those very radical elements in Bavaria which formed the nucleus of the budding Nazi party. They wanted a new society; so did he. They considered themselves idealists; so did he. They were also men, in the overwhelming majority, who had proved themselves on the field of battle. So they were much that he was not. Despite his squeamishness, prudery, and self-doubts, he joined them. He had something to offer: the diligent, patient, step-by-step administrative intelligence of a minor clerk, but nonetheless a clerk with ambition.

It is generally accepted that the catalyst who brought Himmler together with the group of ex-soldiers and fiery students in Munich at the time was Captain Ernst Röhm, a pudgy, violent homosexual who had been extremely active in military and political circles since the end of World War I. In late 1918 Röhm had served on the staff of the Twelfth Bavarian Infantry Division in Himmler's hometown of Landshut. In May 1920 Himmler had received his weapons from the very unit of which Röhm had been Armaments and Equipment Officer, the Twenty-first Rifle brigade in Munich. In 1922 the Reichswehr, or Army, had appointed Röhm as a secret quartermaster to the undercover defense organizations with which official Army circles had been flirting for some years. It is believed that the two men, Röhm and Himmler, did not meet until January 1922 when a meeting of one of these defense organizations took place in the Arzberger Keller, a Munich beer hall. The meeting itself was called a gathering of a *Schützenverein*—a rifle club—to disguise its real purpose. It is probable that Himmler had run into Röhm on a previous occasion. His diary for January 26, 1922 reads: "Captain Röhm and Major Angerer were also there; very friendly. Röhm pessimistic as to Bolshevism."

Nineteen twenty-two was a significant year for Himmler. He passed his agricultural examinations on August 5 and secured a job as agricultural assistant in a chemical factory in Schleissheim. Not long after, on Röhm's strong recommendation, he joined Röhm's paramilitary organization, the Reichskriegflagge. Röhm played an important part in enlisting the support among the disaffected men of the day, in nationalistic organizations dedicated to the overthrow of Bolshevism and the rescue of the Fatherland from the provisions of the Treaty of Versailles. He was a highly decorated soldier for whom Himmler had profound respect. Their relationship may well have been inspired by the attraction of opposites, for nothing could have been further from Himmler's temperament than the homosexual-cum-adventurer, whose rank and experience would have been a compelling influence on the young Himmler. This did not prevent the young clerk with the middle-class background from having Röhm assassinated twelve years later, when Röhm and his SA became an embarrassment to the revitalized Nazi party, now most anxious to obtain a more respectable image.

Being a member of the Reichskriegflagge did not offer enough to satisfy Himmler's quest for virility. He could shoulder his rifle on Saturday mornings, don his gaiters and light-gray windbreaker, and take part in parades. But the first occasion on which Himmler must have felt part of some great historic event was when Hitler attempted his famous Beer-Hall Putsch on November 8, 1923. While Hitler was regaling the local Bavarian dignitaries at the Bürgerbräukeller with a fiery speech announcing the start of a national right-wing revolution, it was Röhm's assignment to occupy the War Ministry building in

Munich. Himmler enjoyed the special prestige of acting as standard-bearer in this enterprise. A surviving photograph shows a blurred picture of the young Himmler outside the War Ministry, looking somewhat out of place in his military regalia, holding the old imperial war flag only a few steps away from Röhm himself.

It would be difficult to describe this event as Himmler's first taste of battle. He did not set foot in the Bürgerbräukeller, neither did he participate in that famous event known as the Blutmarsch—the march of blood—which was to be dignified by Nazi propagandists throughout the history of the Third Reich. Nonetheless Himmler's participation in the proceedings evoked enthusiastic response from certain of his female admirers. One of them, Maria R., wrote: "Troops of the Reichskriegflagge in front of the War Ministry. Heinrich Himmler at their head carrying the flag; one could see how secure the flag felt in his hands and how proud he was of it. I go up to him incapable of speech, but ringing in my ear is:

> 'Be proud I carry the flag.
> Have no cares—I carry the flag.
> Love me; I carry the flag.' "

Maria R. also wrote, "This letter is for my friend Heinrich. Let it be a small indication of our fervent gratitude and faithful memory of that deed which gave us a few moments when we learned to hope once more."

This is all very surprising. Apart from the fact that Himmler was physically not a very prepossessing specimen, he had really not done anything other than clutch a flagpole. Perhaps the fact that at the time he was surrounded by leading figures in the nationalistic movement (including Count du Moulin-Eckhardt and Röhm himself) produced a certain celebrity by association.

Hitler's ill-timed, ill-organized putsch foundered. During the winter of 1923/24 Himmler found himself without a uniform and without anybody to lead him, for both Röhm and Hitler ended up in jail. What was probably even worse, he lost his job and simply could not find another. His loyalty to Röhm, however, remained untarnished. He rode out to Stadelheim prison with some newspapers and oranges to visit his former chief. On February 15, 1924, he wrote: "Talks for twenty minutes with Captain Röhm. We had an excellent conversation. . . . He still has a good sense of humor and is always the good Captain Röhm."

The failed putsch resulted in the banning of the Nazi party. Those who were not jailed for their participation in it were compelled to reorganize themselves politically. This they did within two *"völkisch"* ("pure German") groups, most of whose energies were exhausted in heated dispute with each other. Himmler joined the National Socialist Freedom Movement led by the slightly deranged General Ludendorff —a wise choice nonetheless, because another member was Gregor Strasser, a chemist from Landshut. Strasser was a highly intelligent man with a keen nose for smelling out administrative talent. He saw certain qualities in Himmler which he decided to put to use. In May 1924 there were to be elections for the Reichstag. Previously the right-wing extremists had spurned participation in the elections because they felt this might associate them with the machinery of the Weimar Republic, which they felt to be the root of all ills. But putsch-making had proved an abortive exercise. They therefore decided to attempt to disrupt parliamentary government in Germany from within the Reichstag and fielded a large number of would-be deputies. Strasser intended to conduct a vigorous election campaign and placed Himmler in charge of propaganda in Lower Bavaria.

The unemployed would-be soldier suddenly found himself provided with a motorcycle and with the authority to run about Lower Bavaria making speeches and drumming up enthusiasm for the Nazi cause. To this task he applied himself with remorseless disregard for his health.

Since Gregor Strasser is accepted to have been one of the abler and more coherent of the early Nazi politicians, it is difficult to understand his choice of the young Himmler as his political agent. For to be an administrator is one thing; to be a public speaker is another. There was nothing in Himmler's presence to suggest a glimmering of that charismatic appeal, that happy turn of phrase which is the precondition of the successful public orator. Why then was he selected? Probably because Strasser was impressed with Himmler's obvious loyalty and desperate need of funds. And he need only use Himmler as a supporting speaker. Somebody of more prominence would always precede him. This would in no way antagonize Himmler; the world was full of men who appeared to have more enterprise, more energy, more masculinity, than he. All he asked of the world was that it show him his place. He would then make the very most of it. And above all, what must have determined Strasser in his choice of Himmler was the knowledge that his agent would be addressing peasants, a task for which he was eminently qualified. He had, after all, had an agricultural training and knew something of the problems of the farmer. Since his political "education" consisted in absorbing a series of catch phrases such as *Zinsenknechtschaft*—interest slavery—

he would speak a language which might well endear him to the bigoted and anti-Semitic peasants of Lower Bavaria.

For Heinrich Himmler, now twenty-three years of age, the appointment undoubtedly meant taking the first step on the rungs of the political ladder. And what an irresistible chance it offered him. He could now actually be on a platform, however makeshift, in the position of a teacher instructing his students, just like his father. What is more, people would listen to him! With an opportunity like this, what did it matter how much territory he covered or how hard he pushed himself? He had his brief, he had his audience, he knew where he stood. At the end of a day's rushing around Lower Bavaria addressing a mere handful of peasants, he would make entries into his diary which aggrandized his activity. He was now spreading "political enlightenment."

In addition to public speaking, Himmler managed to get some written pieces published in local newspapers. In February 1924, while speeding about the countryside, he found time to draft an article entitled "Letter from Munich" which appeared in a newspaper known as the *Rotenburger Anzeiger,* and which was heavily racist in tone. Some of his speeches bore the title: "The Enslavement of the Workers by Stock-exchange Capitalists" which to the uninitiated might sound Marxist in implication. But they had little to do with Marxism and reflected rather the suspicion with which the farmer regarded the strange dealings that took place in the large towns. This rift between country and town life was very probably the basis of Himmler's anti-Semitism. One saw significant numbers of Jews only in towns, and towns were where all the social ills which affected the lives of the peasantry germinated. Towns and Jews were thus linked in his mind, in sharp contrast to the honest and simple existence of the farmer at his peaceful work, exploited by the quick-thinking, doubletalking middlemen who "understood" and were "responsible" for the "system."

The virtues of the country and the vices of the towns are themes to which Himmler repeatedly returned in his conversations with one of his few confidants, his Finnish masseur, Felix Kersten. Fortunately, Kersten kept a diary of his talks with Himmler which contain many entries relating to Himmler's obsession about the purity of country life. On February 7, 1941, almost at the height of his power, he said to Kersten, "Look at the peasants in Bavaria. Do you think they run to a doctor the moment there's something wrong with their cattle? Of course not—still less so on their own account. They'll treat a cut, for example, with plantain and wait to see what good that does . . . they drink an infusion of wormwood and gentian to cure their own aches and pains. . . . But ask in towns about such herbs; nobody will have the least idea of them or of their healing properties." And again in December 1940 he told Kersten, "In these weeks of winter when Nature draws right back into herself, man has to do the same . . . he must share in the rhythm of Nature . . . to experience the winter solstice. . . . Country men understand that perfectly; they lie behind the stove and "laze," as the townsman calls it. People in towns know nothing about all that—to them one day is the same as another and they carry on their pursuits indifferent to whether Nature is in blossom or fruit or has surrendered to her winter sleep."

In the summer of 1941 he told Kersten, "Men must be led away from the narrow limits of great cities to surroundings in keeping with their nature. . . . The Roman lawyer is closely bound up with the town where everything is atomized. The countryside has offered the longest and most obstinate resistance to the compulsion of Roman Law." And on July 17, 1942, he said to Kersten, "Cowards are born in towns, heroes in the country." All this indicates the true origin of Himmler's social thinking. The same type of perplexity existed in America in the 1930s, when farmers in the depressed areas would refer to New York as "Jew" York.

Himmler was not only teacher, publicist, and propagandist, he was preacher as well. On February 24, 1924, after speaking at a packed hall in Hellheim, he and a fellow speaker, Dr. Rutz, moved among the crowd to provide *Einzelaufklärung*—individual enlightenment. "Bitterly hard and thorny," he wrote in his diary on this day, "is this duty to the people." These are words written with the tired satisfaction of the evangelist. On the following day he lectured peasants at Rohr for one and a half hours. "At the end," he wrote, "came a buyer for a Jewish hop dealer, and the peasants soon made short work of him." The implication is that Himmler's audience threw the intruder out.

"I have a terrible amount to do," Himmler confided in a letter to his friend Kistler. "I have to direct and build up the organization of the whole of Lower Bavaria, in every sense." In the elections Strasser's movement gained almost two million votes and entered the Reichstag with thirty-two deputies. But where did this leave Heinrich Himmler, once the celebrations were over? Until the next election the momentum of his work would fall. Moreover the very movement on whose behalf he had worked so diligently was again beset with internal strife. In a further letter to Kistler he protested, "We *völkisch* are making efforts which will apparently never bear fruit in the immediate future," and he went on to say that he felt he was supporting a potentially lost cause. For Hitler had not yet cemented the different warring factions within the nationalistic movement. He was not released from Landsberg prison until December 1924. He resolved to make a clean sweep within the movement and by February 27, 1925, had united under his own leadership the entire body of Bavarian right-wing factions to form a new National Socialist German Workers party. Himmler's former boss, Gregor Strasser, had not forgotten the sterling work Himmler had done before the May 1924 elections, and appointed him as his secretary in the late summer of 1925. Behind the St. Martin's Church in Landshut Himmler was installed in a sparsely furnished room. He was to assist Strasser, whose function it was to run the party propaganda machine in Lower Bavaria.

Yet Strasser had his eyes firmly fixed on the situation in North Germany. Unlike most Bavarians, he saw the future of the movement in the eventual establishment in Prussia, at the seat of national power in Berlin. When Strasser moved to Berlin, Himmler was left without a daily contact with some person who could give him direction. Without direction he was useless. Thus it was that at this time he began to move within the orbit of the one man who could provide him with continuous leadership: Adolf Hitler.

It is not known exactly when the two men first met. In the confused welter of conflicting right-wing political organizations prior to the Beer-Hall Putsch of 1923 there can be no doubt that Himmler had heard Hitler speak. But it was not until Hitler had been released from jail and had reorganized the political fortunes of the different nationalistic factions that Himmler started to be impressed with him. This speedily turned into adulation, and Himmler was later to refer to his early years in Hitler's movement as "glorious days. We members of the Movement were in constant danger of our lives, but we were not afraid. Adolf Hitler led us and held us together. They were the most wonderful years of my life." Hitler spoke with the certainty of a messiah. If Himmler wanted to be led, he could find no more persuasive leader. Moreover, loyalty was one quality Hitler prized most highly. The diligent and enthusiastic Himmler was rewarded with new titles and new offices. In 1925 he became Deputy Gauleiter of Upper Bavaria and Swabia, then Deputy Reich Propaganda Chief and, in 1927, Deputy Reichsführer-SS.

To his new political offices Himmler added new intellectual pursuits. He became obsessed with the mystic relation between blood and soil. In an undated memorandum he wrote, "The yeoman on his own acre is the backbone of the German people's strength and character." The good society accordingly draws its strength from the superior biological strain of the independent farmer. Somewhere or other within the background of all great men, so Himmler thought, must lurk this fine peasant strain, firmly linked to the soil from which it sprang. The land became for Himmler the source of all honesty and purity, whereas cities were the refuge of all that was morally sick and tainted. This is a theme which was later to be taken up by the journalists who contributed to the newspaper of the SS, *Das Schwarze Korps*. The black-clothed, country-oriented SS men would walk up and down fashionable Kurfürstendamm in Berlin of a Sunday afternoon and look with hatred and disgust at the burghers dressed in their Sunday finery eating cakes and drinking coffee at the pavement cafés. They saw Jews everywhere; Jews became the embodiment of city life and thereby were the source of all moral corruption. There is a curious parallel between the writings and attitudes of the early Zionists and the editorials of *Das Schwarze Korps*. Both want a return to the land; the Zionists in order to change the economic image of the Jews as purely townsfolk, the SS in order to maintain racial purity. It is easy to dismiss this ideology as nonsense, but not so easy to refute the tremendous appeal of the land to vast numbers of people in the twentieth century. Himmler wanted to set up farmers' schools throughout the countryside, to instruct the inhabitants in the true way of life. The male teachers would have qualities of leadership and show pupils the present world's fabric of "lies and frauds." The female teachers would be "lively, clean-living women, with true maternal instincts, free from the diseases of today's degenerate city women, strong and gracious, leaving the last word to the man in the everyday things of life." Himmler's radicalism, if it can be so called, is therefore the radicalism of the middle class. His women are pure, they are free of disease, and they have true maternal instincts. Nothing could summarize more succinctly the constant impact on Himmler of his Bavarian bourgeois background. His women even know their true place, since they must leave "the last word to the man in the everyday things of life." These blond, plump, dirndl-skirted fräuleins, smelling cleanly of soap and flowers of the meadow, were to lead the new generation on the road to a purer society. The trouble was, where were they to do this? There was not enough room within the frontiers of the Reich itself. Like thousands of other Germans, Himmler considered his country to be overpopulated and robbed of territorial and other assets by the Versailles Treaty. So he looked eastward. The vast steppes of Russia offered the most obvious solution.

As Himmler took almost everything he heard literally, he must have been aware of that verb used by his leader, Hitler, with such astonishing frequency: *beseitigen*. (It means to eliminate or wipe out.) While other Nazis thought that the use of *beseitigen* in Hitler's speeches was capable of various interpretations, Himmler knew what was intended. If Jews and Slavs were to be *beseitigt,* it meant they were literally to be wiped out.

Himmler became an insufferable pedant. When people spoke to him he developed the habit of tapping his fingertips together patiently. Then he would deliver his lecture rather in the manner of a good-natured headmaster. Equipped with a magnifying glass, he would stare for hours at photographs of would-be SS applicants. Did their facial structure seem to be of the right type? Was there any evidence, during the past two centuries, of any non-Aryan strain in their pedigree? Like some fanatical cultivator of obscure orchids making hourly sorties into his hothouse to add a bit of fertilizer here, a drop of water there, Himmler addressed himself to the question of human cultivation. He did so with absolute certainty in the probity of his aims and the necessity of his mission. He was taking part, so he thought, in a grand experiment. His was a historic task. If one had told him that his theories constituted sadistic rubbish, he would have responded with mild astonishment. As far as he was concerned, he was a good man doing a good job. Moreover, there was certainly nothing in it financially for him. At no stage of his career did he ever draw a salary commensurate with his high position. He lived modestly and cautiously, a clerk who knew his place. He had the good fortune, as he repeatedly remarked, to have as master "the greatest genius of all time," Adolf Hitler. He would have denied, with some justification, that he had ever attempted to seek self-glorification. Incapable of a grandiloquent gesture, the only thing he ever did which appeared to transcend the confines of his bureaucratic nature was to establish at Wewelsberg a large castle, which was to be the seat of his New Order, the SS. When he was eventually compelled to visit the sites connected with his sociobiological theories, he had to struggle to choke back nausea, just as many others did who were as bourgeois as Heinrich Himmler himself. When Himmler said life was difficult, he meant that you needed a very firm hold on yourself not to fall prey to pity for your victims, the racially inferior beings who must be wiped out if the purer strain was to survive. He repeatedly told his men that they needed an extra degree of toughness to execute their historic task. For those who had had training in the Freikorps, his words were unnecessary; they were not inhibited by the Christian habit of soul searching. For later entrants into the SS, there were some whose squeamishness had to be overcome.

The various titles which Himmler acquired during 1925 from a grateful Führer were certainly satisfying for the status seeker, but hardly remunerative. His work was also extremely time-consuming, and after his abortive overtures to Maja Loritz in his student days, there are few references in his diaries to women, apart from brief character studies. But at some time in 1926 he found himself in the famous German spa Bad Reichenhall. A sudden downpour drove him into the lobby of a fashionable hotel. There he almost collided with somebody, and in an excess of middle-class propriety he swept off his rain-soaked hat, thereby drenching his victim. She was Margarethe Boden, a blond, blue-eyed woman of some thirty-three years, the daughter of a West Prussian landowner. During World War I she had worked as a nursing sister. After the war she had moved to Berlin, had an unsuccessful marriage, and opened a nursing home with money inherited from her father.

Heinrich Himmler fell in love. Marga, as she was called, was a truly Nordic type, but in the eyes of the Himmler family she was totally unsuitable for their son. She was eight years his senior, Protestant *and* divorced. Himmler simply could not take her home to meet his parents. "I would rather," he confided to his brother Gebhard, "clear a hall of a thousand Communists single-handed." It is doubtful that he received much sympathy from Gebhard, since he himself had hardly been supportive of his brother's courtship of Paula Stolzle. It is also amusing that Himmler should have dreamed up the fantasy of dealing summarily with a thousand Communists "single-handed"; he would probably have fallen over a few chairs on the way. But clearly the self-image as Teutonic warrior had by now taken a firm hold on the young man's imagination.

In the end, love triumphed and Heinrich took Marga home. After warnings, exhortations, and finally disbelief at what was taking place around them, Himmler's parents gave in and left the couple to the consequences of their decision. Heinrich and Marga were married on July 3, 1928, but they could hardly live on Heinrich's income from his political activities. Marga sold her clinic in Berlin and with the proceeds they purchased some land near Munich at Waldtrudering. They then constructed a small wooden house and Heinrich built a chicken coop which he intended to be the first of many for a projected chicken farm. They bought fifty laying hens. And then they waited. While they were waiting, Himmler's political career continued to make demands on him. As far as he was concerned, there was no choice. Politics must take precedence over chickens. He was always away, leaving Marga with the problem of trying to make ends meet. On May 6, 1929, therefore, ten months after their wedding, she wrote: "The hens are laying frightfully badly; only two eggs a day. I worry so much about what we're going to live on and how we're going to save for Whitsun. Something is always going wrong. I try so hard to save. . . ." And on another occasion: "You have not written; that's naughty. . . ."

In fact, from very early in their relationship Marga adopted the tone of a slightly disapproving mother toward Himmler. Some biographers have maintained that this was probably what attracted Himmler to her. They point to the fact that she was eight years older than he and suggest that she was a mother figure to him. In such letters as have survived, written almost exclusively from Marga to Heinrich, she likes to use the word *naughty* both to describe her own as well as his behavior: "Darling, the wicked husband always has to worry about saving, because you know the naughty wife always spends every penny she has." This cloying and puerile style may well have diverted Himmler at the beginning but certainly it began to irritate him as their relationship progressed. Her attitude marred Himmler's self-image, and so he started to stay away from home for longer spells, even when political duty did not call. After the birth of their only child, a girl called Gudrun, they lived apart. This did not prevent Marga from entertaining hopes that they would eventually be reunited. "When the elections are over we can have a few years of peace. And you will be with me all the time." And: "You naughty soldier of fortune—surely you must be in this part of the world sometimes!" When the playful tone of these letters failed to have the desired effect, they became slightly more peremptory and petulant in style. "Sometimes I get very sad sitting here at home all the time. Only today I was thinking how we might celebrate your birthday. Darling—let's go to some exhibition together; we've never done that." Also, "Things are not good with me. What is going to become of me?"

Himmler had of course dropped her. If he had not accumulated titles, assiduously collected contacts, and made his way step by step upward within the Nazi hierarchy it is possible that he would have responded more favorably to the entreaties of his wife. But away from that defunct, unprofitable chicken farm, he could be a man. He had a uniform, he had titles, and he seemed to be where History was being made. Furthermore, he had been brought up to believe that women should know their place. Had his life outside his marriage been unsuccessful, he might have stayed on the chicken farm and he and Marga might have become a pair of agreeable cranks, cultivating organic foodstuffs, pottering about in a vegetable garden, and joining folk-weaving societies.

2
CONSOLIDATION, GROWTH, AND INTERNAL STRIFE

SS or Schutzstaffel means Protective Squad. The initial function of its members was to act as Hitler's personal bodyguard; hence their title. But their activities far exceeded this limited brief and to understand them fully their antecedents need to be examined.

It is fair to assert that the SS, like the SA, or Sturmabteilung (Storm Detachment), was born in the First World War. It was the brainchild of a certain Captain Rohr of the Imperial German Army, years before anybody had ever heard of Adolf Hitler or Heinrich Himmler. During World War I, when the battle assumed the proportions of a war of attrition with both sides virtually immobilized in the trenches, the German General Staff realized that some rethinking had to be done about the concept of mobile warfare on which it had been reared. Certain Army commanders began to experiment with small highly mobile units which they called Stosstrupps—Storm Troops. Their function was to break through the trenches and thereby act as the spearhead of a new attack. They had a limited success in the Argonne as early as the autumn of 1914, but it was not until Captain Rohr came on the scene that they assumed the importance for which they were later to be renowned.

Captain Rohr perfected the idea of training superbly fit fighting men whose assignment was to thrust through the enemy lines (*stossen* means literally to thrust) and force a gap through which the regular infantry could proceed. So effective were these squads in the battle of the Somme in 1916 that in October of that year, the Army High Command ordered each of its armies to build up what had now come to be called Sturmbataillone on the Rohr model. These Storm Troops were a cut above everybody else in the Army. They received special rations and equipment and extra leave. They were authorized to carry pistols, which beforehand was the prerogative of officers. Moreover, they wore the coveted Deaths' Head insignia, which had previously been used only by the aristocratic cavalrymen. Not for them the life in the trenches. They trained in relative comfort far behind the lines and were only brought up to the front when they had a job to do. In many Sturmbataillone, men could be heard addressing their officers with the familiar pronoun *du,* an unheard-of breach of discipline in the old Prussian Army. They had a certain swagger. They were told they constituted an elite and they came to believe it. Their literary spokesman was Ernst Jünger, who himself commanded a Sturmbataillon. He was later to write: "Combat during the World War had its great moments. Everyone knows that who has ever seen these princes of the trenches in their own realm with their hard-set faces and bloodshot eyes; brave to the point of madness, tough, quick to leap forward or back."

The Stosstrupps or Sturmbataillone were commanded by young officers, lieutenants, or captains in prime physical condition. Their men were totally devoted to them. A biography of one storm troop leader called Markmann, states: "Markmann knew precisely how he stood with his men. To them he was not their commanding officer; he was their Leader! And they were his Comrades! They trusted him blindly and would have followed him into hell itself if it were necessary."

The Sturmbataillone anticipated the Schutzstaffeln in several ways: in selection of personnel, in relationship between leader and led, in the setting up of the idea of an elite, and finally in a kind of blind savagery which was taken over from the heightened conditions of war into peacetime bourgeois life. Their members did not consider that the war had ended in November 1918; it had simply been transferred to another front, namely the fatherland. The enemy this time consisted of traitors, signatories of the treaties of Versailles and St. Germain, workers who had gone on strike, and sundry others who had undermined the war effort. While brave soldiers had done their duty gloriously on the front, the *Etappe,* or rear, was full of traitors, so they thought. The German armies had been well and truly beaten on the battlefield, but their soldiers were encouraged to believe that they had been let down at home. The executive committee of Germany's Social Democratic party published a pamphlet in November 1918 which contained the following astonishing intelligence: "SOLDIERS! A new Germany greets you! Perhaps you do not return as victors who have completely crushed the enemy to the ground . . . but neither do you return as the vanquished, for the war was stopped at the wishes of the leadership of the Reich. . . . So you can hold your heads high." The seeds of the notorious *Dolchstoss* legend, the belief that German armies were stabbed in the back by traitors at home, were therefore sown not only by right-wing extremists but by German socialists themselves. They, too, refused to swallow the unpalatable truth of Germany's military defeat.

It was not long before the returning soldiers were called upon to maintain order within the new Republic. Although the Army had effected an orderly withdrawal from the front, it had not arranged proper demobilization. Thus were born the volunteer formations, or Freikorps. They were paramilitary organizations formed sometimes at the request of the government, sometimes on the initiative of the Army itself, and sometimes as an expression of patriotic fervor of junior officers. They had, in theory, a twofold function. The first was to crush the menace of Bolshevism at home. The second was to protect German frontiers from the encroachments of the Poles to the east. The collapse of German arms in 1918 rekindled the old enmity that existed between Poles and Germans in disputed areas on Germany's eastern frontiers. The Poles had been waiting for the appropriate day to reclaim their land from the German invaders. In doing so they uprooted thousands of Germans whose families had lived in these areas for generations, but this did not deter them; the time was ripe for retribution.

Within Germany there was a very real threat of some form of Bolshevism. Even before the war had ended there had been a left-wing mutiny in the Navy, and in the months after the war various uprisings of a similar nature had taken place.

During the course of 1919 advertisements like the following appeared in many German newspapers and on posters:

COMRADES
The Spartacist danger has not yet been removed.
The Poles press ever further onto German soil.
Can you look on these events calmly?
NO!
What would your dead comrades say?
Soldiers arise! Stop Germany from becoming the laugh-
                          ingstock of the world. Enrol NOW in
THE HULSEN FREE CORPS
Recruiting offices: Bauer Café, Unter den Linden,
Potsdam Beer Gardens. . . .
VOLUNTEERS FALL OUT!
Patriotic Germans, join the fierce and foolhardy
LUTZOW FREE CORPS.

If there were patriotic and ideological motives for joining the Freikorps, there were also very persuasive material and psychological ones. In the defeated Germany of the time, a man who joined the Freikorps was at least clothed at government expense, could expect to receive a daily pay of 30 to 50 marks, and could also rely on 200 grams of meat and 75 grams of butter each day. One volunteer, a member of the notorious Ehrhardt Brigade, wrote in his memoirs: "The Bavarian Government added another 5 marks a day to our base pay. We got plenty of beer and cigarettes and a quarter-liter of wine daily. We had a good time." The Ehrhardt Brigade was very intimately involved in that ludicrous attempt at a coup d'état known as the Kapp Putsch, a rightist attempt to contain the threat of left-wing elements in Germany. It foundered because the workers achieved sufficient unity of purpose to counter with a very effective general strike. The government of the time had no option other than to rid itself of the very forces it had been using "to maintain internal security." On March 17, 1919, the Ehrhardt Brigade was ordered to leave Berlin. It did so in a very ugly mood. A crowd formed along Unter den Linden and watched in silence as the volunteers marched out of the capital. Brigadier General John H. Morgan, a member of the Inter-Allied Military Commission of Control, was present. No band played. Nothing could be heard but the sound of marching boots. A small boy in the crowd of onlookers laughed, the tension proving too much for him. Two members of the Ehrhardt Brigade broke ranks, knocked the boy down, and beat him with their rifle butts until he was quite still. Nobody else moved, though someone had the courage to hiss. An officer barked a command and machine guns opened fire on the crowd. Then the Brigade formed ranks and marched in impeccable order through the Brandenburg Gate.

This story has been recounted because it is an example of the gratuitous brutality which characterized the Freikorps. It helps to endorse the hypothesis that psychological motives outweighed patriotic or material ones for those who applied for membership. There can be little doubt, as one reads of their activities, that the majority of volunteers were desperados who would have followed any cause as long as it offered them the chance of brutal action. Yet the movement, for such it was, produced two writers of considerable distinction who attempted to provide ideological background for the Freikorps. They were Ernst Jünger and Ernst von Salomon. Von Salomon wrote: "Anyone who judges Freikorps fighters by the standards of the civilization it was their task to help to destroy is utilizing the standards of the enemy."

This very nihilistic statement is of interest because it suggests that the Freikorps had its own standards which those nurtured on the middle-class values of Western civilization are unable to understand. If it had standards, what were they? The answer, in the very sobering light of subsequent history, must be that the Freikorps did not produce standards; it only produced men of action for whom sadism was both the means and the end of their existence.

Even more vociferous than its experienced members—those who had actually seen service in the trenches—was the new generation of students which had been too young to serve in the war. The young von Salomon, the young Heinrich Himmler, ached to be given the opportunity to crush the traitors at home, Bolsheviks and Jews, and to teach the Poles a lesson on Germany's eastern frontiers. The ratio of officers to men in the Sturmbataillone had often been as high as one to four, and all over Germany in the years 1918–1921 there appeared young lieutenants and captains who had previously commanded Sturmbataillone and who now formed their own corps, each with its own banner, each member swearing loyalty to its own leader. In the two years or so from the end of World War I, it was well nigh impossible for any self-respecting young middle-class boy in Germany to resist the overtures of the Freikorps. In the summer of 1919 an independent socialist Reichstag deputy, Hugo Haase, asserted that an illegal army of over one million men existed in Germany, though Noske, Minister of Defense, estimated its real strength as closer to 400,000.

The Freikorps anticipated almost everything which was to happen under the general direction of the SS in Europe during World War II. The only difference was one of organization. The SS streamlined and coordinated a series of attitudes to which sporadic expression was given by the Freikorps in Germany, Poland, and the Baltic states between 1918 and 1921. All the hatred, brutality and ruthlessness were there to see twenty years before the mass murders of World War II took place. Himmler and his civil service applied technology and the full weight of the State to prejudices and attitudes which had existed previously.

Among the first of the political murders perpetrated by members of the Freikorps were those of Karl Liebknecht and Rosa Luxemburg, leaders of the German Communist Party. In January 1919 the method of their disposal was to set a pattern which was often to recur during the years of the Third Reich. Having been clubbed by a rifle butt, Liebknecht was driven along the Charlottenburg Highway in Berlin. At a lonely spot the car stopped and his captors asked him if he could walk. He managed to stumble forward for a few paces and was shot "while attempting to escape." An officer of the same unit, in this case the Volunteer Division of the Horse Guards, emptied his pistol into the head of Rosa Luxemburg, whose body was found floating in a Berlin canal some days later. Sometimes summary justice was dispensed in drumhead courts-martial. Naval Captain Ehrhardt's Brigade set up a notorious *Vehmgericht,* a makeshift court based on medieval practice, which assigned to itself the function of murdering a number of "enemies of the nation." Among its victims was Walter Rathenau, who had once written, "I am a German of Jewish descent. My people is the German people, my fatherland is Germany, my religion is that Germanic faith which is above all religions." Rathenau had served his country well. He had been Germany's Albert Speer during the First World War, for as Director of the Raw Material Department he had supervised Germany's war effort. Furthermore, he was a firm supporter of the Freikorps himself, had made personal contributions toward its maintenance and had helped to raise huge sums on its behalf. He was murdered because he had showed his readiness to sit down with foreign statesmen to discuss methods of paying Germany's war debts, and also because he was a Jew.

During the course of the Baltic campaign in 1919 the Freikorps drew the attention of the world to its successful activities against the Latvians and Russians. The British, who had once turned a blind eye to the victories of these irregular German troops in the belief they were saving western Europe from the "red peril," began to fear a rearmed Germany instead. They then gave their support to the Latvians, whose army was now equipped from British arsenals. The British Navy bombarded German Freikorps units from offshore positions. The German volunteers were driven back westward, their government in Berlin having deserted them for fear of antagonizing the allied powers, who watched the rebirth of German arms with increasing vigilance. The volunteers were honed to an hysterical fever pitch. One of them, Friedrich Heinz, wrote: "The soldiers of the Iron Division and the German Legion unloaded all their despair and fury in one wild power-blow against the Letts. Villages burst into flames, prisoners were trampled underfoot. . . . The leaders were powerless, or else they looked on with grim approval." Ernst von Salomon wrote: "We saw red . . . we no longer had anything of human decency in our hearts. . . . Where once peaceful villages stood was now only soot, ashes, and burning embers after we had passed. We kindled a funeral pyre, and more than dead material burned on it—there burned our hopes, our longings, there burned the bourgeois tables, laws, and values of the civilized world. . . . And so we came back swaggering, drunken, laden with plunder. . . ."

All writers, essayists and journalists who participated in the activities of the Freikorps between 1919 and 1921 protest with all the vigor they can command that they are antibourgeois and loathe the defunct standards of the middle class. For it was the middle class, so they claimed, which landed them into the mess from which grew the Weimar Republic, which in turn signed the Versailles Treaty, which stabbed the Fatherland in the back, and which itself was the tool of the Jews.

The strange aspect of all of this is that most of the leaders of the Freikorps came from the middle class, and in a sense what we can witness in their activities and in the subsequent history of the Third Reich is the spectacle of the German middle class indulging in an orgy of self-destruction, almost of devouring itself because of its burning hatred for its own standards. The world was later to see newsreel pictures of Adolf Hitler, illegitimate son of a minor customs official, seated at the table with his cronies, little finger quaintly bent as he sipped his coffee and ate his cream cakes in emulation of those he had possibly seen at Sachers in Vienna in his impoverished youth. All the while his restless mind turned on thoughts of mass destruction.

There is one other aspect of the Freikorps which is so pronounced that it must be mentioned. Many of its leaders were homosexual; indeed homosexuality appears to have been widespread in several volunteer units. Gerhard Rossbach, who founded the Sturmabteilung Rossbach, was an open homosexual. On his staff was Lieutenant Edmund Heines, who was later to become the lover of Captain Ernst Röhm, the same Röhm whose role in organizing paramilitary formations in postwar Germany was crucial.

These thousands of German men who participated in the Freikorps campaigns have been described on at least one occasion as "Bolsheviks of the Right." They streamed into the SA and the SS as soon as these organizations were formed. It would be foolish to ascribe to them any political ideology which they took seriously. It would be wiser to conceive of them as men of action who did not mind what they did as long as it was brutal and aggressive. It is possible to illustrate the historical links between the Freikorps and the SS by taking a number of personal histories. For example:

Friedrich Alpers:	Member, Märcker Freikorps; became SS-Standartenführer (Colonel) 1931.
Benno von Arendt:	Adjutant von der Heyde Freikorps; became SS-Sturmführer (Lieutenant) 1932.
Robert Bergmann	Member Maltzahn Freikorps; became SS-Standartenführer 1932.
Rudolf Beiber	Member Lichtschlag and Düsseldorf Freikorps; became SS-Standartenführer 1932.
Friedrich Eichinger	Member Lutzow Rifles and von Epp Freikorps; became SS-Sturmbannführer (Major).
Werner von Fichte	Member Ehrhardt Brigade; made Inspector of SA and SS in Westphalia 1932.
Karl Fritsch	Member von Epp Freikorps; then Major-General in SS.
Wilhelm Reinhard	Founded Reinhard Freikorps; subsequently became SS Brigadier General.
Karl Wolff	Company Commander in Hesse Freikorps; became SS Brigadier General and later Himmler's adjutant in SS.

The list could be extended to cover hundreds of names. It is by no means difficult to prove that the stamp of the Freikorps was indelibly unprinted on the SS, which inherited from its predecessor the swastika, the German salute, or *Heil!*, the brown shirt, and many other common features. The difficulty is to disentangle the SS from the general SA or Sturmabteilung.

In the months following the end of World War I, Adolf Hitler became the protegé of the German Army. The aristocratic officers of the German General Staff loathed the Republic, but hated Communists even more. They felt beholden to do what they could to maintain order in Germany despite the severe limitations placed on their activities by the Treaty of Versailles. Each Wehrkreis, or Army Area Command, had its political officers, men who were to watch events and lend support to such organizations who were likely to summon popular feeling to the side of right-wing, patriotic political factions. In Munich in 1919 Captain Karl Mayr, head of Press and Propaganda in Army Group 4 (Bavaria) heard Hitler speak. He was impressed. Undoubtedly this explosive orator could be put to use. One way was to keep Mayr informed on such matters as the program and influence of the various political parties which were springing up in Munich at the time. Among them was a party called the Deutsche Arbeiterpartei (DAP), the German Worker's Party. It was small and consisted of a group of nationalistic and intensely anti-Semitic lower-middle-class men. Hitler became member number seven and soon dominated their meetings. He repeatedly visited the War Ministry in Munich to report in person to his chief, Mayr. He did well. By January 1920 the DAP numbered sixty-four members. Hitler had established himself as its most effective orator, was elected Head of Propaganda, and promptly changed the name of the party to the National Socialist German Workers party, the NSDAP.

Mayr then left the scene and his place was taken by Ernst Röhm, who until this time had busily collected weapons and created arms dumps up and down the countryside against the day when the hated Republic could be brought down. But in the summer of 1921 the government in Berlin succumbed to Allied pressure and agreed to disband the various volunteer units which men like Röhm had taken such pains to establish. It appeared for a while as if all Röhm's work had been in vain. What remained were groups of disaffected and disgruntled officers, leftovers from the Freikorps, without unity and with little in common except a general hatred of the Weimar Republic and an inability to readapt themselves to civilian life.

Röhm needed a catalyst to cement these men and give them a common purpose. He found this in the person of Hitler, for he, too, had quickly appreciated the compelling influence Hitler appeared able to exert over his audiences. But Hitler needed protection, Röhm argued, otherwise his enemies might disrupt his meetings. The first squads employed as guards at meetings at which Hitler spoke were provided from the Nineteenth Trench Mortar Company under a Captain Streck. These were renamed the party's "Gymnastic and Sports Section" so as to allay the suspicions of the Allied Control Commission, and finally, when the time appeared ripe to Ernst Röhm, received the name Sturmabteilung (SA), or storm detachment. The SA was officered by men from the old Freikorps, principally from the Ehrhardt Brigade. They reworded their old sailor songs to suit the occasion:

Hakenkreuz am Stahlhelm,	Swastika on our helmets,
Schwarzweissrotes Band,	Black-white-red armband,
Sturmabteilung Hitler	Storm Detachment Hitler
Werden wir genannt.	Is our name.

Yet from the earliest moment, the SA had sown the seeds of its own destruction. Its members did not mind beating people up at political meetings; that, after all, was what life was all about. Their experiences in the Freikorps had taught them that. What they abhorred was politicians, and they drew no fine distinctions. Of course, Reds were beyond the pale, but if a right-wing politician, even an extremely patriotic and nationalistic one, was verbose, they had little patience for him. As Colonel Kriebel, one of their members, said: "The politicians must keep their mouths shut." SA men felt they owed allegiance only to their own leaders.

Hitler felt this in his bones. He needed the SA, for they provided free publicity. They were noisy, they marched about the streets, they drew public attention to him continuously. But if ordered by their officers to shoot him, they would undoubtedly obey. It took Hitler thirteen years to settle accounts with them. This took the form of murdering most of their leaders on the Night of the Long Knives, June 30, 1934. But until then they made him uneasy, and justifiably so. He placed his trusted Hermann Goering at the head of the SA in 1922, but this was not enough for him to sleep peacefully at night. Gradually the idea occurred to him that he needed some counterweight within his organization, some possibly small but totally reliable body which owed allegiance to nobody but Hitler himself. Thus was born the Schutzstaffel. It must forever remain Hitler's personal corps. There must be no Ernst Röhm or Hermann Ehrhardt or ex-Freikorps leaders in the way. Its very motto *Meine Ehre heisst Treue* —Loyalty is my Honor—must mean loyalty to one man: Adolf Hitler. To his close confederates one evening in January 1942 Hitler confided, "I told myself I needed a bodyguard, even a very restricted one, but made up of men who would be enlisted without conditions, even to march against their own brothers, only twenty men to a city (on condition that one could count on them absolutely) rather than a dubious mass." The "dubious mass" to which Hitler referred was of course the SA, among whose leaders were many men who claimed the exclusive allegiance of their troops, a situation totally unpalatable to Hitler.

In March 1923 a few men assembled and swore to protect Hitler with their lives if necessary. They called themselves the Stabswache, or Staff Guard, and they were issued with field-gray overcoats, black ski caps decorated with the silver Death's Head button reminiscent of the Sturmbataillone of the First World War, and armbands with a black-bordered swastika. All these signs distinguished them from the regular SA men.

This bodyguard was short-lived. The leader of the Ehrhardt Brigade, Captain Ehrhardt, whose alliance with Hitler had always been uneasy, broke with him in the spring of that year and withdrew his men from the SA. Hitler then formed the Stosstrupp Adolf Hitler. A photograph exists showing some twenty men in the rear of a converted army truck bearing the license number IM-4425 and carrying a large sign announcing that they are the STOSSTRUPP ADOLF HITLER MUNCHEN. It was taken at the time of the Munich Putsch in the winter of 1923. The fact that they were called a Stosstrupp shows their debt to the Rohr units of World War I and indicates that they considered themselves an elite, ready for any type of action. Who were these men? We know something about them. "Ulrich Graf," writes Hoehne, a historian of the SS, "was a butcher who had made quite a name for himself as an amateur boxer. Emil Maurice, Hitler's bosom companion, was a watchmaker who had been convicted for embezzlement. Christian Weber had been a groom and was now earning a pittance in the Blauer Bock in Munich."

After the failure of Hitler's ill-timed and inept Beer-Hall Putsch of November 1923 the Nazi party entered the doldrums. It was not rescued until some time after Hitler's release from Landsberg prison when his capacity for intrigue enabled him to combine the various right-wing factions that had once been the Nazi party. The court which had tried Hitler and his associates after the attempted putsch had also banned the SA. It preserved its identity by the simple expedient of changing its name to "Frontbann." With Hitler in jail, Röhm arranged a loose assembly of the remnants of the SA and various patriotic associations from all over Germany under the aegis of the Frontbann. When Hitler was released from prison in December 1924 he was far from pleased with what he saw. The energetic Röhm seemed to be going his own way. It was time, Hitler decided, to split with him. He wrote him a farewell note in April 1925 which contained the sentimental phrase "In memory of glorious and difficult days which we have survived together."

It was now Hitler's prime purpose to supplant the SA of which Röhm had been undisputed organizer, with an organization whose exclusive loyalty to himself could not be challenged. In the same month, April 1925, he instructed Julius Schreck—an ex-member of the Stosstrupp Adolf Hitler—to form a new bodyguard, and in the month of May 1925 this became known as the Schutzstaffel, subsequently abbreviated SS.

Schreck's recruiting ground was the Torbräu beer cellar in Munich. This is where the first Stosstrupp Adolf Hitler had been assembled and this is where Schreck applied himself to creating its 1925 counterpart. He soon collected eight trusties largely from the old Stosstrupp. Their uniform was slightly changed. They wore a brown shirt and, more significantly, a black tie. Not for Schreck the fussy pedantry of his successor Himmler. He understood by "elite" a bunch of dedicated roughnecks who asked no questions and did what they were told. You did not need to study Nordic runes to find the right men. They were available in any German city, and in September 1925 he issued Circular 1 to all local party groups urging them to set up Schutzstaffeln. All that was needed, so instructed Schreck, was a leader and ten men. Possibly Berlin by virtue of its size, could have two leaders and twenty men. Entrants had to be healthy, and "habitual drunkards, gossip-mongers, and other delinquents" could not be considered. These standards were liberal compared with those imposed by Himmler in later years.

The years between Schreck's leadership of the SS (1925) and that of Himmler (1929) were difficult for the Nazi party because they coincided with that period of relative economic growth which brought expansion and an apparent return to normalcy to Germany. National Socialism only flourished within general economic bankruptcy. The Party made only hesitant progress until Himmler's arrival, which enabled both it and Himmler to cash in on the advantages of mass unemployment and its concomitant, the "red menace." The story of the SS during these four years is one of ever-changing leadership.

In April 1926 the ex-leader of the Adolf Hitler Stosstrupp returned from Austria, to which he had fled with a host of similar political refugees after the failed Putsch of 1923. His name was Berchtold. He did not last very long. At the Party rally in Weimar in July 1926 Hitler announced that the SS was his elite organization. This it may well have been, but it did not prevent the Führer from considering the position of its leader as a card to play for the repayment of favors. Although Berchtold was appointed in an excess of sentimentality at the reappearance of an "old fighter," the offer of the position to Franz Pfeffer von Salomon represented a totally different strategy. The various Nazi and SA groups in North Germany viewed with mistrust and suspicion the activities of this ex-corporal, who was not even a German citizen. The appointment of Pfeffer, a North German, as head of the SA and SS was Hitler's attempt to enlist the support of non-Bavarian Nazis. It endorsed the view, generally felt, that although SS men might consider themselves a cut above the rank and file of the general SA, they nonetheless toed the line when they received orders from the SA. Pfeffer was given the title of Oberster SA-Führer (Supreme SA Leader) on November 2, 1926. Berchtold was placed firmly under him, but obtained for his wounded pride the title of Reichsführer-SS. Hitler had sacrificed his elite organization for what had seemed at the time a higher purpose: keeping on the right side of the North German Nazi faction. Thus the title of Deputy Reichsführer-SS which Heinrich Himmler acquired in 1927 may be seen in the relatively unimportant light in which Hitler considered it: a small reward for a small man. Many years were to pass before the title would come to mean terror and death.

Berchtold did what he could to preserve the special role assigned to the SS. He stated boldly: "Neither the HQ of the local group nor of the Gau is to interfere in the organizational problems of the local SS," and "The SS is a completely independent organization within the Movement." These injunctions fell on deaf ears. Local party bosses went their own way and SS officials found themselves consigned to backwaters. Berchtold left in a fit of pique and was replaced by Erhard Heiden in March 1927. The SA continued to grow under the leadership of Pfeffer, who resisted any attempt made by Heiden to permit the SS to increase in some parity. Moreover, in Pfeffer's view, in towns where the SA was below strength, the SS had no right to exist at all. It was clear that the high-sounding titles of the SS leadership covered a paucity of purpose and importance, so that to look for a career within it indicated poor judgment.

When Himmler took over his appointment as Deputy Reichs-führer-SS his organization was only allowed to have up to 10 percent of the strength of the SA. In 1928 Himmler was accordingly Deputy National Leader of 280 men. Not a very prepossessing situation. At home in Waldtrudering the chickens were not laying, Marga was nagging, and certainly in his work his chances within the Nazi hierarchy did not look auspicious. Furthermore, a gigantic gap existed between his ivory-tower investigations into racial theory and the daily work he had to offer his men. They delivered propaganda material, sold space in the Nazi paper *Der Völkische Beobachter*—on the whole they were a group of delivery boys. What held them together and why did Himmler not start looking elsewhere, along avenues which offered better prospects?

Partially the SS man was satisfied with the knowledge that he belonged to an elite. As early as September 1, 1927, Heiden had ruled: "The SS will never take part in discussions at meetings. No SS man will smoke during a lecture and nobody will be allowed to leave the room." Himmler had the attitude of the ever-patient frog who will stare at a fly interminably; then suddenly the tongue darts out, and the victim is seized. He was prepared to watch and wait; when the time was ripe his insatiable appetite for further titles and offices would be appeased. On January 6, 1929, Hitler appointed him Reichsführer-SS, and at the relatively tender age of twenty-eight, Heinrich Himmler imposed his strange personality on the SS so that from that moment its entire direction and aims became indistinguishable from Himmler's own life. It is astonishing that an organization which developed into such mammoth proportions should have been directed by a man as anxious, indecisive, and sycophantic toward his Führer as Himmler. It cannot be explained by the usual suggestion of mediocrity rising to the surface. It seems that in addition to all the negative, small-clerk qualities Himmler possessed, he had an unquenchable thirst for extra appointments and a fine nose for discerning where and when to be present when these offices were likely to fall vacant. An equally difficult question to answer is how he managed to control men who were undeniably his superiors in their capacity for intrigue or intelligence and who shared with him an overwhelming ambition for self-advancement. How did he control these lions?

In some strange way Himmler had established himself as the true fount of orthodoxy within the SS. The SS has often aptly been compared with a religious order, and it is known that Himmler had studied and was greatly impressed with the Jesuits. He saw life in terms of membership in conflicting orders. Thus Freemasons could not be tolerated because they were an order whose purposes conflicted with those of the State. Similarly Himmler was quite certain that the Jews were involved in a world struggle to assert evil over good. He accepted willingly the idea that they had an organization to assist them in this task. Himmler's own Order, that of the SS, must therefore assume the role of the seat of the true orthodoxy. As its Grand Master, Himmler must be the final arbiter of what was and what was not consonant with the purposes of the Nazi state.

His loyalty to his Führer was beyond question. He would stand to attention and click his heels when answering the telephone from Hitler's alpine residence at Berchtesgaden. At the end of a telephone call from his Führer, he would return to his guests flushed and transported. Anybody therefore who courted the idea of replacing "Loyal

Heinrich," as Hitler called him, had to act with profound circumspection. He might be unseating the Grand Master who alone appeared to know the special mission of the SS, and in doing so would undoubtedly have to reckon with the wrath of Hitler. After the events of June 30, 1934, the Night of the Long Knives, this was a course of action which anybody with some concern for saving his own skin might daydream about but would never translate into action. For this reason, Heydrich, potentially Himmler's most dangerous rival, treated him with respect and concern, in total contrast to his normally unpleasant manner. Lina Heydrich might make jokes in private about Marga Himmler (she used to remark that the latter wore size fifty knickers), but these were for the exclusive delectation of her husband and a few intimate guests, and her husband would ask her to behave with more caution afterward.

From January 1929 until April 1934 Himmler occupied an office at Party headquarters in Munich. When he moved to Berlin in April 1934 he had spent rather more than five years in intrigue, currying for favor in the right quarters, jockeying for position with his rivals, and gradually establishing the basis of his own empire. The story of how he achieved this starting with a small force of 280 men and ending with total command of the police forces of the entire Reich testifies to his considerable gifts at intrigue. The story is concurrent with the demise of the Weimar Republic, the end of a federal Germany, and of the establishment of Hitler's dictatorship.

He was given a small room in the Brown House in Munich in January 1929. He spent his first weeks examining files. By April he had drawn up a report in which he summarized the special elitist functions of the SS within the Nazi movement. He envisaged a vast program of expansion. He submitted his report to Hitler and to Pfeffer, who was still his superior. Pfeffer, who considered Himmler a crank, probably threw it into the nearest wastepaper basket. Himmler's ideas were all out of proportion to the force he controlled, and anyway he was difficult to take seriously. The theories about blood and soil with which Himmler would lard his conversation with other Nazi dignitaries had earned him the reputation of a pedantic nonentity. Certainly he was not one to be taken seriously. Anyone who had the misfortune to find himself sequestered with Himmler for more than fifteen minutes was almost inevitably treated to a lecture on the benefits of herbal treatment and the need for proper racial selection, among various other bizarre theories.

If Himmler was cold-shouldered, he was in no way deterred. Like any other patient schoolmaster he could only do his best to instruct his pupils, and if they proved wayward, all he could do was persevere in the hope that his message would sink in sooner or later.

As long as the number of entrants into the SS did not become suspiciously large, Pfeffer would leave Himmler alone. So in the selection of applicants, Himmler was later to say, "We went about it like a nursery gardener trying to reproduce a good old strain which has been adulterated and debased; we started from the principles of plant selection and then proceeded to weed out the men whom we did not think we could use. . . . I started with a minimum height requirement of five feet eight inches; I knew that men of a certain height must somewhere possess the blood I desired."

But Himmler's appointment coincided with the economic collapse of the Depression, and his office was inundated with applications for membership of the SS. One year after taking office he was able to report to Ernst Röhm, "The SS is growing and by the end of this quarter should have reached two thousand." This in no way endeared him to Pfeffer whose SA men were beginning to show a noisy aversion to their opposite numbers in the SS. In 1930 Himmler won a considerable battle for his organization. His SS men were given a new uniform to distinguish them further from the SA. Gone was the brown. They now wore a black cap, black tie, black-bordered armband, and black breeches. Moreover, the internal structure of the SS was revised. It was now authorized to supplant the small 10-man units by "Stürme" of 70 to 120 men. Black had triumphed over brown, and all was due to the pertinacity of Heinrich Himmler, crank though his opponents may have considered him to be. Orders continued to emerge from the Führer's pen, presumably in response to the urgings of Loyal Heinrich. The SA was instructed to contribute men to the SS, but only "selected personnel" need apply: applicants who satisfied Himmler's genetic prerequisites. This enraged the SA, but Hitler was anxious to form his praetorian guard and ignored the sensibilities of his SA commanders. The SA was an unruly mob and Hitler knew one day he would need to settle accounts. At this stage the system of groupings and titles was created which was to remain a permanent feature of the SS until its demise:

UNIT	TITLE OF LEADER	
Schar: 8 men	Scharführer	(Corporal)
3 Scharen (1 Trupp): 20–60 men	Truppenführer	(Sergeant)
3 Trupps (1 Sturm): 70–120 men	Sturmführer	(Captain)
3 Stürme (1 Sturmbann): 250–600 men	Sturmbannführer	(Major)
3 to 4 Sturmbanne (1 Standarte): 1–3,000 men	Standartenführer	(Colonel)
1 Untergruppe (several Standarten)	Oberführer	(Brigadier)
1 Gruppe (several Untergruppen)	Gruppenführer	(Lt. General)

"The task of the SS," Hitler's order of November 7, 1930, proclaimed, "is primarily to carry out police duties within the Party."

This historic statement was delivered by Hitler at a time when he felt, with considerable justification, that his security as leader within the Nazi movement was very questionable. The leading contestor was Gregor Strasser, Himmler's old employer, who took far more seriously than Hitler the word *Socialist* which formed part of the title of the Party. He envisaged a form of corporate state, generally along fascist lines. But Hitler had never been a socialist and certainly did not want to alienate certain prominent industrialists who had been giving financial assistance to his organization. His security was further threatened by the menacing increase in size and importance of the SA brownshirts, that unruly mob, who felt that they were not receiving sufficient recognition from their wayward leader. Hitler was therefore surrounded with potential pockets of power which could unseat him and this undoubtedly added to his paranoia. The SS was to make sure that nobody interfered with his own destiny as he saw it. That strange conglomerate called the Nazi party contained a vast range of attitudes and convictions. At one stage Goebbels actually proposed that "that petit-bourgeois Adolf Hitler should be expelled from the Party," while Gregor Strasser pressed for an understanding with the Soviet Union. These were dangerous signs for Hitler, for he had accumulated a large amount of goodwill from the German middle class and from the German Establishment by preaching the crusade against Bolshevism. Here was one of the most prominent Nazi Reichstag deputies advocating overtures to Moscow, the seat of what was believed to be the international conspiracy of the Left. Somebody had to bring these disparate elements into line. This was Hitler's notion of the function of the SS.

The world economic crisis produced a wave of unemployment, and vast numbers of Germans became dependent on public charity. The ranks of the SA began to swell and by 1930 achieved a membership of 100,000. In Berlin, Hitler's influence was at its weakest. In South Germany his fortunes were controlled by such faithful followers as Himmler, but in the north, where the Party had its most radical supporters, his position was tenuous. The leader of the Berlin SA, an ex-Freikorps man and sanitary engineer named Kurt Daluege, had distinguished himself as a ruthless and brutal organizer. Hitler decided he would prove a useful ally and should be weaned away from the SA into the SS. This was achieved in 1929. But although Daluege was nominally responsible to Himmler, he considered that he need only consider orders which originated from Hitler. Daluege's brief was to keep watch on potentially dangerous circles within the SA and report to Hitler. He and his staff of particularly reliable SS men had much to tell. A great many SA men who had streamed into the movement from the working classes thought Hitler was betraying them. He was, after all, flirting with the ultraconservatives of the Deutsch-National party in his maneuvers to enter the government and destroy the Weimar Republic from within. The typical SA man could not be expected to understand the niceties of the political game his Führer was playing. It was also becoming abundantly clear that Hitler was negotiating with precisely those circles of industrialists and aristocrats which the SA was most anxious to unseat. They demanded an explanation of his activities and when this was not forthcoming sent a deputation to Munich to confront Hitler and the Party bosses. It was a difficult moment for the Führer, as it happened shortly before the Reichstag elections of September 1930. Nonetheless he refused to see the deputation. When the list of Nazi candidates was published it was clear that the radical element had been excluded. In late August many Berlin SA commanders handed in their resignations, and their followers refused to assist the Party in the campaign. It was even more damaging when Goebbels as Gauleiter of Berlin, organized a mass meeting in the famous Sportpalast, the Berlin SA withdrew in a body and the meeting was left to the mercy of anti-Nazi hecklers. The time had arrived for Daluege's SS men to restore order. They were poorly rewarded for their efforts. Those of them who maintained guard outside Goebbels's Headquarters were beaten by enraged SA men. Open warfare now existed between the SA and SS.

What was Hitler to do? An agitated Goebbels made his way to Munich to give his Führer a report on the impossibility of maintaining order in Berlin. The Party appeared to be split down the middle.

Hitler's first step was to dismiss Pfeffer. He had outlived his usefulness. Was there nobody around who could pull the dissidents together and present some semblance of unity to the nation? There was no point in sending Himmler, as he would be torn to pieces by that unruly mob. Then Hitler had an inspiration. What about Ernst Röhm? If anybody could be relied on to retrieve the situation it surely must be the old Stabschef to whom the SA after all owed its very existence. Röhm had spent several years on a German military mission in Bolivia. But his parting words to Hitler had been: "You have only to give me the word, 'Be at the Siegestor at 6:00 A.M. on such and such a day with your men, and I shall be there.'" Hitler recalled Röhm. But even he was unable to contain the hysterical anti-Hitler mood within the rank and file of the SA. In April 1931 the SS again entered battle with the SA in answer to the threat that a large SA faction under Stennes no longer accepted orders from the Führer. The Stennes "Putsch," as it came to be called, ran out of steam when the SA minions were cut off from their supply of funds. Their coffers emptied and Hitler was able to announce his undisputed hegemony over the Party, much to the annoyance of other political factions in Germany who had been assured of a Nazi party torn by fratricide.

Hitler announced that he had overcome the threat of a Stennes revolt because of the loyalty of his SS. From that moment the SS became the mainspring of Hitler's security system. At an SS leaders' conference on June 13, 1931, Himmler was able to declare: "Our Führer knows the value of the SS. We are his favorite and most valuable organization because we have never let him down."

There is jubilation in these words. But Himmler was not happy at so far a remove from the scene of activity. Bavaria, where he reigned, was a long way from Berlin. He must extend his power to Prussia and the whole of Germany if his special mission were to be fulfilled. For the moment, however, he satisfied himself with providing Hitler with intelligence reports that reached him from all over the Reich— most were concerned with the state of the Party and the activities of the SA.

Himmler's first action was to draw a smokescreen over the work of the SS. This was totally consonant with his Führer's picture of a political situation in which he was surrounded by enemies. Nobody outside the SS was permitted to discover what the SS was doing. In March 1931 Daluege, as head of the Berlin SS, issued the order: "Even in the face of unjustified criticism, SS men and SS commanders are strictly forbidden to converse with SA men and commanders or with civilian members of the Party. . . . Should criticism be leveled, SS members will leave immediately and silently commenting only that the SS carries out Adolf Hitler's orders." This was music to Hitler's ears. Himmler added fuel to the fire by reporting the world Bolshevik conspiracy to be everywhere. In June 1931 he wrote to his SS leaders, "Our enemies' efforts to bolshevize Germany are increasing. Our information and intelligence service must aim to discover and suppress our Jewish and Freemason enemies." In October 1931 he reported: "In certain towns the Communist party has attempted to infiltrate some of its men as spies into SS formations."

During the summer of 1931 the SS enjoyed the services of a new recruit, a man named Reinhard Heydrich, who had been dishonorably discharged from the Navy. He soon showed himself to have a special aptitude for intelligence work, came to collaborate with Himmler in Munich, and finally helped him set up the SD—Sicherheitsdienst, or Security Service of the SS. Himmler and Heydrich had the same sort of background. Both were of the middle class, their fathers schoolteachers. But this is where the similarity ended. Heydrich had a lightning intelligence whereas Himmler's was plodding and methodical. Heydrich was a particularly athletic man, a fine violinist, an expert fencer and skier, blond and tall. He was given the rank of Sturmführer (Captain) and he and Himmler amassed a vast amount of information on Hitler's enemies, both real and imaginary. The Führer was so impressed that he entrusted members of the SS with the mission of ensuring his personal safety. In January 1932 Himmler became head of security at the Brown House in Munich. Therefore menacing SS guards would be seen at each Nazi meeting and outside each Party building.

The increasing status and importance of the SS was undoubtedly aided by public knowledge of the fact that the SA, under its leader Ernst Röhm, was administered to a large extent by homosexuals. An elaborate pimping service had been developed to satisfy the appetites of Röhm and his cohorts and some of the details leaked to the non-Nazi press. As relations between the SA and SS deteriorated, many Germans began to look upon the SS as guardians of national morals.

Nonetheless, despite his increasing favor with the Führer, Himmler did not consider himself anywhere near the top of the ladder. Events in Berlin appeared to constitute the real pacesetter, and in Berlin Daluege was in charge of the SS. When on January 30, 1933, the Nazis emerged as the largest single party in the nation and Hitler was finally installed as head of a new cabinet as Reich Chancellor, Himmler was not offered a ministerial position. It is very probable that this was due to the fact that he did not push himself forward to the same extent as the other men who had risen to prominence within the movement, such as Goebbels, Goering, and Frick, who were rewarded with high office. Himmler was, and remained, a colorless sycophant, industrious and loyal, but of little presence. In March 1933 in his native Bavaria, it was Franz Ritter von Epp who was appointed as state governor, a title to which Himmler must assuredly have aspired. All he got out of the reshuffle in Bavaria was the rank of "Acting Police President" of Munich. Other men would have rebelled, or remonstrated with the Führer. Not Heinrich Himmler.

Even more disconcerting for Himmler was the chain of events in Berlin. Goering had become Minister-President of Prussia and was only too ready to collaborate with Daluege, who ran the Berlin SS.

He detested Himmler, whose primness and servility were anathema to him. Daluege, no mean conspirator in the battle for power, soon showed how low in the scale of life he considered his nominal superior, Reichsführer-SS Heinrich Himmler, to be. Something had to be done. Down in Munich Himmler had urgent talks with Heydrich. The question as to who ran the SS had to be settled. Daluege must be brought to heel. How should this be achieved? Heydrich had meanwhile been promoted to Standartenführer (Colonel). In full regalia he was sent to Berlin for a confrontation with Daluege, who of course as Gruppenführer (Lieutenant General) outranked him. Himmler instructed his trusty Heydrich to set up an information service to keep him informed on Daluege's movements and activities. The SS had begun to spy on itself.

Once in Berlin, Heydrich told his wife, Lina, who was pregnant at the time, to rent a house in the West End. He then presented himself at Daluege's headquarters and waited for admission in an outer office, only to be told that Daluege was unable to see him. Heydrich made repeated visits but was rebuffed on each occasion. He then had to decide whether to stay on in Berlin and complete the second part of his brief—that is, to keep watch on Daluege—or to return to Munich and inform Himmler of the position. He chose to return.

There is of course no record of the conversation which took place between "Reichsheini," as Himmler had come to be called ("Heini" is a nickname for Heinrich) and Heydrich on the latter's return to Munich. An intelligent guess is that they jointly decided that they must install themselves with all despatch in Berlin, bring the dissident Daluege to heel and assume command of all the police and security forces in the Reich.

3

THE TRIUMPH OF
BLACK OVER BROWN

The bitter thoughts which dogged Reinhard Heydrich when he returned to Munich in the Spring of 1933 after his insulting treatment at the hands of Daluege, reflected far more than wounded pride. In a larger sense they presaged a series of events which were to effect radical political changes in the years to come.

National Socialism was a philosophy of action. It did not provide its supporters with a constitution or an intelligible set of political guidelines after the assumption of power. Its theoreticians, the Führer himself in *Mein Kampf* and Arthur Rosenberg in his *Myth of the Twentieth Century,* had bequeathed verbose and largely unreadable tracts to whoever had the patience to read them. They were hardly a plan for action. The only knowledge the followers of national socialism had was loudly announced by propaganda chief Josef Goebbels in 1928 during an election campaign: "We join the democratic process in order to destroy it." You did not need to be a prophet to discern from Nazi literature Hitler's intention to extend the German empire to the east, but you would look in vain for any concrete formulas for political organization which might form the basis of a new state.

The Nazis inherited the detritus of the Weimar Republic. Its constitution had been framed by men who considered they had designed the most flexible instrument of government ever conceived. It was a model of legal provisions designed to protect the democratic process. Unfortunately at any one time there were up to thirty different political parties. In consequence its governments, though almost continuously led by members of the Social Democratic party during its short life, were coalitions, which foundered one after the other. Social unrest at home, inflation, mass unemployment, the payment of huge reparations, all played their part in bringing about the demise of Weimar, despite the lofty intentions of its founders.

The only certain knowledge any government had was that it inherited that most valuable asset, the Prussian Civil Service, a body of men who were supposedly selfless in their dedication to the State, a tradition born under Frederick the Great and enhanced by the work of reformers in the nineteenth century. They stayed at their posts after the Nazi *Machtergreifung,* the seizure of power, in January 1933.

They were a thorn in the side of aspiring Nazis. These old men with their legalistic minds would not always do what they were told by Hitler's brownshirted leaders. Instead of adopting the slogan "If you can't beat 'em, join 'em," the Nazi leaders pursued a different tactic: "If you can't beat 'em, form your own ministries."

In the years between 1933 and 1939, therefore, a series of parallel organizations was set up in Germany alongside the old ministries. Neurath might continue in the Foreign Office, but Ribbentrop founded his own bureau. Local and regional police forces might continue to function, but the Nazis had created their Gestapo and SS as counterweights. With the passage of time the old ministries atrophied and the new departments created by the Nazis flourished. But this was not the end of the problem. Nobody had told Nazi leaders what they should do. It was left to the personal power aspirations of each man to impose his special stamp on his ministry and then to watch carefully among his opponents in case they attempted to encroach on what he considered his special preserve. Thus, a series of separate empires was established. Jealousy between the new leaders was rife. They adopted the policy of following the dictum "When in trouble, run to Adolf." Hitler's rooms at the Reich Chancellory were besieged with visits from his old warriors who sought his signature on documents testifying that such and such a province of activity was the exclusive preserve of the latest claimant. Each man's success or failure to achieve these signatures was determined by his current standing with the Führer. This was a difficult thing to gauge. Hitler was a whimsical man. He would sign in quick succession documents which were often in direct contradiction to each other. Furthermore, he believed most profoundly in sowing confusion among the ranks and juggling with his supporters to ensure that none of these separate empires within the Nazi State would ever constitute a threat to his leadership. When Dr. Todt died, Speer, Goering, and Himmler all appeared at the Obersalzburg to claim their inheritance from the Todt empire, which, concerned as it was with the construction of the Autobahnen and employing as it did millions of foreign laborers, would provide very useful pickings for them.

It was a difficult game to play and demanded at times a delicate touch and at other times a heavy hand. To play it, you not only had to watch the activities of the old civil service, you had to have your spies firmly planted in the offices of your Nazi opponents. Some were more adept at the game than others; possibly none so successful as Heinrich Himmler. If you had been one of the older members of the Reichstag—indeed even if you had enjoyed high office under the Weimar Republic and had engaged for tactical reasons in periods of flirtation with the Nazi movement—you were continuously outmaneuvered. If your name was Franz von Papen and you had held such offices as Chancellor and Vice Chancellor, you were in a constant state of amazement at the trickery and skullduggery which went on around you. This was because the game of power within the Nazi State had no rules; at least certainly none which you might understand if you had been raised with a respect, however nominal, for the Rule of the Law. It was a pragmatic and day-by-day affair. You would start your day by making certain you were still in favor with your whimsical Führer. Woe betide you if you made the mistake of sending a deputy up to the Obersalzburg to present your case to Hitler. He loved new faces and would confer far-reaching powers on whoever happened to be at hand. The trusted subordinate you sent up to see him might return as your boss. And you must never discuss money matters with Hitler. He had no patience for them. If you had plans which involved digging deep into the public purse, you must find your own ways to achieve this. The thing to do was insert some innocuous sentence in whichever document you placed before Hitler authorizing you to lay your hands on vast sums, and hope that his roving and restless mind would not detect this stratagem.

Within this strange and demanding situation, the duo of Himmler and Heydrich decided to capitalize on their assets. In 1933 they had made little headway in Berlin. But Hitler trusted them implicitly. Even the worst paranoiac must have somebody to trust, and in Hitler's case it was his SS. This was in fact their only asset, and until the time became ripe for further expansion they could do nothing but consolidate their standing with their Führer.

One certain device to get Hitler to place even more responsibility on the SS was to draw his attention at every opportunity to the existence of plots, whether real or imaginary, to assassinate him. Hitler was only too ready to give credence to any story which suggested that his life was imperiled. At Cabinet sessions he would ask, for example, what had happened to various quantities of high explosives which had been reported as missing. In March 1933 the Cabinet minutes report Hitler as saying: "During recent years 150 tons of explosive have been stolen, of which only 15 tons have so far been recovered."

Where were these explosives stolen from? Were they from industrial sites, from Army depots, or could they have been taken from one of the various arms dumps which Ernst Röhm had accumulated for his SA? Himmler added fuel to this fire. In that same year he arrested Valley, the assassin of Eisner, on the grounds that he had "planned a coup against the Reich Chancellor on his own admission." Agents of Soviet Russia were also lurking at every street corner, claimed Himmler. At the end of March he proclaimed: "Three Soviet agents placed hand grenades near the Richard Wagner statue where Adolf Hitler's car was certain to pass." Each time Hitler entered or left the Chancellory, he looked suspiciously at the guards, for these were provided by the Reichswehr, the Army. Who could tell whether or not the Army was not part of the plot to do away with him? Surely these guards should be replaced by his trusty SS. Himmler was only too ready to agree. SS-Gruppenführer Sepp Dietrich was instructed to organize a Headquarters Guard. In September 1933 at the Nuremberg Party rally, Hitler christened this new unit of 120 men "Leibstandarte Adolf Hitler"—the Adolf Hitler Bodyguard.

Sepp Dietrich was in Berlin guarding the Chancellory, but Himmler was still in Munich, his influence restricted to Bavaria. He began to cast about the other German *Länder,* or states, to see if he could extend the influence of his SS in them. In the summer of 1933 he installed Politische Bereitschaften—Political Emergency Units—in the state of Württemberg to assist the local police in controlling anti-Nazi factions. The ripe plum of Berlin and Prussia was not ready for the picking; there he was outranked and outgeneraled by Goering, Goebbels, and Daluege. In Bavaria itself, however, his position became unassailable. On April 1, 1933, he assumed the office of Political Police Commander. Since only a fortnight earlier he had been Acting Police President of Munich, it can be seen how effective Himmler's measures had been in securing rewards from a grateful Führer. He addressed himself methodically and cold-bloodedly to the task of routing out all pockets of resistance to the Nazi movement. North of Munich was a collection of old stone huts at a place called Dachau. Here Himmler built the first concentration camp; a prison in which communists and social democrats were incarcerated. Every aspect of the organization of this camp was controlled with bureaucratic efficiency. Forms appeared in triplicate, statistics were carefully maintained, and the ruthless machinery of the police state began to emerge. Himmler, the clerk *par excellence,* had begun to put his stamp on the character of the Third Reich. Police colleagues from the other *Länder* looked with astonished approval at their Bavarian

counterpart. The would-be schoolmaster in Munich received acco-
lades from his fellow bureaucrats. He ran a well-oiled machine, kept
countless orderly files, and maintained an apparatus of informers and
agents which proved the envy of most of them. Lest any among them
were in any doubt as to Himmler's final aim, he informed them, "I
want to found a real Reich police force from these sixteen separate
Länder forces. A national police force is the strongest lynch pin a state
can have." In the state of Hesse he found a useful ally in the person
of Dr. Werner Pest, who led the Police Section in the Hesse State
Ministry and who expressed himself ready to assist in forming a national police force.

To get into Berlin and Prussia, Himmler had to come to terms
with Goering. This was far from easy. Goering considered him a
pedantic upstart. Furthermore, he himself wanted to run a Reich
police force, and as Minister-President of Prussia, a state which covered more than half the area of the Reich, he had a much more
effective launching pad than Himmler. He also founded the Geheime
Staatspolizei, Secret State Police, or Gestapo, and made it answerable
only to him. In comparison, Himmler's activities in the south were
modest. But Goering's anti-communism was not given sufficient rein
by the Gestapo he had founded and the Prussian police he had inherited. To do an effective job he claimed to need more men, and he
determined to use the Berlin SA as an auxiliary force. Here he
unleashed forces that even he was unable to control. The Berlin SA,
containing as it did the most brutal and discontented men in Germany, began a reign of terror which exceeded that of the early 1920s.
They founded their own prisons in disused buildings, constructed
makeshift concentration camps, and terrorized the populace. Their
victims were not only Jews and Communists, but anybody who represented the vestiges of middle-class order. Stories of savagery in Berlin
and all over Prussia gained wide currency. Goering had lost control.
In the Cabinet, in answer to the protestations of men like von Papen,
even Hitler, possibly in a show of histrionic talent, thumped his fist
on the table and promised to put an end to the *Schweinereien* (ob-
scenities) perpetrated by his SA squads.

Goering's failure to keep his SA auxiliary force under control was
the real reason behind Himmler's eventual entry into Berlin. Not that
Hitler was particularly upset by the behavior of the SA in their exercise of terror. What was far more insupportable was the existence of
rumors that the SA leaders, and in particular Ernst Röhm, had ambitions of merging with the Army. The SA men, enraged at Hitler's apparent role of negotiator with the old conservatives of Weimar,

looked to Röhm rather than Hitler as overlord in the new Germany.

If the police forces in the different states were to be centralized under one aegis, it was clear that only one organization was ready to arrange it. When Wilhelm Frick, Minister of the Interior, drew up a memorandum reorganizing the entire police system of Germany, it was to Himmler as head of the SS that he turned, undoubtedly with Hitler's knowledge and approval. Between November 1933 and January 1934 Himmler assumed leadership of the police in one state after another. This defederalization, which took the form of Frick's "Law for the Reconstruction of the Reich" and was submitted to a passive Reichstag in January 1934, really put the legal seal on events which had already taken place. As far as the German police forces were concerned, the only ones not under Himmler's control were those of Prussia and Schaumburg-Lippe. The Reichstag was passive since Hitler had used the simple expedient of placing his parliamentary opponents in prison.

Goering was far from happy at this turn of events, but his alliance with the brownshirted mobs of the SA, however temporary, had emasculated his ability to negotiate. Some four million SA men continued to march all over Germany terrorizing local populations. It was in Goering's better interests to give up the battle for leadership of a national police force. On April 10, 1934, Himmler became head of the Gestapo with Heydrich as his immediate deputy.

His first function was to deal with the SA, and in his view this meant asserting the superiority of the black of the SS over the brown of the SA.

The sequence of events terminating in what has come to be called The Night of the Long Knives mirrors most effectively the disintegration of the Weimar Republic. The ostensible victim was the SA under its leader Ernst Röhm. He now controlled a military force of rather more than four million men, officered by ex-soldiers, most of whom had done service in the Freikorps. It was public knowledge that Röhm's design was to emerge as head of a newly constituted national army, one which would be imbued with the zest of the Nazi movement. Röhm had even independently entered into secret talks with the military attaché of the French embassy to sound out their opinion of his plans. In all of his dealings Röhm considered himself to be a patriotic and profoundly convinced Nazi and at no time did he ever question his final allegiance to Hitler. This faith was hardly reciprocated by the Führer, who saw in Röhm the greatest potential challenge to his leadership. For his pains Röhm also incurred the wrath and suspicion of the leadership of the Army, ever anxious to continue in its exclusive role as guardian of the Reich's forces. The older generals, reared in the demanding traditions of the Prussian General Staff, looked on his machinations with increasing hostility. One among them, von Reichenau, did in fact negotiate with Röhm and earned himself the reputation of being a Nazi as a result. Reichenau's main motive, though he was passionately right-wing himself, was to bargain with the devil in order to destroy him. After the event, the Army was only too ready to congratulate the SS for the surgery it undertook to rid the General Staff of its main competitor.

At first Himmler was far from happy to enter a conspiracy which had as its end the murder of Ernst Röhm. It was Röhm who had introduced the young Himmler into the movement in the early days. Himmler had always respected the swashbuckling captain whom he had stood beside during the abortive Munich Putsch of 1923. But Heydrich was not deflected in his pursuit of power, by such sentimentality, despite the fact that Röhm and Himmler had been joint godfathers to his child. It was not long before Heydrich had persuaded his vacillating superior that his better interests lay in aligning himself and the entire SS and SD within the anti-Röhm camp. Once he had so committed himself, Himmler became as uncompromising as Heydrich.

Hermann Goering also possessed a fine nose for determining which way the wind was blowing. He brought all the weight of his authority as Minister-President of Prussia on the side of the conspirators and held his Prussian police unit "General Goering" in readiness.

It was now the job of Himmler and Heydrich to accelerate the course of events. They pretended to unearth plot and counterplot. They "discovered" arms dumps, and where they could find no "evidence" of a projected coup d'état by Röhm and the SA, they invented it. Goering stood ever ready at Hitler's side to authenticate this "evidence" and even to enlarge on it.

Within this situation Hitler behaved in a curiously ambivalent fashion. At one moment he would claim to disbelieve that his SA was guilty of such intransigence. At another he would rage against the army of traitors with which he appeared to be surrounded. He was accustomed to playing one Party faction against another. His paranoia deeply entrenched, he knew his enemies were legion. Persistent rumors and the thinness of the "evidence" provided by Himmler did not lessen his sense of impending disaster. He knew that action was needed but until the final moment appeared uncertain of the form that action should take.

While the Führer bent with the wind, Himmler, Heydrich, and

Goering spent their time making lists of those who must be assassinated. The criminality of the Freikorps of 1920 found its counterpart in the list-making of 1934. The idea of trials for the accused or of any of the paraphernalia of the due process of law would again be abandoned. The difference between 1920 and 1934 was that in 1934 the forces of the State itself were to take the initiative and act as marauders. This was a vital distinction. The inhuman act was to be perpetrated by the State itself. The forces of authority, so firmly entrenched in the German national consciousness, were to be mobilized in acts of uncontrolled fury.

The lists which the leading personalities in the conspiracy drew up, were movable affairs. Names would be added, then crossed out. The surgeon-in-chief was Heydrich. As far as he was concerned, everybody in the Army, the government, the SA, or in intellectual life who in any way had expressed resentment was a potential rival in the SS's bid for power. Therefore they had to be eliminated. For Heydrich only one instrument was suitable: the scalpel; and he prepared himself for its indiscriminate use.

The excitement gathered momentum during the month of June 1934. In the final week of that month Hitler attended the wedding of an old Party member, Terboven, in Essen. The conspirators were delighted to see their indecisive Führer leave Berlin. "I had the feeling," said Viktor Lutze, Röhm's opponent within the SA, "that it suited certain circles to aggravate and accelerate the affair just at this moment when the Führer was absent from Berlin and could therefore neither see nor hear things for himself, but was dependent upon the telephone."

Lutze was right. While Hitler attended the wedding reception in Essen he was called to the telephone. Himmler was on the line from Berlin. He startled Hitler with massive verbal "evidence" of an SA putsch in the offing. Goering only waited for Hitler to replace the receiver to add the weight of his knowledge to Hitler's heightened suspicions. A visitor then entered Hitler's hotel suite. It was Paul Koerner, Goering's secretary at the Prussian State Ministry. He had additional news. There could be no doubt that the SA was on the brink of revolt. Hitler had wavered long enough. His problem now was to find some ruse to assemble his SA leaders at a point where they could be murdered. During the evening of June 28 he placed a call to Röhm, then holidaying at Bad Wiessee in Bavaria. He instructed Röhm to summon all SA leaders to Bad Wiessee for a meeting with their Führer at 11:00 A.M. on June 30.

So innocent was Röhm of Hitler's real intentions that he did not read the writing on the wall. His conscience was clear, he had served Hitler well and faithfully. He spent June 29 taking long walks with his aide-de-camp. One by one, the old guard of the Nazi party now enjoying high rank in the SA arrived at the Pension Hanselbauer at Bad Wiessee where they were greeted by their Chief of Staff, Röhm.

Sepp Dietrich, commander of the SS Leibstandarte Adolf Hitler, was then given his orders. He must assemble Leibstandarte units near to Bad Wiessee using the utmost discretion, and then await further orders.

Two further messages reached Hitler at that state. Both were untrue but they did achieve the desired effect of producing a state of frenzy in him. Himmler telephoned again on June 29 and confirmed that the SA's putsch preparations were completed and they planned to take over all government buildings the following day. The second message came from Wagner, Gauleiter of Bavaria. The SA in Munich, he said, were massing in the streets to demonstrate against the Führer and the Army.

At 2:00 A.M. on June 30, 1934, Hitler, ashen with rage and fatigue, climbed into a Junker at Bonn airport and left for Munich. Two escort cars took the Führer and his party from Munich to Bad Wiessee. Their occupants stormed into the Pension Hanselbauer, where all were fast asleep. Hitler himself woke up Röhm, called him a traitor, and announced that he was under arrest. Röhm vigorously denied all accusations. One by one the other rooms were entered. The captured SA leaders were assembled and transported to Stadelheim prison while SS units searched Munich for other members of the mythical putsch. Meanwhile Hitler made his way to Party headquarters in Munich and instructed Goebbels to proceed with the "action" in Berlin. This was the moment for which Himmler and Heydrich had been waiting. Out came the lists and throughout the entire Reich began that series of murders for which the Night of the Long Knives became notorious.

In Munich Sepp Dietrich was personally instructed by Hitler to make his way to Stadelheim prison, "select an officer and six men and have the SA leaders shot for high treason." The list of these leaders was handed to Dietrich by Martin Bormann. It was 6:00 P.M. before Dietrich reported to Stadelheim. The prison governor believed in protocol. He studied the list and told Sepp Dietrich that it had not been signed. He refused to release the prisoners until the document had been graced with this "proof" of authenticity. So Dietrich returned to the Brown House. There he found Gauleiter Wagner, who in addition occupied the post of Bavarian Minister of the Interior.

Wagner obligingly wrote at the foot of the list: "By command of the Führer, the men whom SS-Gruppenführer Dietrich indicates are to be handed over to him."

In the courtyard of Stadelheim prison, an SS officer read out to each SA leader the following message: "The Führer and Reich Chancellor has condemned you to death. The sentence will be carried out forthwith." Only Röhm was excluded; his turn was still to come.

Meanwhile in Berlin, Himmler, Heydrich, and Goering had embarked with all haste on their bloody exercise. Hauptsturmführer Kurt Gildisch of the Leibstandarte was summoned to Heydrich's office and received the following staccato message from his superior, a message which Heydrich was to repeat with nauseating regularity in his curiously high-pitched voice throughout the course of that day: "Putsch by Röhm. State of emergency. Order from the Führer. Immediate action." Heydrich called men of Gildisch's squad, backed by Gestapo officials and members of the SD, one by one into his room and gave them their assignments, all of which were accepted without demur. Trucks and police vehicles thundered through the streets of Berlin, the SA headquarters were cordoned off, the series of murders was under way. Initially Himmler stationed himself in the offices of the Minister President of Prussia, Goering. When von Papen, at the time Vice-Chancellor, therefore a senior member of Hitler's Cabinet, arrived, he barged into Goering's office and demanded to know why he had not been apprised of the course of events. While he was so occupied, three members of his staff at the Vice Chancellory were shot.

WIR MISTEN AUS! So had run one of the Nazi party slogans pasted up on the streets of Berlin during an earlier election campaign. This slogan is a somewhat crude way of indicating that the Nazis were intent on cleaning out the public stable and removing from it all the filth which had accumulated there. No better way of translating this slogan into practice could have been devised. Most of the prominent men in public life throughout the Reich were to be the victims of Himmler's assassins in one of the bloodiest actions in history. General Kurt von Schleicher, inveterate Reichswehr schemer and one-time Chancellor, was shot at his desk. His wife, who threw herself across his body in an attempt to save him, suffered the same fate. Major General von Bredow, a high official of the Reichswehr Ministry, was shot through the head. Gregor Strasser was shot from behind a few hours after he had been released from a Gestapo prison. As the startling news filtered through to the sacred precincts of the Reichswehr Ministry, it might be expected that the old officers would rise and attempt to contain the murders which numbered so many of their own colleagues among its victims. This was not the case. Von Rei-chenau, a firm believer in radical action to cleanse the state of its more questionable servants, did not find it abhorrent if certain members of his caste were killed without trial. "In word and in deed," ran his communiqué issued on the afternoon of July 1, 1934, "von Schleicher has acted against the State and its leaders. When police officers came to arrest him he offered armed resistance. There was an exchange of shots as a result of which both he and his wife, who placed herself in the line of fire, were mortally wounded."

Once furnished with their orders issued by Heydrich, Himmler, and Goering, the SS units ran riot. Old scores were settled, personal battles resolved. It was impossible to keep track of the murders. Until this very day nobody knows exactly how many people met their deaths during the forty-eight hours which started at 6:00 A.M. on June 30, 1934. Hitler, in a later address to the Reichstag, admitted a total of 79. Other estimates have been as high as 600.

Goering, who liked to present himself from time to time as the symbol of moderation and conviviality, realized as the day progressed that matters were getting out of hand. The SS had run wild. He had to stop them before the entire Reich was taken over by these amoral protegés of Himmler and Heydrich. As von Papen left his Ministry he heard Bodenschatz, Goering's aide-de-camp, shouting: "We'll see who is in command here, Minister President Goering or the SS!" Goering started to cross out names on the lists which had come into his hands. But his caution was short-lived. When Hitler flew in from Munich, where he had left Sepp Dietrich in charge of an extermi-nation squad, he seemed singularly anxious not to do away with Ernst Röhm, and he continued to save Röhm from the executioner's bullet. His motives for this are obscure. Possibly that tortuous mind, during the flight from Munich, had exercised itself with the picture of Goering and Himmler acquiring too much power as the result of the recent killings. It is even possible that somewhere in that dark soul there lurked a vestige of sentimentality toward the Chief of Staff of the SA. In any event, to Goering's and Himmler's repeated inquiries as to whether Röhm was dead, Hitler continued to shake his head. This was a situation which they found intolerable. If their actions were to have any justification they had to adhere to their story that they had prevented a Putsch organized by Röhm. How could they murder everybody else and leave the arch-conspirator Röhm free? It would make nonsense of the devious work in which they had been engaged for months.

For many hours Hitler would not be moved. He adopted a reflective, statesmanlike pose and to those around him he even assumed the role of moderator, doing his best to control the wayward spirits of Goering and Himmler. True, he had personally ordered the massacre of a handful of SA leaders in Munich, but he could claim that events in Berlin and Prussia were the work of Goering and Himmler. For these events they could shoulder the responsibility, while Hitler might watch them with grudging disapproval.

When they had finally persuaded Hitler that Röhm must die, the Führer insisted that he be given the option of committing suicide. If Röhm selected this course of action it would add substance to an eventual claim that he had killed himself because of his intention to conduct a Putsch, an intention which the Gestapo had unearthed.

SS-Brigadeführer Theodor Eicke was instructed to perform this delicate task. He reported with two other SS officers outside Röhm's cell at Stadelheim. The door was opened. Röhm sat there sweating heavily, stripped to the waist. Eicke said, "You have forfeited your life. The Führer gives you one more chance to draw the conclusions." He gave Röhm a loaded pistol, closed the door, and waited outside. Ten minutes passed, fifteen, but still no sound of a shot was heard. Eicke reopened the door and shouted, "Stabschef, get ready!" Two shots were then fired by one of the SS officers and Röhm's last words as he slumped to the floor, were, *"Mein Führer, mein Führer!"*

Eicke telephoned Berlin to announce the success of his mission. Thereupon the murders were resumed. At the Columbia House in Berlin, one of the largest SS prisons, the shooting continued into July 2. According to SA-Gruppenführer Schreyer it only stopped during the morning of July 2 and just in time to prevent his own assassination. As he was being led from his cell toward the execution block an officer of the Leibstandarte rushed in and shouted, "Stop! It's all over. The Führer has given his word to Hindenburg that the shooting is finally over."

The shooting did in fact die down. But how were the nauseating actions of the previous three days received in Germany?

In the barracks of the Army, high-ranking officers raised their glasses to the success of the operation. Major General von Witzleben even expressed regret that he had not personally witnessed the scenes of execution. The Minister of Defense, General Werner von Blomberg, committed himself to print and in an order of the day stressed that "the Führer had attacked and crushed the traitors and murderers with exemplary courage and soldierly decision." There were of course those who viewed the events with profound misgivings. But in the main Germany breathed a sigh of relief. It looked as if the radical, threatening, and disorderly mob of men who constituted the Sturm-abteilung had now been removed. Of course the most desperate measures had been undertaken to effect this removal, but possibly this was the end of violence. Even Count von Stauffenberg, the one man who came nearest to killing Hitler in the plot of July 20, 1944, considered the Night of the Long Knives as "the lancing of a boil." The general feeling was relief that finally order had been reestablished throughout the Reich and people could now address themselves to normal pursuits. The Cabinet, headed by Hitler, placed its legal seal on a law drafted by the Chancellor and Führer which stated tersely and unequivocally, "The measures taken on 30 June, 1 and 2 July to suppress treasonable activities are legally considered to have been taken in emergency defense of the State." The German people could eagerly grasp the implications of Hitler's statement that "in this hour I was the supreme judge of the German people." Was it not clear that if you had a rotten tooth in your mouth its extraction often proved painful?

The German people were to pay dearly for this shortsightedness. The real victors of the Night of the Long Knives were the SS. Army officers might clink champagne glasses in the belief that they had finally overcome the threatened incursions of the SA. What they did not realize was that their claim to be the exclusive armed force in the Reich was now to be challenged by a far more ruthless, methodical, and efficient organization than the SA. They now had Himmler and Heydrich to contend with, whose SS had entrenched itself most firmly in the favor of their Führer. They were to be his executive arm, and in the pursuit of what they interpreted as his wishes they were totally merciless. Eighteen days after the killing had stopped, on July 20, 1934, Hitler announced, "In view of the great services rendered by the SS, particularly in connection with the events of 30 June, I hereby promote the SS to the status of independent organization within the framework of the party."

Little more than a year had passed since Heydrich had been spurned by the powers in Berlin. He and Himmler were soon to show how they interpreted the Führer's decree. The SA was now publicly accepted as a group of potential criminals. But they did not lie down quietly, and as a result of pressure some of the old Nazi SA members managed to exert on Hitler they were permitted, in August 1934, to clean their own stable. A special SA court was established with the function of hunting down so-called accomplices of Röhm who had not been trapped in the net of events earlier in that fateful summer. The Führer issued an order on August 9, 1934, instructing this Court to consider "all circumstances by which SA leaders have rendered themselves unworthy of membership of the SA Leaders Corps, such as life style, immorality, materialism, embezzlement, drunkenness, and debauchery."

In fact the activities of this Court turned on a different issue. As testimonies were gathered, its inspectors found themselves inundated with a series of splenetic outbursts about the actions of the SS during the June/July murders. Some older SA men, ever obedient toward higher authority, did their best to accept their now subservient role to their SS masters. One reported plaintively, "I issued strict instructions to my men to comply with the orders of the SS. . . . The treatment of the older SA men by the SS, many of whom were *mere boys,* was shattering. . . ."

This is an interesting comment. If many SS men were mere boys, it shows that the old guard which had seen service on the front in the First World War and within the subsequent Freikorps was being gradually replaced by a new generation. This new generation, which had not known battle, received its standards and its ethos from the weird schoolmasterly quasi ideology of Himmler. The future belonged to them. They were now entirely clothed in black. They wore a black cap and chinstrap with the silver Death's Head insignia. Over a brown shirt was a black jacket. A black tie, black belt, black breeches, and black jackboots completed the picture.

Black had finally triumphed over brown.

4

THE OCCUPATION
OF GERMANY

Historians normally use the word *occupation* to signify the coercive administration of one country by another. In the case of Germany in the years immediately following the Nazi seizure of power in January 1933, while the apparatus of the police state existed and became more and more firmly entrenched, a kind of voluntary occupation took place. The only opposition of any substance to the extension of Nazi power came from its victims: Jews, left-wing political parties, and to a lesser extent the Protestant and Catholic churches.

Although the Nazis had established what was called a political party, they liked to describe their organization as a movement. "Make Way, You Old Ones!" ran the title of an article written by Gregor Strasser in the 1920s, and in his book *Hitlerjugend* (Hitler Youth), Baldur von Schirach, leader of the Hitler Youth, had proclaimed: "The Nazi Party is the Party of Youth." Youth movements of the most disparate kinds had existed in Germany for many years before World War I and had considered themselves as representing the vanguard of a national revival. While the other political parties were encumbered with a past which associated them indissolubly with the failure of the Weimar Republic, the Nazis had no such encumbrances. They were new and vigorous and employed new techniques. If a generation gap existed in Germany in the 1930s it was effectively mobilized as an instrument of propaganda by Goebbels, who saw in youth the most tenacious embodiment of radicalism within the nation. Other parties might cling to the outmoded standards of a defunct bourgeoisie, but Baldur von Schirach announced: "Faust, the Ninth Symphony, and the will of Adolf Hitler are eternal youth and know neither time nor transience."

If the Nazis represented novelty, dynamism, get-up-and-go, what did the other parties have to offer? Only the cumbersome machinery of the democratic process of Weimar, defeat and humiliation in the war, the burden of reparations payments, and mass unemployment.

For a youngster in the 1930s there was only one possible choice, and this in a physical sense, for once the Communist party had been outlawed, no other party which could lay claim to any form of radicalism which might engage their support was permitted to exist.

It was in the universities themselves that the Nazis gained their strongest hold. As early as 1931 Nazi support in the universities was twice as strong as in the country as a whole, and in an appeal to the electorate on March 3, 1933, no less than three hundred university professors declared themselves in favor of Hitler. In November of the same year the famous surgeon Sauerbruch and the philosopher Heidegger publicly demanded an "understanding attitude" toward Hitler's policies. They may have been bewitched by the propaganda techniques of the present, but they were undoubtedly aided by the work of scholars of the past. Since the days of the Napoleonic invasion of Germany, successive generations of German historians, poets, and thinkers had implored a somewhat passive nation to assert its historic role in Europe, its *Sendung,* or mission.

Where support did not exist for them, the Nazis installed their own professors. The most macabre warning of what was really taking place occurred when some 20,000 books written by "un-German" writers were publicly burned to the accompaniment of torchlight processions and military music played by the bands of the SA and SS. This book burning presaged a return to medieval standards. Wilhelm Frick, Minister of the Interior, proclaimed, "An end must be put once and for all to the spirit of subversion which has gnawed for long enough at Germany's heart." It was not appreciated at the time that the road from burning books to burning people was a relatively short one.

Curiously enough the lowly status of women as breeders and homemakers in the Third Reich in no way impaired their enthusiasm for the new movement. At newsreel pictures of Hitler's birthday celebrations, at Nuremberg Party Day rallies, women were present in the thousands, many of them weeping at this divine proximity to their Führer. It has frequently been maintained that Hitler's public speaking offered him a vicarious sense of potency that he was unable to realize in his sexual life. If the tears, fainting fits, and joyful response he evoked in women as he whipped himself onward to rhetorical climax are studied, they reveal the probable authenticity of this analysis. In any event, women appeared only too ready to abandon any civic rights, any feeling of equality they might have entertained, in favor of the specific and exclusive roles the Nazis had assigned to them. They were to produce children and run a tidy home, and as

Heinrich Himmler himself once said, "Who will ever ask in three or five hundred years' time whether a Fräulein Müller or Schulze was unhappy?" Julius Streicher, notorious Jew-baiter of the regime, appealed to German women; "Never become ladies! Remain German girls and women!" By this Streicher was waging war on the use of cosmetics and the adoption of "airs and graces" by women, a form of petit-bourgeois puritanism in which many of the Nazi leaders indulged.

More culpable, because they were ostensibly less susceptible to propaganda tricks, were the conservative elements in Germany, from industry, banking, and the Army. A typical parade in the early days after the Nazi accession in January 1933 would inevitably contain representatives from these reactionary circles. In the group surrounding the Führer were the top-hatted figures from the Ruhr and the resplendently uniformed generals. They gave Hitler the respect and authority he so desperately needed in the early years of his rule. They endorsed his every step. Government by decree, the dissolution of the trade unions, the disappearance of freedom of speech and assembly, their passive acceptance or actual endorsement of the crimes committed on the Night of the Long Knives, were of enormous assistance to him. They committed all these blunders in the belief that it was still possible to harness the power they had helped to unleash, but they were continuously outmaneuvered by Hitler. In many respects their aims were not dissimilar to those of the Nazis. The generals were only too ready to lend support to a movement which aimed at expanding the Army; the industrialists could see nothing wrong in the removal of the troublesome trade unions. Of course you had to pay a price. Jews were beaten up and there was a large element of rowdyism within the Nazi movement which conservative snobbery could only abhor. But on the whole these excesses would be removed; Hitler, so they thought, would simmer down.

There were three major legal steps taken to endorse Hitler's construction of an authoritarian State. The first occurred on February 28, 1933, and was a direct result of the burning of the Reichstag. On the evening of February 27 a red glow could be seen over the rooftops of Berlin. Someone had set the Reichstag on fire. It is now generally accepted that this was engineered by a squad of SA men who had entered the German parliament via underground tunnels which connected it to the presidential palace of Goering. But at the time the entire apparatus of the Nazi machine was invoked to hurl abuse at the Communists who had, so they claimed, emerged in their true colors as destroyers of the Republic. On the day after the fire, the aged President Hindenburg was prevailed upon to sign a decree "For the Protection of the People and the State" designed as a "defensive measure against Communist acts of violence endangering the State." The decree stated: "Restrictions on personal liberty, on the right of free expression of opinion, including freedom of the press, on the rights of assembly and association; and violations of the privacy of postal, telegraphic, and telephonic communications; and warrants for house searches, orders for confiscations as well as restrictions on property, are also permissible beyond the legal limits otherwise prescribed." This body punch at the Weimar constitution suspended all of its provisions for individual and civil liberties.

The second act of the Nazis was the promulgation of the "Law for the Removal of Distress of People and Reich" on March 23, 1933. Hitler needed a two-thirds majority to make this effective. By incarcerating all Communist deputies in prison he was able to push it through the Reichstag which had assembled at the Kroll Opera House. For four years this law removed from the Reichstag almost all of its powers and transferred them to the Cabinet. The Reichstag was now thoroughly emasculated. Only one deputy rose to protest at this measure, Otto Wells, leader of the Social Democrats. He spoke quietly and convincingly, announcing that the government might rob the Social Democrats of their power, but their honor was untarnished. In his reply, Hitler screamed, "You are no longer needed! The star of Germany will rise and yours will sink! I do not want your votes!"

Finally, one year after taking office, on January 30, 1934, Hitler celebrated the anniversary by issuing a "Law for the Reconstruction of the Reich." All the sovereign powers of the separate German *Länder* were transferred to the central government and the state governors placed under the administration of the Ministry of the Interior, headed by Wilhelm Frick. It is a piece of historical irony that Adolf Hitler was able to achieve what even Bismarck and Wilhelm II had been unable to effect, namely the centralization of Germany under one administrative edifice. Germany was now no longer federal.

To set the final seal on this sequence of events, a law was passed which stated tersely, "The NSDAP is the only political party in Germany. Whoever undertakes to maintain the organizational structure of another political party or to form a new political party will be punished with penal servitude up to three years or with imprisonment of from six months to three years, if the deed is not subject to greater penalty according to other regulations."

It will be clear that this tumultuous reversal of German political and civic life placed an enormous strain on the entire apparatus of the new state. And none were to bear this strain with more initiative or enthusiasm than the SS. The form this initiative took reflected the differing personalities of the two leaders of the SS, Himmler and Heydrich. Heydrich was a man animated solely by cruelty. His subordinates often referred to him as "the blond beast," and Hitler in his speech at Heydrich's funeral, called him "the man with the iron heart." Heydrich reached his decisions with lightning determination, in direct contrast to the plodding pedantry of Himmler. It was Heydrich's belief that the SS man should receive his military training with live ammunition and that any SS officer candidate should be able to place a hand grenade on his helmet, remove the pin, and stand to attention while the bomb exploded. A particularly adept fencer himself, his entire career in many ways mirrors the actions of a high-speed fencing match, with rapid exchange of thrust and counterthrust. At whatever he turned to, Heydrich found it necessary to excel. In many ways he succeeded. A man of this type would obviously never accept the position of number two to Himmler, and it is not too far-fetched to claim that he considered himself Hitler's logical successor.

Why was it, then, that in the battle for power, Heydrich always appeared to defer to Himmler? And why was it that whenever he was seen together with Himmler he adopted the formal pose of a subordinate who knew his place?

The answer which has obtained the widest currency is that Himmler "had something" on Heydrich. This "something" was the knowledge that Heydrich had a Jewish ancestor. Should he not toe the Himmler line, so the argument ran, Himmler would publish the true facts about Heydrich's background. Heydrich himself had endeavored to destroy all the evidence which pointed to the fact that his maternal grandmother was Jewish. Nonetheless he was forced to take legal action against various individuals on the grounds that they were slandering him. The effect of all this, so the theory continues, was that Heydrich became a split personality. On the one hand he was extremely ambitious, cruel, and vain. On the other he was driven by self-hatred—induced by the knowledge that his blood was "impure." In exterminating Jews, therefore, Heydrich was eradicating from himself that aspect of his makeup which he found most repellent. This theory has been embellished by one memoir which recounts how, at the end of an evening spent at the Berlin nightclubs he frequented with his anxious subordinates, Heydrich returned home, caught a glimpse of himself in the bathroom mirror, and actually shot his own image.

As an attempt to offer a general theory for the behavior of Heydrich during his years of power, this notion is decidedly suspect and threadbare. If he was a schizophrenic, he must have been one before he joined the Party or bothered to examine his ancestry in such minute detail. Yet Himmler was convinced that Heydrich suffered great anguish at having had a maternal grandmother who was Jewish. To his masseur, Felix Kersten, Himmler confided, "He suffered constantly; he never really found peace. Something was always upsetting him. Often I have tried to talk to him and help him, even against my own convictions, pointing out the possibility of overcoming Jewish elements by the admixture of better German blood, citing himself as a case in point. He was often very grateful to me for such help . . . but nothing was any use in the long run." This cordial picture of Himmler as benevolent psychotherapist might go some way to explaining Heydrich's relations with Himmler, but as an explanation of Heydrich the man, more convincing evidence must be produced.

If we are looking for causes for his behavior, we might more profitably turn to the fact that he was dishonorably discharged from the Navy. He had volunteered for General Maercker's Freikorps at the age of sixteen, in 1920, and two years later had only one aim, to enter the Navy and become an officer. A voracious womanizer, Heydrich later caused the daughter of a director of the massive German industrial complex I. G. Farben to become pregnant, but refused to marry her. He had already turned his attentions elsewhere—to Lina von Osten, whom he was eventually to marry.

The father of the pregnant girl had high connections in the Navy. Heydrich was summoned to appear before a Naval Court of Honor to give an account of himself. His demeanor before his superior officers was offensive. He could not—so he maintained—marry the girl, because any girl who gave herself to a man before marriage was obviously not somebody a German naval officer could marry. This inverted logic infuriated the President of the Court, Admiral Raeder, who thereupon ordered Heydrich to be cashiered. Heydrich thus found himself at the age of twenty-seven excluded from that band of ultraconservative naval officers whose company and status he so desperately craved. He became one among the millions of unemployed. It was his wife, Lina, whose ambitions almost matched his own, who arranged an introduction for Himmler and who thereby was responsible for the start of Heydrich's career as the police technologist in chief of the Nazi State.

Once in the saddle, Heydrich whipped himself along at breakneck speed. As long as he stood high in the opinion of Himmler he was in a safe position, for Himmler enjoyed a special position at Hitler's Court. Heydrich did not seek notoriety. He might inspire the anxiety of his fellow SS officers, but he hardly ever allowed his picture to appear in the pages of *Das Schwarze Korps,* the magazine of the SS. Only rarely is there reference to him there. Let Himmler continue to make his pedestrian pronouncements in that ill-organized and crudely written periodical. All that Himmler could find to say in the issue of January 7, 1937, in an editorial comment was: "The year 1937 will be the first year of the national police force of Adolf Hitler. One of its greatest tasks will be the solution of the problem of the unnecessary loss of German life through road accidents. . . ." More and more Himmler seemed set on the pursuit of odd studies, Nordic runes, Germanic ancestry; more and more did he address himself with pedantic satisfaction to the examination of the Freemasons.

For such ideological claptrap Heydrich had no time. While the Reichsführer-SS occupied himself in this fashion, Heydrich introduced *Schutzhaft,* protective custody. While previous police forces had confined themselves to the examination of crimes and the pursuit of the guilty, Heydrich formulated a new concept in police procedure. The thing to do was to prevent crimes from happening at all. *Schutzhaft* was the device which would achieve this. All police units were requested to submit to him a list of known and "potential" criminals, and names of known and "potential" enemies of the regime. These vague categories covered anybody the local Gestapo and SD agents might capriciously decide ought to be included. They were liberally provided with search and arrest warrants which came into eight categories:

1. Arrest
2. Arrest, if no fixed address
3. Report place of residence
4. For deportation
5. Search for missing persons
6. Recover lost papers
7. Unobtrusive observation
8. Professional criminal—arrest

Nobody in Germany was safe from Heydrich's agents. Neither did these agents have to account to anybody other than Heydrich for their actions. Furthermore, possibly guided by the reading of detective fiction, of which he was inordinately fond, Heydrich ordered that at any meeting which he attended only two people were to be present, namely himself and one other.

While Heydrich extended the police empire of the SS within Germany, with the connivance and blessing of his superior Himmler, the Reichsführer-SS was busy in other areas. He issued an invitation to a number of industrialists, landowners, and scholars to meet him personally and listen to an address he intended to make. His speech was well attended. He informed his audience that no State could function without an elite, that in National Socialist Germany that elite would be provided by the SS. Obviously, to fulfill its mission, the SS required as members the best elements in society, "genuine military tradition, the bearing and breeding of the German nobility, and the creative efficiency of the industrialist, always on the basis of racial selection." The speech was an open invitation to all present to join the SS. According to a later report, the result was general astonishment. This did not, however, prevent the overwhelming majority of those attending from seizing the opportunity of becoming members of that select body which was subsequently called Freunde des Reichsführer-SS—Friends of the Reichsführer-SS. Nothing titillates the sensibilities of men more than the knowledge that they are entitled by birth, social standing, or individual achievement to constitute an elite. Himmler's concept paid a very handsome dividend. Entry into what had been considered as an exclusive Order now became available to those men in Germany who considered themselves members of the governing class. What was more, they could wear a uniform, and in the Germany of the 1930s a man who did not possess a uniform definitely felt out of things. Blue-blooded aristocrats could now be seen in SS regalia: the Grand Duke of Mecklenburg, Prince zu Waldeck und Pyrmont, Prince Christof and Prince Wilhelm of Hesse, Count Bassewitz-Behr, Count von der Schulenberg, and Prince von Hohenzollern-Emden.

From German industry and commerce the new recruits included Dr. Heinrich Buetefisch of I. G. Farben, Hans Waltz, a director of Robert Bosch, Friedrich Flick and representatives of the Deutsche Bank, Norddeutscher-Lloyd and Hamburg-Amerika shipping lines, the Dresdner Bank, the Dr. Oetker food company, Siemens-Schuckert and Mitteldeutsche Stahlwerke. Many of them considered membership in the circle of Friends of the Reichsführer-SS as a means of protecting themselves from the encroachments of the State in economic affairs. It was not long before they were advised that moneys should be made available "for the cultural, social, and charitable activities of the SS." An account was opened at the J. H. Stein

Bank into which money poured and was then transferred to the SS coffers at the Dresdner Bank.

For those who paled at the thought of donning the Death's Head uniform of the SS, an indirect avenue of membership was opened, for they could become *Fördernde Mitglieder,* or sponsoring members, and could demonstrate their support of the SS by making financial contributions. Each SS unit or Standarte had its own "FM" organization and each SS man was expected to act as recruiting agent. By the end of 1934 there were almost 350,000 sponsoring members.

By entering the marketplace in this fashion, Himmler could no longer control selection of candidates effectively. Old SS men would complain that some of the industrialists were ex-Freemasons and that an overwhelming number of people associated with the SS had not the slightest understanding of what National Socialism was all about. This was a problem which the purist Himmler could not properly resolve throughout his reign. The larger his organization became, the more difficult it was to screen applicants properly. But he urgently needed the money and social "face" of his new recruits, and in this area he allowed a degree of opportunism to determine his activity.

The SS now addressed itself to the German nation as a whole. For the small-minded, bigoted types the magazine *Das Schwarze Korps* presented the worst features of yellow journalism. For example, an issue of February 1937 contained a double-page spread showing pictures of blacks at a dance hall in Harlem dancing the "Lindy Lou." Accompanying captions referred to the obscene and bestial nature of this dance and also asserted that in the home of the great American democracy these blacks would need only to leave the dance hall and walk round the corner to be lynched. While the petit-bourgeois prudes of the countryside and suburbs could regale themselves with this intelligence, the leaders of Germany from industry, commerce, and the rural aristocracy could be comforted in the knowledge that they had joined an elite organization, an Order, for which their breeding and attainments had qualified them.

The years between the accession of the Nazis (1933) and the outbreak of the Second World War (1939) also saw the entry into the SS of that sinister breed, the SS intellectuals. Typical of this class was Otto Ohlendorf, an economist who had for some years been trying to induce one university after another to include the study of the political ideology of fascism in their curriculum. These efforts were blocked by succeeding professors who failed to see the benefits of incorporating this new technique of study into the standard courses of the social sciences. He entered the SD, the Security Service, where for a time he tried to bring his expertise as an economist into play. His superiors had little time for this rather gifted pedant, and he ended up running a type of information service. He assigned to himself the task of testing the mood of the country rather in the manner of what were later to become political surveys. His motives were always in keeping with those of the intelligence service in general, namely to assess public reaction to police and propaganda techniques and to unearth those suspected of not endorsing all aspects of the new policies. Unfortunately for Ohlendorf, who in some respects was incredibly naive, his intelligence reports often had the effect of enraging men high up in the Nazi hierarchy. It was possible, for example, by discreet questioning, to ascertain exactly how effective Goebbel's propaganda methods were up and down the country, as the war progressed. Sometimes the results were very poor indeed, and Ohlendorf, firmly convinced that he was acting with probity and efficiency, would draw attention to this fact in his reports, which gained wide circulation in the various ministries. Goebbels's opponents in the rival satrapies were delighted, and gloated at the adverse publicity their rival had earned. But Goebbels himself was furious, and applied pressure via Hitler and Himmler to put a stop to Ohlendorf's work. To add to his craving for experience, Ohlendorf sought action with the Einsatzgruppen, the extermination squads of the SS, later on in the war. When tried at Nuremberg War Crimes Tribunal, and accused of having personally killed 150,000 people, he interrupted the prosecutor to contest this figure and to announce that in fact the figure was several hundred higher. This is probably the best example of Ohlendorf's amorality. It never occurred to him that human beings were the victims of SS tyranny. He was blinded by that characteristically Teutonic drive which considers that as long as a document was franked by an official stamp and bore a signature it was blessed with that authority which was its only prerequisite.

The vast encroachments of the State into every province of German life required a gigantic civil service. This need could by no means be met by new recruits among Nazi supporters. Accordingly large numbers of civil servants who had enjoyed a career under the republican governments of Weimar were transferred to the new departments and reconstituted ministries. The Gestapo was not manned by a new breed. It took over large numbers of officials who had previously been on the payroll of the criminal police. There were of course some who entertained misgivings about the new methods being employed, but the overwhelming majority continued to execute their functions with that attitude of blind obedience so assiduously fostered by Himmler. The idea of service to the State, so firmly entrenched in German history, remained paramount and robbed them of any initiative they might have displayed by arguing about the legality of the orders they received.

Where such questions were asked the answer was speedily supplied by new forms and new official stamps to allay their suspicions. The crudity of Heydrich's use of protective custody even provoked the Minister of the Interior, Frick, to write on January 30, 1935, "I have drawn attention to the comparatively large number of persons in protective custody in Bavaria; I have had no satisfactory explanation from the Bavarian Political Police, nor have I seen signs of any serious effort to reduce the number of prisoners. . . . I cannot allow such a situation to pass without comment. . . ." Himmler had no time for such encroachments on his territory and contented himself with the laconic comment: "The prisoners will remain."

Many officials from various ministries would remonstrate orally and in writing with Himmler about the barbaric events occurring in the concentration camps as a result of pressure they themselves were under each time they attended a State function. Wherever they went, they were besieged by foreign statesmen and foreign journalists who pestered them with stories which were gaining wide currency about the cruelty of concentration camp life.

Within the camps themselves the Jews constituted by far the greatest number of inmates. This was Hitler's method of venting his pathological spleen on them. His reading of that notorious forgery, *The Protocols of the Elders of Zion,* which was a spurious attempt to demonstrate that the Jews were conducting a conspiracy to dominate the world, had left no doubt in his mind that they must be eliminated. And he had no time for that sporadic outburst of localized anti-Semitism which is called a "pogrom." While still in the employ of the German Army, in 1919 in Munich he wrote a letter to a certain Gemlich which contained the following statement: "Anti-Semitism for purely emotional reasons will find its final expression in the form of pogroms. The anti-Semitism of reason, however, must lead to the systematic combatting and elimination of Jewish privileges. Its ultimate goal must implacably be the total removal of the Jews." The necessary consequence of "rational" anti-Semitism was the establishment of the slaughterhouses of Auschwitz and Treblinka. Here it was no longer a matter of spontaneous outbursts against the Jews, but a technologically sound implementation of the plan to wipe them out entirely. A new breed of obedient "idealists" like Himmler and Hoess, who was later to be commandant of Auschwitz, was needed to put the plan into operation.

Hitler's passionate involvement with the mythical Jewish world conspiracy had one other curious result. In a conversation with Hermann Rauschning reported in a volume called *Hitler Speaks,* the following exchange took place:

Hitler: I have read *The Protocols of the Elders of Zion.* It simply appalled me. The stealthiness of the enemy and his ubiquity! *I saw at once that we must copy it*—in our own way, of course. It is in truth the critical battle for the fate of the world.

Rauschning: Don't you think you are attributing rather too much importance to the Jews?

Hitler: No, no, no! It is impossible to exaggerate the formidable quality of the Jew as enemy.

Rauschning: But the *Protocols* are a manifest forgery. . . . It is evident to me that they can't possibly be genuine.

Hitler: Why not?

The most telling phrase in this exchange was Hitler's determination to copy the "stealthiness and ubiquity of the enemy." The instrument of this was of course to be the SS, and in order to fulfil its historic task *it* must be ubiquitous. To achieve this the SS became a huge overlapping and unwieldy institution. To stress the need for the SS to combat anti-Germanic elements in society, even that gifted string puller Heydrich, who infinitely preferred to operate behind the scenes, emerged early in 1935 to address himself to the world at large: "The enemy motive forces will always be the same: world Jewry, world Freemasonry, and the clergy." These were visible enemies, but there were an infinite number of undercover enemies "who work outside the law. Their objective is the destruction of the unity of our leadership, in Party and State. . . . The ramifications of this network are enormous." From this picture of conspiracy and counterconspiracy which was the Nazis' paranoid version of world history, the SS attempted to build up its various formations and give them appropriate assignments. This was not achieved without difficulty; however, the difficulty did not result from any obstacles which might have been imposed by a twentieth-century State with a respect for the Rule of Law, but rather emerged from competition among those within the SS itself. They were all greedy to acquire additional offices.

What did the public prosecutors make of this astonishing situation? How was it possible that the activities within the various concentration camps could be effectively screened from them? Those who still retained a certain probity would continuously nag at Himmler to produce evidence for the incarceration of so many people without trial. One of the more persistent was Walter Steppe, a senior State Attorney. Himmler decided the most suitable course of action was to make an ally out of this irritating man with his insistence on legal formalities. He persuaded Steppe to join the SS, arguing that from within it Steppe would surely be in a better position to assess the situation. Only one year later Steppe became Deputy Head of the Political Police.

So effective was the SS use of cajolery and threat that the German judges themselves abandoned their posts. On May 2, 1935, the Administrative High Court of Prussia ruled that the actions of the Gestapo could not be contested in the administrative courts. In other words, if you had some grievance against the Gestapo, your only course of action was to register a "disciplinary complaint" with the Head of the Gestapo. The SS became answerable only to the SS. "In the National Socialist State," it was ruled by the Hamburg Administrative Court on October 7, 1935, "the Legislature, the Administration, and the Judiciary cannot be legally opposed . . . the Judiciary cannot therefore invoke another point of view and disavow action by the State taken as a political measure."

This is tantamount to saying that if you had a relative who had been shot in a concentration camp, you might lodge a complaint with the Political Police, but this action would be as meaningless as if you had complained verbally to the SS man who had actually pulled the trigger. He acted in the interests of the State, and since he represented the Law, his actions were beyond criticism. "Provided the police are carrying out the will of the Leadership, they are acting legally," said Dr. Werner Best, legal expert of the SS, a man most adept at surrounding inverted logic with legal smokescreens.

The huge apparatus of the SS by 1937 showed signs of weakening itself through internal strife. Although firmly in the hands of Himmler and Heydrich, at the secondary level of leadership there were the rumblings of internecine battle. Heydrich decided it was high time to define the relative functions of the different departments. The SD (Security Service) and the Gestapo (Secret State Police) began to look like mirrors of each other. It was possible that the entire edifice might disintegrate because of an internal war between disaffected functionaries. On July 1, 1937, Heydrich put his thoughts on paper. "There must be no rivalry," he asserted. "Neither is senior or junior to the other; they are mutually complementary. Duplication of work must be avoided." This was easy to say, but difficult to put into practice. He allocated Marxism, treason, and emigrés to the Gestapo. The SD was responsible for science, Germanism and folklore, art, education, Party and State, constitution and administration, Freemasonry and religious sects.

Even to the warped minds of Nazi-oriented officials this was far from clear. What about the Jews? Who was to get them? Heydrich declared that the SD was to deal with "general and basic questions" and the Gestapo would attend to "all individual cases in which secret police measures enter into consideration."

This gobbledegook was an endemic feature of SS organization. Heydrich's obscurantism would only allay their suspicions for a few minutes while they attempted to decipher all his verbal acrobatics. One thing appeared clear to the bright young intellectuals of the SD: the Gestapo was getting all the action and the SD seemed to be consigned to work in the field of ideology. This was unacceptable to them. The Gestapo, after all, was manned mainly by erstwhile police officials like "Gestapo Mueller," who had been in his time a Bavarian separatist, had made disparaging remarks about the Führer himself, and who had no time for National Socialist ideology. It was clear, so argued the SD men, that only officials fully imbued with the ideological spirit of National Socialism could be entrusted with the overriding aim of establishing the Germanic state on earth. But the SD remained thwarted in its goal of infiltrating and gradually taking over the functions of the Gestapo. It therefore hunted about for new areas of activity. One immediately suggested itself: foreign espionage. Here it might run afoul of the Abwehrdienst, the Army counterintelligence service, but that was something it took in its stride. Its enthusiasm was not matched by any particular skill. It managed to unearth, in clumsy fashion, a secret radio station near Prague which regularly transmitted broadcasts against the regime to Germany and was led by an old enemy of Hitler named Otto Strasser. It established an intelligence network in Palestine whose purpose was to foment the already existing antagonism between Arab and Jew.

It did not become possible to allocate functions properly, but Himmler and Heydrich decided the whole machine must be brought under one umbrella. Step by step they worked toward this goal. On September 27, 1939, an organization emerged with the unwieldy title of Reichssicherheitshauptamt—Reich Main Security Office. It was a monolith of gigantic proportions. It was so top-secret that it was forbidden to use its name on its letterhead. The administrative mess was "departmentalized" in the following way:

Department 1: Administration and Legal under Werner Best
Department 2: Ideological Investigation under Franz Six
Department 3: Spheres of German Life under Otto Ohlendorf
Department 4: Suppression of Opposition under Heinrich Mueller
Department 5: Suppression of Crime under Arthur Nebe
Department 6: Foreign Intelligence Service under Heinz Jost

These high-sounding titles were clearly a smokescreen hiding a bureaucratically top-heavy rabbit warren.

For example, Departments 4 and 5 must have overlapped, since if "opposition" is a "crime," who would deal with an "opponent" or "criminal" who had voiced a grievance against the regime? And what is the difference between "Ideological Investigation" (Department 2) and "Spheres of German Life" (Department 3)? An attempt has been made to show in the form of a chart (see pages 213–18) how the overall administration of the SS worked, but it gives a totally confusing picture. And this is because the SS, from its inception, was a hotbed of competition in which each department spied on the others. This confusion manifests itself in all the spheres of activity of the SS, in its military, police, ideological, and economic undertakings.

5
THE PREDATORS

Heinrich Himmler's obsession with the Jesuit Order and the Freemasons led him to the conclusion that a very distinctive uniform must be provided for his SS men. It must at once express the individual's position within the hierarchy and distinguish him from the mass of the German populace. It must also cater to Himmler's love of mysterious signs and badges.

A member of the Security Service wore on his tunic a diamond-shaped emblem with the initials SD. An "old fighter" had the right to wear an aluminum chevron on his right forearm. An officer up to the rank of Hauptsturmführer (captain) wore six silvered threads on his shoulder tab. A major or colonel had only three threads, but these were plaited. From brigadier general upward a man was entitled to wear three double-plaited silver threads. If you were an outsider, still somewhat confused, about the rank of the man who stood before you, you needed considerable knowledge of collar decorations to assist you in your scrutiny. From colonel upward you had to look at both collar patches. A mysterious combination of oakleaves, stars, and wreaths had to be deciphered before you could properly work out the rank.

Himmler's puritanism made him particularly averse to accepting known homosexuals into the SS. Neither did he have any time for what he described as the "professional unemployed." "A man who changes his job for the third time," he said, "we shall expel. We have no use for loafers."

Every SS applicant had to show proof that neither he nor his wife possessed any Jewish ancestors. An Aryan pedigree had to be produced which demonstrated that for ordinary applications blood had been "pure" since 1800 and for officer candidates since 1750. Furthermore, a final test was imposed on all aspiring candidates by Professor Bruno Schultz of the SS Racial Commission. They had to satisfy three basic criteria before earning the right to don the SS uniform. They must have the correct racial appearance, their physical condition must be such as to satisfy the SS medical inspectors, and their "general bearing" must be satisfactory. Professor Schultz came unstuck on the first category, "correct racial appearance." One of his five acceptable racial groups was described as "harmonious bastard with slight Alpine, Dinaric, or Mediterranean characteristics." This misuse of language masquerading as science did not cause Professor Schultz to blush. It is also quite clear that the overwhelming majority of Israeli-born Jews who are often blond and blue-eyed would have been looked upon quite favorably by SS examining committees. Himmler liked to pontificate about the correct proportions between limbs and trunk in the body of the SS man. There must be "no disproportion between the lower leg and the thigh, or between the legs and the body. Otherwise extra bodily effort is needed to perform long marches."

Assuming you had presented an acceptable pedigree and had satisfied the racial and physical requirements of the SS, you had to undergo a further series of tests. Only on successful conclusion of these could you swear the *Sippeneid,* the Kith and Kin Oath.

As an SS candidate of eighteen you were permitted on November 9 to wear a uniform, but without any collar patches. November 9 was the anniversary of the Munich Putsch. A provisional SS passbook was handed to you on January 30, the day which commemorated the Nazi Machtergreifung, or seizure of power, in 1933. But on the Führer's birthday, April 30, you actually received your collar patches and a permanent SS passbook. It was then that you made your oath as an SS man:

Ich schwöre Dir, Adolf Hitler,	I swear to Thee, Adolf Hitler,
Als Führer und Kanzler des	As Führer and Chancellor of
deutschen Reiches	the German Reich
Treue und Tapferkeit.	Loyalty and Bravery.
Ich gelobe Dir und den von Dir	I vow to Thee and to the
bestimmten Vorgesetzten	superiors whom Thou shalt appoint
Gehorsam bis in den Tod,	Obedience unto death,
So wahr mir Gott helfe.	So help me God.

It is astonishing that an organization as anticlerical as the SS should have adopted this biblical type of language; but then it was headed by a man driven by guilt over having abandoned his Catholicism.

If you aspired to become a member of the Allgemeine-SS, or General-SS, you had to master the SS catechism, which consisted of a series of questions and answers along the following lines:

Q: Why do we believe in Germany and the Führer?
A: Because we believe in God, we believe in Germany which He
   created in His world and in the Führer Adolf Hitler, whom He
   has sent us.
Q: Whom must we primarily serve?
A: Our people and our Führer Adolf Hitler.
Q: Why do you obey?
A: From inner conviction, from belief in Germany, in the Führer, in
   the Movement, and in the SS, and from loyalty.

Like Eliza Doolittle in *Pygmalion* rehearsing "the rain in Spain
stays mainly on the plains," the above litany had to be word-perfect.
Again, the parallels with a religious order are quite obvious. Before
the candidate received that most precious object, the SS dagger, he
had to swear another oath, committing himself and his descendants to
a marriage only if "the necessary conditions of race and healthy stock
are fulfilled" and after permission had been granted by the
Reichsführer-SS himself or his representatives at the Reich Main Security Office.

Himmler's failure as a chicken farmer in Waldtrudering in no way
embarrassed him when he applied the methods of poultry breeding to
human beings. The question remains, however, of just how wooden
and machinelike his men became as a result of their indoctrination.
They have been depicted as totally devoid of independent thought.
Yet certainly during the war, visiting lecturers would complain that
the SS men infinitely preferred joining German Army units in beer-
drinking sessions to sitting quietly while further quasi-scientific mon-
ologues were conducted on the nature of Germanic runes or the latest
findings in the history of the Aryan race. Perhaps their behavior in
the concentration camps as guards has its origins in some other as-
sortment of psychological behavior patterns. No body of men has
been subjected to such close scrutiny by professional psychologists.
The theory has even been advanced that their sadistic behavior resulted from the habit of swaddling infants in Germany. This restric-
tion on their physical movement produced a situation in which, once
liberated, they could find that release denied them as babes in arms,
in acts of spontaneous sadism. Yet any single theory of psychological
cause and effect must be misleading, because the SS counted among
its hundreds of thousands of members the most disparate types imagi-
nable.

At no time did their Grand Master ever consider that he was on
the wrong track. He had set out to establish a new breed of men and

had fixed ideas on how this was to be achieved. Yet any acceptance of his version—that is, that by continuous indoctrination you could produce the desired results—must be suspect. The Totenkopfverbände, or Death's Head Units, which policed the concentration camps, were composed mainly of country boys and men, and they had disliked Jews many years before anybody had asked them to swear a Kith and Kin Oath or recite a new catechism. The service of Himmler and the Nazi theorists lay in the fact that they lent the approval and organization of the State to systematizing a haphazard form of anti-Semitism which had been active for years.

The chief ideological pillar of National Socialism was its racial theory and for this reason the catch phrase *Die Juden Sind Unser Unglück* (The Jews are our misfortune) needs to be examined carefully. For the uninitiated it simply meant that it was unfair that the Jews appeared to exist in disproportionate numbers in banking, commerce, journalism, the liberal professions, and the arts. But for the Nazis it indicated something far more sinister. It meant to them that German society was a basically healthy organism constantly at the mercy of a bacillus which would eventually destroy it. This bacillus appeared in the form of the Jews, whose declared intention through their international connections was to undermine the strong races, primarily the Teutonic race, and rule the world. To do this they undoubtedly needed an international organization, but this they had, and to the Nazis and theorists of the SS, this had been abundantly proven by the document entitled, *The Protocols of the Elders of Zion*. It would be difficult to overestimate the importance of this tract since the middle of the nineteenth century in propagating anti-Semitism. It was believed implicitly by all the professional haters of Jews in Germany, from Hitler and Himmler on down. It also gained considerable currency in France (where it originated), Russia (where it was used to initiate pogroms), the United States (where it was chiefly disseminated by Henry Ford), and England, where even the London *Times* asked whether the government should not set aside some research money to examine its authenticity.

The circumstances of the origins of this "evidence" of a Jewish world conspiracy are so bizarre that it seems impossible that anybody could have taken the document seriously.

In 1868 the German journalist Hermann Goedsche, who was on the staff of a respectable, conservative Prussian newspaper called the *Kreuzzeitung*, published a novel called *Biarritz* under the pseudonym "Sir John Retcliffe." The novel contained a chapter entitled "In the Jewish Cemetery in Prague," which is devoted to the description of a nocturnal secret meeting. At eleven o'clock the cemetery gates creak open, there are sounds of clothes rustling, and suddenly a white figure is seen making its way toward one of the tombstones. It kneels, touches the tombstone three times with its forehead, and begins to pray. Gradually it is joined by twelve other figures, all of whom perform the same ritual. By midnight all are assembled. The clock strikes and a blue flame illuminates the thirteen figures. The Devil, speaking from the depths of the grave around which they are assembled, says: "I greet you, heads of the twelve tribes of Israel." The men then give an account of their activities in the preceding century, that is to say, since their last meeting. The head of the tribe of Levi is pleased to announce that Israel is now able to raise its head again, thanks to the accumulation of gold. Reuben indicates that by means of manipulation of the stock exchanges, all the princes and governments of Europe are now in the debt of the Jews. Judah states that owing to Jewish mass-production methods, all independent craftsmen are reduced to the status of factory workers. Simeon puts forward a plan for the division of the huge landed estates which will become their slaves. Aaron is the specialist at undermining the work of the Christian church by spreading freethinking and skepticism. Issachar has as his target the vilification of the military class and the patriotism it represents. His purpose is so to infiltrate the patriotic forces of each country so that they will become the passive slaves of the Jews, who of course have no territorial allegiance. Zebulon asserts that the Jews must always appear to be on the side of the forces of radicalism, because in this way the Jews can use revolution as a front to cover their real activity, which is to obtain ever greater sources of power and wealth. Menassah speaks most persuasively of the great need of the Jews to capture the press in each country so that news can be manipulated to spread unrest. The meeting closes with the decision to meet again, as is their custom, in one hundred years, by which time the grandchildren of the assembled tribal heads will enjoy the benefits which would accrue to them as a result of the activities of their fellow Jews in the intervening century.

Biarritz was a novel. But only four years after its appearance in Germany, in 1872, the chapter "In the Jewish Cemetery in Prague" was published in St. Petersburg as a leaflet which claimed the story was based on fact. In 1871 the story appeared in France and was presented as a serious piece of historical study. In 1896 the French writer François Bournand reproduced the speech in his work *Les Juifs et nos contemporains* with a covering note which read, "The program of Jewry . . . is expressed by the Chief Rabbi John Readclif [!] in a speech made in 1880."

Wherever anti-Semitism reared its head, the "Rabbi's Speech" appeared in one form or another. And wherever the established order was challenged it could be "proved" by reference to one or other of the remarks of these "heads of the tribes of Israel." Therefore Bolshevism became part of the Jewish conspiracy, Freemasonry with its strange rituals was simply a front of the Jews, and under the Nazis the Christian churches themselves had become so infested with the virus spread about by the Jews that they had become their secret weapon.

What, it may be asked, has all this to do with the SS? The answer has been given by Hitler himself. He told Hermann Rauschning that he believed implicitly in the Jewish world conspiracy. Moreover, it was his avowed intention to copy it. He had been impressed with their "stealthiness" and "ubiquity," weapons which had proved so effective that they must form the very basis of Nazi techniques themselves. His own SS must practice stealth and must be everywhere, but for a far different purpose from that of the Jews. The machinations of the Jews were directed to undermining the mission of the pure Teutonic race. The activities of the National Socialists were to be applied to rescuing the world from the Jewish conspiracy. This was the Germanic mission of the twentieth century, and most certainly, if the Germans did not perform this historically necessary function, the entire world would be subjugated under the yoke of the Jews.

To the SS men the implications were enormous. Imbued with the theories of social Darwinism, they were instructed to treat the Jews literally as a form of virus. It was a precondition of their own survival. They were surgeons who had to cut away what was rotten in the body politic.

To Himmler this exercise in social surgery was a religious task. To execute it properly he needed to surround it with the ritualistic trappings he had enjoyed in his Catholic childhood. He set up a museum dedicated to Masonic uniforms and regalia. His chief work was the establishment at Wewelsberg of a castle which reflected the reading he had done on King Arthur and the Knights of the Round Table. The leaders of the SS were entitled to assemble at a large oak table in a dining room measuring 100 by 145 feet. They sat in high-backed chairs made out of pigskin, on each of which was a silver disk on which the selected "knight" had his name engraved. Here the chiefs of the SS were compelled to sit in the company of their Grand Master for hours of contemplation and meditation. While they did so, their underlings in the concentration camps committed the most bestial acts of sadism on their miserable captives. Each "knight" had his own quarters in the castle at Wewelsberg. Leading down from the dining room was a flight of steps into a crypt which contained twelve stone pedestals. If an Obergruppenführer were to die, an urn containing his ashes was placed on the appropriate pedestal. The smoke was directed upward into the vents in the ceiling so that those assembled could watch the spirit ascend into a type of Valhalla. Wewelsberg had been specially chosen because it had been named after a robber-knight called Wewel von Buren, and at the time of the Huns it had offered an outpost of resistance against their incursions. In Himmler's mind the next assault on Teutonic values would come from the east, from the Slavs who were tools of their Jewish masters and part of the vast Judeo-Bolshevik conspiracy. Himmler's own quarters were located in the southern wing of the fortress. There he ordered a large hall to be built which contained his very extensive collection of weapons, a large library, and a Court of Honor which was to act as the highest SS court in the land.

The castle at Wewelsberg and its trappings eventually cost a total of $3.7 million, a significant sum, because it was the one area in which Himmler's pettifogging attitude toward expenditure was surmounted by his sense of mission. Himmler's attitude to money was that of a minor bureaucrat: each pfennig must be accounted for. The castle was the one grandiose gesture of his life. He believed that the life styles of the old Germanic tribes lived on in the SS. His favorite historical character was Henry I of Saxony who had conquered the Slavs. On the thousandth anniversary of his death, Himmler visited his tomb at Quedlingberg cathedral and undertook to complete the divine work his predecessor had started. At the stroke of midnight each year on July 2, Himmler would commune in silence with King Henry. According to his masseur, Felix Kersten, Himmler came to believe that he was the reincarnation of the old Saxon king.

Despite the earnest intentions of Himmler, the typical SS man had little time for the mystical groping of their leader into the Germanic past. The Head of the SS education office, Standartenführer Caesar complained in January 1939 that "boredom with these subjects is gradually becoming noticeable among the men, and so instruction has been extended to cover the basic concepts of National Socialist ideology."

In fact Himmler was on the wrong track. The staging of the Nuremberg Party rallies, based as they were on a combination of the sort of choreography perfected in Hollywood by Busby Berkeley, the catch phrases of Propaganda Minister Josef Goebbels, and the inspired architectural insights of Albert Speer, were far more effective in creating that brand of fanaticism which was an endemic feature of the Nazi scene. The cranky scholarship of Himmler never exerted the influence he would so dearly have loved it to have. Schoolmaster Himmler was able to indulge his obsession with tribal images from the misty past of German history, but his strange preoccupations were not shared by the rank and file of the SS.

In the SS marriage ceremony Himmler wanted to fill the gap created by his aversion to the established religions and yet retain its ritualistic trappings. To this end, he founded an Order of Germanic Clans which was governed by a form of paganism. If you were an SS man between twenty-five and thirty, you were expected to marry, but you and your fiancée had to complete a questionnaire prepared by the Reichssicherheitshauptamt. You had to supply renewed proof of Aryan background and send a snapshot of yourself and your fiancée in a bathing costume. Himmler or his subordinates would then study the photographs and decide whether you both qualified for entry into the SS Clan book. You would have your marriage at a registry office, but this must be followed by a ceremony presided over by the local SS unit commander at which special SS marriage vows were sworn. An SS factory at Allach near Munich provided the couple with gifts as they produced children. A silver beaker was given to them on the birth of their first child, together with a silver spoon and a shawl made of blue silk. If they were extremely fertile and went on producing children, for every fourth child (!) they were given a candlestick which bore the inscription: "You are only a link in the Clan's endless chain."

Himmler could not persuade his men to abandon the celebration of Christmas. He invented a ceremony which he hoped would replace it, called the Festival of Midsummer. Midsummer plates and candlesticks were generously distributed from the factory at Allach, but the Festival of Midsummer never really caught on. Furthermore, large numbers of SS men continued to have religious marriages.

The notion of issuing a candlestick for every fourth child did not have the effect of increasing the birth rate among the SS, for this remained only marginally higher than the national average. Neither did the institution known as Lebensborn, which offered the SS man the opportunity of having children with specially chosen Aryan girls without the burden of marrying them, result in the large-scale production of bastards.

One particular branch of the SS, the Waffen- or Armed-SS, gained considerable notoriety during World War II. To an extent these troops were the brainchild of a former World War I officer named Paul Hausser who established a series of cadet schools in which training methods made the most stringent demands on all who attended them. The SS recruit would start his day at six in the morning. Immediately upon arising he underwent one hour's intensive physical training. This was followed by a breakfast consisting of nothing more sustaining than porridge and mineral water, to comply with Himmler's passion for implementing his dietary theories and also because the SS had acquired the Matteoni and Apollinaris factories which produced these commodities. Training on the handling of the newest weapons followed breakfast, and at least three times weekly the morning was interrupted by lectures on the purpose of National Socialism or talks about Hitler's life.

After lunch an inordinate amount of time was spent on the barracks square in drilling. "Square-bashing" assumed punishing proportions. Assuming the recruit was still able to stand at the end of this routine, he was ordered to scrub his quarters clean, polish his rifle, and remove any particle of dust which might still remain in the compound. The entire camp was then given a thorough inspection by his superiors. So was he. At the end of this demanding day he must appear with his short hair well slicked down, his face scrubbed, his uniform neat. His pockets might contain his paybook, a small amount of paper currency which did not cause his pockets to produce any unsightly bulges, and one prophylactic, with which he was to make his way into the nearby village to seek out a suitable partner. As an anticlerical organization, the SS had no church parade on Sunday. Each recruit had to suffer surveillance by the officers before being allowed to spend his free time out of the barracks, and at least one out of three failed to meet the standard imposed.

The object of this Spartan training was to produce a race of men whose obedience was unquestioning. In one of his more impassioned moments the Führer was heard to utter confidently, "And if I tell my SS troops that they must fight tanks with walking sticks, they will run out and do what they are told!"

In fact the Waffen-SS distinguished itself during the fighting in World War II, but the regular Army never really accepted it. From time to time Hitler accorded Waffen-SS units the right to join the Army at maneuvers, and this was always reported with great pride in *Das Schwarze Korps*. As the war progressed the Waffen-SS always managed to obtain the latest in weaponry, much to the annoyance of the Army. Claus von Stauffenberg, who was shot after his failed attempt on Hitler's life on July 20, 1944, once lectured officers at the General Staff College and said: "What is the difference between an SS Division and an ordinary Army Division? SS has no divisional chaplains and better weapons!"

Himmler tried to come to terms with the Wehrmacht. As early as January 1937 he told a group of senior officers: "The next ten years will see a war of annihilation conducted by the subhuman enemies of the entire world against Germany, which is the kernel of the Teutonic race, as guardian of the culture of the human race. They will mean the existence or nonexistence of that white race of which we are the leading nation." He went on to draw attention to the need of special policing forces to assure the success of this Germanic mission. At the time there were only three Standarten which had the strength of an infantry regiment: the Leibstandarte Adolf Hitler, the Germania, and the Deutschland. But with the outbreak of the war Himmler feared that many of his precious SS men might be lost to him. He arranged that a man could not automatically be drafted into the Wehrmacht if the Waffen-SS claimed him first. One additional factor kept the SS man from duty within the general armed forces. That was Hitler's wish to keep them apart. On August 17, 1938, the Führer issued a decree which stated that the SS-Verfügungstruppen (out of which the Waffen-SS was created) were to be "a unit of the Party, exclusively at my disposal." Hitler's purpose in reaching this decision was to have at his right hand a mobile force of highly trained men on whom he could rely completely, for within the Army itself there were still many generals who were not totally obedient to him.

The effect of Hitler's decree of August 17, 1938, was to allay the suspicions of the Wehrmacht. If the SS were not to be incorporated within the Army, the generals who controlled the regular fighting forces would not be under continuous surveillance. It gave them the illusion that they still retained a certain degree of mobility within the Nazi regime. They would certainly not be surrounded by Himmler's spies. Accordingly the attitude of the Wehrmacht softened, and within a few weeks of the publication of Hitler's decree, young SS officers from the Hausser cadet school at Bad Tölz were seconded to the Army for six month periods.

It was only during the war itself that officers of the Wehrmacht came to learn of the foul acts of the Waffen-SS and of the extermination squads of the general SS in their mass murder of civilians. "You are not a soldier; you are a butcher," said General Hoepner to Theodor Eicke, ex-commander of the concentration camp service and now leader of an SS Division in the French campaign.

The reputation of the Waffen-SS as a superb fighting force in no way reflected good generalship, for the men who were given a leading role in SS divisions were often either former police officials or sadistic butchers. What Hausser had managed to achieve was the development of a hard core of superbly fit fighting men who believed they constituted an elite. It was these men who were prepared to make a last-ditch stand when the fortunes of the Reich suffered severe setbacks in 1945; it was these men on whom the years of indoctrination had wrought their tragic effects. The young fanatics had enjoyed incredibly rapid promotion. Fritz Witt became a major general at the age of thirty-four. His successor, Kurt Meyer, who distinguished himself by his indiscriminate massacre of Canadian prisoners, was even younger.

In strategy the Waffen-SS was mediocre. Its chief asset lay in providing leadership at junior-officer level. Square-bashing at Bad Tölz, National Socialist indoctrination, and the knowledge that Heydrich had once startled von Papen by telling him at the dinner table, "I feel nearer to God in an airplane than in a church," failed to produce necessary expertise in tactics or strategy.

There is a further group of men within the General-SS who acquired leading roles in the administration of the occupied areas of Europe and whose actions must be recounted. These men were basically administrators, almost without exception of middle-class origin, who acted as if they were executives in some giant industrial corporation. When tried at Nuremberg they conveyed the impression of dedicated businessmen who happened to find themselves in a new type of corporation dedicated to redrawing European frontiers and reorganizing the European economy.

Ulrich Heinrich Emil Richard Greifelt, the son of a pharmacist from Berlin, joined the Nazi party in 1933 and was therefore called a *Märzveilchen*—a "March violet"—a term applied to those people who jumped on the Nazi bandwagon when it had achieved a measure of success. In August 1914 he was head of his class at the Lichterfelde Realgymnasium. He started his service in the First World War as an aircraft observer, and when the war ended was a staff officer with the German military government at Riga. At the close of hostilities he joined the Freikorps Deutsche Schutzdivision, but when this unit was incorporated into the Army he returned to Berlin to marry. Here he cast about in those difficult days for some form of employment. For a year or two he worked in an economic agency of the government. This did not seem to offer much of a future financially, and he obtained a position with a Berlin firm that manufactured appliances and was run, ironically enough, by a family called Israel. His industry was rewarded and he was eventually made factory manager. Israel Brothers went bankrupt in 1932, together with countless other firms which suffered the same fate in the Depression. Greifelt was unemployed for more than a year, but this did not drive him into the Nazi camp. He happened to run into his old commander from Riga, who now occupied a high post in the SS and who, according to Greifelt, "reawakened my longing for the comradeship of military service as exemplified in the front-soldier Adolf Hitler." This "reawakening" had promising results. He became the adjutant of his old superior officer in the SS and thus terminated his year of inactivity. His diligence was rewarded, and when his superior died, Greifelt was offered the position of manager of the SS office in Coblenz, which he accepted. There were aspects of SS life which Greifelt did not enjoy, particularly its anticlericalism. Also he began to pine for Berlin. He even tendered his resignation, but it was refused, so he claimed, and the SS obligingly transferred him back to Berlin. Because of his earlier years in industry, Himmler considered Greifelt to be something of an economist. He promised him rapid promotion on his staff as economic adviser to the Four Year Plan, the scheme to revive the flagging German economy. By June 1939, at the age of forty-four, Greifelt had the rank of SS Colonel. To his family, Greifelt would express intense annoyance at the very mention of the words *concentration camp* and claimed that at no time did he ever consider himself a policeman. Nonetheless he eventually carried the title of Major General of the Police because of his excellent work in the "resettlement" program. The "resettlement" program was an attempt to carve out large areas of Eastern Europe with a view to settling Germans and ethnic Germans in them as farmers. Some of the town planners within the SS envisaged a string of garden cities all the way from the Baltic to the Black Sea in which Germans could till the soil and live the life of a yeoman farmer which had so intrigued the theorists of the SS, such as Walter Darré, head of the SS Race and Resettlement Office.

There was one basic obstacle to this plan. The area was already inhabited.

To put it into practice, therefore, the current occupants had to be "resettled," which in SS terminology meant they had to be put to death. Greifelt therefore was a man who "grew into his job," acquiring a certain administrative expertise, but active in the field of mass murder. This does not appear to have made the slightest difference to him. It was simply a factor in the situation and had the same significance that the existence of unpleasant competition within the marketplace might have for any ordinary businessman. In other words, Greifelt had become an amoral technocrat.

Another example of the dedicated technocrat from the middle class which the SS seemed to attract was Richard Hildebrandt. He ended up holding very high office. He was Superior SS and Police Leader of Danzig and West Prussia from 1939 to 1943 and Chief of the SS Race and Settlement Office from April 1943 until the end of the war. He finished his schooling in May 1915 and thereafter spent four years in the Field Artillery, emerging in 1918 as a Lieutenant in the Reserves. He then began his university education. For three years he attended the universities of Cologne and Munich where he studied economics, history, languages and art history. In 1921 he became a business correspondent. He joined the Nazi party as early as 1922, and when it was banned after the Putsch of 1923, he transferred his allegiance to the extreme right-wing Bavarian movement known as the Bund Oberland. In 1928 he decided to try his luck in the United States, and after roaming around found an office job in New York City. There he joined a small group of men who had founded the New York National Socialist movement. But he was keen to return to Germany and did so in 1930. He secured a position with the Nazi party in Munich and transferred to the SS in 1931. Here he became adjutant to Sepp Dietrich, who executed the SA "traitors" in Stadelheim prison on July 1, 1934.

Hildebrandt was an energetic and enterprising young man. He managed the SS offices in Goerlitz and Breslau, served with the SS in Coblenz, and transferred to Wiesbaden in 1937. He was known to be severely critical of any corruption or carelessness.

There can be no doubt that Greifelt and Hildebrandt were definite products of the German middle class. They had both been exposed to a reasonably high standard of education and had occupied managerial positions. Their conduct during the war shows that they enjoyed their roles in the expansionist program of a mammoth business corporation. For their efforts they were rewarded with rapid advancement and additional titles, just as they might have been in business. They had nothing in common with the street toughs of the SA or brownshirts. They turned a blind eye to the mass murder their colleagues within the SS were perpetrating, and if they were challenged at their impersonal view of the sufferings they and their kind inflicted on millions of their victims in Eastern Europe, they shrugged and claimed that you could not create a new social order painlessly. These were, in the words of one of them, "the hard consequence of the war with Bolshevism." And if "the problem of partisan resistance was a difficult one," as another maintained at his trial, surely there could be nothing wrong in dealing with it radically, even if this meant killing millions of men, women, and children. Indeed at the Nuremberg trials each of the SS defendants justified his behavior during the war with great tenacity. They had acted, so they claimed, in a spirit of self-sacrifice and had done their jobs conscientiously. They were only too ready to agree that "the war entailed much suffering," but by phrasing it in this passive way, they implied that they could not be regarded as active instruments in that process. They were victims of the war as assuredly as were those who had been killed. Their real enemy was Heinrich Himmler, the boss, who had no real understanding of administration, of how to run the business. The operation could have been far more streamlined were it not for the pettifogging duplication of offices engineered by Himmler, and his waste of time and labor on historical research. If they had been given the chance, they would have had a board meeting at which they, the real technocrats of the SS, would have been able to offer their advice on how to make their "business" run more smoothly.

At the outbreak of the Second World War, therefore, the SS was an amorphous mass of Spartan soldiers, concentration-camp guards, police informers, professional torturers, strange cranks who pursued quasi-scientific racial and dietary theories, sneaks, spies, businessmen *manqués,* and occasional warped idealists.

Such were the predators. We must now examine their prey.

6

THE PREY

We have been concerned so far with political intrigue, the pursuit of individual ambition, ideological dispute, and the search for social power at a high level.

Our purpose now is to examine the concrete results of these machinations at an individual level. We have to ask ourselves the question: What was it like to be a victim of the SS? To answer this correctly, we have to put ourselves in the position of an ordinary citizen, and we also have to place ourselves in time. Here we must differentiate between two distinct periods. The first is concerned with the years between the Nazi seizure of power in 1933 and the outbreak of the war in 1939. The second is the period of the war itself, that is to say, from 1939 to 1945. The difference between the two periods can be summed up in one word: genocide.

Let us take the first period: 1933–1939. You are, apparently, an ordinary citizen. You were born in Germany. You might be a Jew, a Jehovah's Witness, you might have been active in any number of political parties including the Communist party, you might have been a journalist or a teacher. Otherwise there was nothing to distinguish you from any other member of the German nation—except for one thing; you were considered by the local Gestapo office to be potentially or actually *staatsfeindlich,* that is, an enemy of the State.

Reinhard Heydrich's institution of Schutzhaft enabled anybody in the local Gestapo office to arrest without warning any member of the public he took it into his head to consider as *staatsfeindlich.*

So here you are, a Jew, or possibly a Jehovah's Witness, fast asleep in bed next to your wife, in 1937. At the favorite time of the Gestapo officials, 3:00 A.M., there is a violent knocking at the front door. You stumble out of bed and open the door, and there stand two menacing figures in black. They inform you that you are under arrest and they allow you a few minutes to throw some belongings into a suitcase and get dressed, while your wife and children stand by you in petrified silence.

You are then roughly escorted to an ordinary police prison. You know, because you have heard similar stories, that your final destination is a concentration camp, but you still entertain some hope that an administrative error has occurred and maybe they have confused your name with that of someone else. You might even, in your hasty packing, have placed in your suitcase your First World War medal, which you believe will finally persuade your prosecutors that they have made a mistake. For how could anybody cited for bravery by his country be considered *staatsfeindlich?*

You languish in an ordinary local police prison for days, weeks, or months, totally at the whim of the officials in charge. This is all part of the "breaking down" process which inspires fear. You might have a cell to yourself, or you might be in a much larger cell with twenty or thirty other mystified companions. But mystification soon is replaced by terror, because the very same police officials who had represented order and security in the years before the Nazi accession to power would now beat you indiscriminately—certainly for no reason that you could ascertain. Your wife, your relatives might make repeated efforts, by direct application or via some Nazi party member with whom some relationship had persisted, to discover the nature of the charge and when you might be brought to trial, but all to no avail. All such applications were dismissed. Dr. Werner Best, the SS legal expert, had already made it clear that since the Gestapo acted as an arm of the State and since the State could do no wrong, it was clear that if you were arrested there must be adequate grounds for this act, and that was the end of the matter.

One day, out of the blue, a police guard opens the cell door, hauls you out, and informs you that your trial is the next on the list. According to his personal whim, he might then beat you about the head and body or subject you to psychological cruelty, holding the carrot of freedom before you only to withdraw it later. But after this process he would hand you a red document and order you to sign it. It was a *Schutzhaftbefehl,* or an order for protective custody. This official-looking document bore the bureaucratic title "Form D-11." It would contain some details of your background and generally ended with the terse phrase ". . . . because of the suspicion of high treason is to be detained in protective custody," or ". . . is to be detained in protective custody because of the danger that he might otherwise misuse his personal freedom to engage in acts detrimental to the National Socialist State."

Because there was no alternative, you signed the form. Then a few days or possibly a few weeks passed. There was, of course, no trial. Suddenly your belongings were returned to you, and you and twenties, hundreds, or thousands of others were collectively transported to the concentration camp designated for you. Many of your companions had not even signed or seen Form D-11. The method of transport to the camp was almost inevitably by rail. The journey could take a few hours or a few days. Packed up to 150 at a time into cattle or goods wagons, without food or water, you were shunted around Germany. Sometimes a change of trains was indicated, and this involved crossing streets from one station to another. In this event, you were chained to each other, and coaxed along by your bullying guards you would move from one terminus to another.

Finally, totally exhausted, you arrived at the station nearest to the camp assigned to you. The truck doors were opened and those still capable of movement were hauled out and cuffed and kicked into waiting trucks. If no transport was available, you completed your journey to the camp on foot. Most of the elderly people who made their way on foot were soon forced to jettison their luggage, as they needed all their strength to obey the continuous commands of the accompanying guards to keep moving. If you fell on the way, you were more than likely to be shot out of hand. Many were, and as you witnessed this, you devoted what strength you still possessed to completing the march. You might breathe a sigh of relief at finally ridding yourself of your cumbersome suitcase, but this relief was short-lived, since you were instructed by the guards to walk with your arms held high above your head. According to Dr. Eugon Kogon, who himself survived incarceration at the Buchenwald camp, no fewer than 240,000 people made this forced march from the railway station at Weimar to the camp itself, on a concrete road which camp inmates had themselves constructed.

You finally arrived at the camp. At this point you had your first exposure to the SS at its lower level, since you were closely examined by SS noncommissioned officers, generally of the rank of Scharführer. Their first act was to walk up and down the lines of the new prisoners and sort out some, according to individual whimsy, for savage beating. If you had a beard, you were more than likely to be seized by it and forced to the ground while your body was systematically kicked by the guards. When the guards had tired of this, they commanded the entire assembly to perform the *Sachsengruss* or Saxon Greeting, which involved doing knee bends with your arms behind your head for hours on end. If you fell over during this painful and physically demanding exercise you were either beaten or shot "while attempting to escape." This explanation was laconically entered into your file, because despite the brutalization of life, the SS under Himmler maintained very orderly files throughout its existence.

If your arrival at the camp was toward nightfall and if you formed part of a large transport, you were not allowed entry into the inner compound of the camp until sometime during the following day. You spent the night in small cells which were so overcrowded that you had to stand erect all through the night. Prisoners were beaten savagely in order to force more and more of them into each cell. The door was then locked and the air vents were sealed off, and the shortage of oxygen soon became evident. After two or three hours most of the occupants fainted—without sinking to the floor, however, since there was insufficient room. After morning roll call had taken place in the main square of the camp, the cell doors of the new arrivals were torn open and the SS guards then kicked and buffeted the prisoners along the passageways to their first screening in front of the Political Division of the SS.

At this screening you were classified. Colored triangles were issued which would thereafter adorn your prison clothing. Preventive detainees were classified in the following way:

Red signified that you were a German "political" detainee.
Purple indicated that you were a Jewish political detainee.
Green indicated that you had committed or were suspected of having
     committed a criminal offence.
Black signified that you were "asocial."
Yellow over white indicated that you were a Jewish person who had
     committed a "racial offense," meaning that you had employed
     or had had sexual relations with an Aryan.
Brown indicated that you were a gypsy.
Mauve designated you as a homosexual.

Details of birth, marriage, and general background were entered into your file, the main features of which were transferred to a large card index, so that despite the enormous number of victims the SS bureaucrats had under their charge, it never took more than a couple of minutes to unearth the relevant details of each and every one of them.

This information was not exacted from the prisoner in an atmosphere of bureaucratic calm. The NCOs of the SS used this opportunity to deprive the new arrivals of what small vestige of self-esteem they might still have preserved despite the period of brutal imprisonment, the forced marches, the denial of food and water, by savage beatings and psychological abuse. A favorite example of the latter, according to Dr. Kogon, was to ask each prisoner why, in his view, he had been arrested. Since the overwhelming majority had no idea and simply stammered an inadequate reply, they were accordingly awarded twenty-five strokes with the lash for their "recalcitrance." Jews were especially chosen for the harshest treatment. Instead of asking for the maiden name of your mother, the SS guard typing away in front of you would scream: "Which whore shat you into the world?" On one occasion at which Kogon was present, this question was addressed to a miserable man who delayed his replies to such an extent that he received many cruel blows. Once he had pulled himself together, he revealed that he was one of six children and that Hitler himself had rewarded his mother with the Mother's Cross in Gold for her efforts at producing soldiers for the greater good of Germany.

Once the personal details had been exacted from each new arrival in the way described, they were entitled to enter the main compound of the camp. They then had to walk through the principal gate, over which there was always some suitable inscription. At Buchenwald, iron letters declared: "To Each His Own" (*Jedem das Seine*), while at Auschwitz you learned that *Arbeit macht frei,* which can be loosely translated as "Work liberates," or "Work redeems."

Once through the gate the process of physical weakening continued. Hours of the "Saxon Greeting" with your face turned toward the nearest bunker were spent while the guards battered you about according to their whim. When the guards had tired of this, the prisoners were then addressed while they stood in rows as to what they may and may not do. An enormous number of trivial departures from what was permitted carried an instantaneous death sentence. To complete the picture, a set of gallows was installed in the main square. Then the inmates were forced at the double into collective ablutions, they were shorn of all their hair, and their clothing was issued to them once they had run naked from the washing area to the stores. Such minor possessions as the inmates still had at this stage were taken, labeled, and stored away. In each camp there were always stout fellows from the SS Death's Head Units who would perform small favors in exchange for sums of money or small personal belongings. Wedding rings, watches, and jewelry might be exchanged for a pair of shoes in slightly better condition than the prisoner might otherwise have received.

At this stage the prisoner was assigned to a specific block where he might spend his nights in bunks of two and three tiers each equipped with a straw sack. In the summer the day began between 4:00 and

5:00 A.M. and in the winter between 6:00 and 7:00 A.M. Thirty minutes were allowed for washing, eating—breakfast consisted of gruel—and preparing one's bed for inspection. If your straw mattress was creased or its angles not sharply defined, you were beaten mercilessly. Then followed roll call in the main square. Searchlights from the various surrounding towers beamed down on the community of thousands, standing there in rows. This lasted until daylight permitted work to start. At this point the SS guard in charge bellowed: *"Arbeitskommandos austreten"*—"Working parties fall out!"—and all present ran to collect their appropriate tools, generally picks or shovels. As they passed below the sign above the main gate, each prisoner had to remove his cap in deference to the slogan, and then, kicked and cuffed by the accompanying guards, the working parties made their way to the appropriate quarry or stretch of road on which they were to work.

The most arduous physical labor was then undertaken until the late afternoon, with possibly a half-hour break in the open air, under all weather conditions, where a further portion of gruel was distributed. Men in the peak of physical condition could not stand this regime for long; exhaustion or death took their daily toll. Work stopped in summer at about 8:00 P.M. and in winter at 5:00 P.M. Then followed the evening roll call. This was a matter which generally lasted several hours, because to the NCOs of the SS, numbers had to tally. Inmates had to stand in the snow and ice until the primitive accountancy had been performed. On one occasion at Buchenwald in midwinter in a temperature of fifteen degrees below zero centigrade, the entire camp stood in the square for nineteen hours until the figures tallied.

At the end of the evening roll call, public punishments were performed for those who had in some minor way transgressed the rules of the camp. If the guards had not yet tired of their amusement, the exhausted prisoners were compelled to sing some nursery song for an hour or two. Finally they received their evening meal, normally consisting of a small piece of bread from their daily ration, possibly some margarine, and a spoon of cheese curds. After further punishment by the omnipresent guards, the prisoners returned to their beds.

This, then, was a typical day in the life of an inmate of a German concentration camp in the late 1930s. This is what it was like to be a victim of the SS, the New Order founded by Heinrich Himmler, an unsuccessful chicken farmer from Bavaria. And terrible as it was, it was an improvement on what was to succeed it, namely the gas ovens of Auschwitz and Treblinka.

The SS in setting up concentration camps entered big business. Not only were the camps self-financing, they produced enormous profits for the administrators. The inmates built roads, produced goods, and had their assets commandeered by the State. The term *concentration camp* had been coined not by the Germans, but, as Hermann Goering was repeatedly to say during his trial at Nuremberg as a war criminal, by the English. For it appeared that during the Boer War in South Africa, the English had set up temporary camps to house prisoners of war and had given them this label. But here the similarity ended. In Germany they were a permanent feature of the social system and constituted a systematic attempt to undermine any possible source of opposition to the National Socialist regime.

There can be no doubt that the rank-and-file element of SS guards was selected from the most primitive sections of society. There can also be no doubt that these men did not need any indoctrination by the National Socialist ideologists to fulfil their task. Their brutality and sadism existed long before the pundits of the Nazis published their literature. These qualities existed in the Freikorps, as we have seen. But such was the degree of alienation from normal moral standards which characterized the SS that a man like Rudolf Hoess, who was commandant at Auschwitz when hundreds of thousands of innocent people were murdered in the gas ovens, could claim that during his service with the SS Death's Head Units, which policed the camps, he had always witnessed the beatings with a feeling of repugnance and had never personally participated in them. What can this mean? Surely that there is a difference between the spontaneous acts of gratuitous brutality described above and the highly technical work of mass murder in which Hoess was engaged. In his memoirs Hoess uses his feelings of repugnance at witnessing individual savagery as a kind of moral escape route. It is as if he is saying that he wished to be charged only as a technologist doing his job. He is willing to participate in a debate over the moral value of what his job involved. But he sides with us in expressing aversion for the system of brutalization which existed in the prewar concentration camps.

If we accept that the guards of the Death's Head Units belong to a different species of man, we shall commit a serious moral blunder. Even Kogon, who has summarized his experiences in Buchenwald in the most systematic fashion in order to subject the SS to sociological scrutiny, claims that these guards came from the most barbaric elements of society. This is tantamount to saying that we could, by wiser administration and saner approach to social problems, eliminate society's more primitive elements. But this, of course, begs the whole question.

The guards whose actions have been discussed performed their function with the knowledge and acquiescence of the more "enlightened" elements in the SS—the desk men in Berlin.

The most profitable source of inquiry into this dual morality we have described lies in an unusual place.

It is in the stomach of Heinrich Himmler.

Himmler had severe stomach cramps which, it can reasonably be claimed, had their origin in a psychosomatic condition. The incidence of stomach cramps increased whenever he was put to a severe moral test. Indecisive, troubled, he found himself at the head of a mammoth organization which was carrying out mass murder in incredibly brutal fashion. From time to time, he would assemble the leading executives in his genocidal undertaking and inform them that they needed an extra degree of courage and determination to carry out their historic task. And they may be sure, so he told them, that they would not be popular for executing their duty. In speaking to them in this fashion, Himmler was also trying to persuade himself. While his brain might accept the situation intellectually, his stomach was unable to take it. He was driven more and more regularly into the soothing hands of the Finnish masseur Felix Kersten, on whom he, or rather his stomach, came to depend. It is almost as though Heinrich Himmler's stomach had a mind, or more appropriately, a mind which concerned itself with morals, which was tortured by nagging doubts as to the rectitude of the course of action on which its owner had set it.

Why, it may be asked, did evil triumph over good in the stomach of Heinrich Himmler?

We need only to look at that physically inept person trying to be a soldier, trying to duel, trying to drink large quantities of beer, tripping over things, trying desperately to be what he considered a real man should be, to discover the answer. Himmler must control his stomach in the same way as he must control his physical ineptitude if he was to embody that true picture of masculinity to which he most assuredly aspired.

7

KRISTALLNACHT

In October 1938 some 17,000 Polish Jews living in Germany were deprived of their Polish citizenship by a cynical measure of the Polish government. An announcement was made to the effect that all their passports were henceforth invalid.

On October 28, 1938, German police officials under the overall direction of the SS main office knocked on the doors of these hapless Jews, who were informed that Poland did not want them, and neither did Germany. Under the general administration of Reinhard Heydrich, thousands of them were rounded up, placed on trains and trucks, and transported to the Polish frontier at Benschen. Here they were unloaded, forced over the fields into Polish territory, and beaten and kicked by Heydrich's officials until they had left German soil. Many were left to die in the no man's land between the two countries.

Among those persecuted in this fashion were a certain cobbler named Sendel Grynszpan and his wife and children. They survived the nightmarish journey back to an unhospitable Poland. Sendel Grynszpan wrote a letter to his seventeen-year-old son Herschel, then living in Paris, in which he described the excesses to which his family had been exposed. He explained that they now found themselves, penniless, back in the country they had left to escape anti-Semitism.

Herschel was a decisive young man. Nobody appeared to be doing anything about this outrage. He determined to exact vengeance himself.

At 7:30 on the morning of November 7, 1938, he went into a shop in the Rue du Faubourg St. Martin and purchased a pistol. At 8:30 A.M. he stationed himself in the courtyard of the German embassy in Paris, in the Rue de Lille. He had made up his mind to kill none other than the German ambassador to France, Count Johannes von Welszek.

At this moment von Welszek returned to the embassy from a morning stroll. Herschel had not the remotest idea what his victim looked like, so he went up to von Welszek and asked him where he might find the German ambassador.

Von Welszek, as a professional diplomat, felt that protocol was not being properly observed. He did not say to Herschel, "I am the German ambassador." Instead, without suspecting anything untoward, he suggested to the young man that he make inquiries of one of the officials. This action was to save his life.

Herschel was directed to the office of a junior counselor at the embassy named Ernst vom Rath, whose function was to receive visitors in the building. Herschel waited outside the door until vom Rath appeared and asked what he wanted. At this point Herschel must have decided that any German would do to make his point; it did not matter whether it was the ambassador or some underling.

He fired twice at vom Rath, who immediately sank to the ground. Hitler sent two of his most trusted doctors to Paris to try and save vom Rath's life, but they were too late, as were many French ex-soldiers who volunteered to donate their blood for the same purpose. Vom Rath died.

When interrogated by the French police, Herschel Grynszpan explained that when he had been informed of the brutal measures employed by the German police in the forced emigration of his family, "I decided from that moment to kill a member of the German embassy as a protest. I wanted to draw the attention of the world to the events which had taken place in Germany, and to perform an act of revenge for the Jews."

On November 9, 1938, two days after Herschel Grynszpan's activities in the German embassy in Paris, Hitler and his cronies were celebrating the anniversary of the Munich Putsch of 1923. While they were at table in the old town hall of Munich, a messenger arrived and whispered in Hitler's ear that vom Rath had died of his wounds. Hitler turned to his neighbor, Propaganda Minister Goebbels, and spoke quietly for a few minutes to him. He then left the table without making his customary speech. Until this day, nobody knows exactly what Hitler said to Goebbels on that occasion, yet whatever it was would bear very heavily on the events of the succeeding days.

The intention was to arrange a "spontaneous" expression of German public outrage at Herschel Grynszpan's action in Paris. But "spontaneous" expressions need some form of organizing, as Heydrich's circular to all German police chiefs was to demonstrate. This circular is so decisive and unambiguous that it deserves quoting in full.

Throughout the Reich during the night of November 9–10 demonstrations are to be expected against the Jews because of the murder of Legation-Secretary vom Rath. These events are to be handled in the following way:

Immediately on receipt of this telex the leaders of political state police units or their representatives must telephone local political organizers [Gauleiters or Kreisleiters] to make known to them the methods to be employed in carrying out these demonstrations. They must be informed that the Reichsführer-SS has issued the following guidelines:

1. Only those measures are permitted which in no way endanger the security of German life or property. For example, synagogues may only be set on fire if there is no danger of fire spreading to adjoining properties.

2. Businesses, apartments, and houses of Jews may only be destroyed, not plundered. The police are responsible for supervising the execution of these orders and for apprehending anyone guilty of plundering.

The name *Kristallnacht* (literally, crystal night) has been given to the events which took place on the night of November 9–10 because of the enormous amount of glass which was broken. But the purpose of the Nazis in setting up what they liked to describe as a spontaneous expression of public outrage was never fulfilled. The whole affair was coordinated via SS headquarters in Berlin. Neither were the directives issued by Heydrich a sufficient deterrent to acts of destruction and plundering. During the course of the night, shops were looted, murders took place, and an enormous amount of damage was done to property.

This all had one curious side effect. For years Nazi economists had been urging patriotic Germans to reduce their consumption of goods so that the economy could address itself firmly to the question of rearmament. "Guns instead of butter" had been one of Goering's most dominant slogans as leader of the Four Year Plan. The acts of vandalism on November 9–10 made a mockery of what had previously been considered to be official policy toward the assets of the Reich. Walter Funk, at the time Nazi Minister for Economics, declared during his trial as a war criminal at Nuremberg: "On the morning of 10 November 1938 while I was driving to my office, I saw evidence of the devastation on the Berlin Streets, and when I reached my Ministry, my officials gave me further information about the acts of the previous night. I attempted to telephone Goering, Goebbels, and even Himmler. Finally, I managed to reach Goebbels and told him that these acts of terror were an affront against me personally, since very valuable and irreplaceable goods had been destroyed and our relations with foreign countries would be seriously undermined." Under prosecution at Nuremberg, Funk warmed to his theme. "Have you gone crazy, Goebbels?" he claims to have asked the Propaganda Minister. "One must be ashamed to be a German. Our entire image abroad is ruined! I am trying night and day to preserve our economic resources and you wantonly throw them all out of the window!"

Somehow the millions of dollars' worth of destruction had to be paid for. Should this be raised by tax? And what about the question of insurance? Were the German insurance companies to carry the burden of paying for the damage of Kristallnacht? And if they did *not* pay, would not their ability to trade abroad suffer as a result? And how on earth was all the glass used in shop windows to be replaced? Most of it was imported from Belgium. The entire productive capacity of Belgium for a very long time would be needed to re-equip German stores.

Obviously, some policy of restitution had to be thrashed out. So, with the consent of the Führer, a meeting was called on November 12, 1938, at which the high-ranking Nazi dignitaries were to sit in committee, under the chairmanship of Goering, to determine the most appropriate solution of all these problems. The minutes have been preserved and make for interesting reading. Among those present were Goering, Goebbels, Heydrich, Daluege, Frick, Funk, and several others, including a representative of the German insurance companies, a man named Hilgard.

The discussion was opened by Hermann Goering, who said: "Gentlemen, I am sick and tired of these demonstrations. You are not damaging the Jews, you are damaging me, for in the final analysis, I carry the responsibility for the whole economy. If Jewish shops are razed to the ground and goods thrown all over the street, the damage has to be made good by the insurance companies. . . . This is insane. . . . The only solution is the complete exclusion of Jews from economic life. Jewish assets must be transferred to the State. They will be compensated. The amount of compensation will be entered into a ledger and we shall pay the Jew a certain amount of interest on the total sum. That is what he must live on."

Conversation then moved to the nature and extent of the damage done during Kristallnacht.

Goebbels: In almost every German city synagogues have been burned down. The spaces left as a result could be used for a variety of purposes. Some towns want car parks. Some want to put up new buildings.

Goering: How many synagogues were actually destroyed?

Heydrich: In total 101 synagogues were burned down, 76 synagogues were demolished, and there are 7,500 businesses destroyed in the Reich.

Goebbels: In my opinion, we should simply dissolve the synagogues. The Jews will have to pay for this. I also think it necessary for us to publish an order forbidding Jews to share a sleeping compartment with a German. . . . This must be expressly forbidden by an order from the German Transport Ministry. . . . We must also issue an order forbidding Jews to use swimming pools or spas.

After some radical anti-Semitic suggestions from Goebbels, all of which were endorsed by the assembled committee, it was decided to summon Mr. Hilgard of the German insurance companies.

Goering: Mr. Hilgard, we have discussed the following matter. As a result of the justified anger of the German people at the Jews, a certain amount of damage has been sustained in the Reich. I assume that some of the Jews are insured. This could actually be quite a straightforward matter, since I could simply issue a proclamation which announces that this damage will not be covered by insurance.

Hilgard: The insurance against broken glass, which constitutes a very large part of the damage, is very largely in Aryan [i.e., non-Jewish] hands. By this I mean the ownership of the buildings, while the Jew is usually only the lessee.

Goebbels: Then the Jew must pay for the damage.

Hilgard: Glass used for shop windows is exclusively manufactured by the Belgium glass industry. We are talking here about damage in the region of [$1,500,000]. . . . The largest claim in this area is that of the store Margraf in Unter den Linden, where damages have been assessed at [$425,000] because the place was totally ransacked.

Goering: Daluege! Heydrich! You have got to get this jewelry back by the most massive raids!

Daluege: This has already been ordered.

Goering: If anybody comes into a store to sell jewelry, and says he obtained it legally, it must be taken away from him immediately without any fuss and bother. . . .

Heydrich: Incidentally, there are about eight hundred cases of plundering in the Reich, but we are already working on retrieving the stolen goods.

Goering: And the jewelry?

Heydrich: That is difficult to say. Some pieces were simply thrown on the street and picked up afterward. The same thing happened at the fur shops. . . .

Daluege: We need the Party to issue an order immediately, asking people to inform the police if a neighbor or somebody suddenly appears in a fur coat, or starts wearing rings. . . .

Hilgard: We are particularly anxious, Herr Reichsfeldmarschall, not to be impeded in fulfilling our contractual obligations . . . we are very active in insurance brokerage abroad and must be certain that confidence in German insurance does not suffer. . . .

Heydrich: We could simply pay out the insurance. Then it could be appropriated. In this way we shall have protected our image.

Hilgard: What Obergruppenführer Heydrich has just said seems to be exactly the right course of action.

Goering: The damages you pay to the Jews must be paid by the Jews to the Ministry of Finance. The money belongs to the State. That is quite clear.

Hilgard: According to my estimates, the total damage in Germany amounts to some [$6,250,000].

Heydrich: Damage to stock, goods, etcetera we reckon to amount to [several hundred million dollars].

Goering: I should have preferred it if you had simply bumped off two hundred Jews and had not done so much damage to goods.

Heydrich: Thirty-five people were killed.

Under the chairmanship of Goering, the committee then discussed various ways and means to exclude the Jews from economic life. Heydrich turned down the suggestion that they should be rounded up in ghettos, because he claimed this would create difficulties for the police. He was far more in favor of having every Jew wear a special badge, and depriving the Jews of any mobility by such measures as appropriating driving licenses. Goering allowed a long exchange of ideas along these lines before returning to the matter in hand, which was, of course, how the damage which took place during Kristallnacht should be paid for. Then he hit on an idea. "How would you view the situation," he asked the others, "if I announced today that the Jews, as punishment, must pay a contribution of [$250 million]? I shall, of course, choose the right words—for example, that the Jews in their totality for their reckless crime, et cetera et cetera, are to pay a fine of [$250 million]. . . . These pigs will not be so quick to commit a crime like this again . . ."

There were those in Germany and elsewhere, who wished most fervently that Herschel Grynszpan, the seventeen-year-old Jewish boy, had not killed vom Rath in Paris. For a short-sighted version of historical cause and effect might lead to the conclusion that if Herschel had not pulled the trigger, Kristallnacht would not have happened, the meeting described above would not have taken place, and the social, economic, and financial consequences might have been avoided.

But this would be a particularly blind analysis of what took place. The economic isolation of the Jews, and their persecution within the Reich's frontiers, were but precursors of their final elimination. Herschel Grynszpan's act did not even accelerate the process. Hitler had known as early as 1919 that he was to liquidate the Jews of Europe. And Himmler had known since his earliest days in the SS that he was to act as the executive arm of this liquidation.

The one document which prevented the 17,000 Polish Jews living in Germany since 1933 from suffering the same fate as the German Jews was a Polish passport. If units of the SS and Gestapo were to knock on their doors at three in the morning, they could produce their passports and demand the rights enjoyed by any citizen of a foreign country who happened to be living in Germany at the time. As long as Germany still maintained diplomatic relations with Poland, the Gestapo officials were bound to accord the Polish Jews the rights of aliens.

The action of the Polish government in October 1938 in invalidating the passports of these hapless Jews delivered them into the arms of the SS. At one stroke 17,000 people became stateless. A stateless Jew was different from a Polish Jew in the eyes of the SS, because he had no authority to protect him. The Polish government of 1938 carries the original responsibility for Kristallnacht. The tormented mind of a seventeen-year-old boy living in Paris can hardly be held to blame.

The language used at the meeting described above, attended by the high Nazi functionaries, shows the extent to which their minds had been infected by the virus of anti-Semitism. The cynical and amoral acceptance by Hilgard (representing the German insurance companies) of Heydrich's proposal to pay out damages to the innocent

Jews whose synagogues had been burned and whose shops had been looted, only to have the money appropriated by the State, demonstrates the readiness with which "respectable" German commercial undertakings abandoned any semblance of propriety under Nazi rule.

Insofar as the history of the SS is concerned, its activities in the Kristallnacht episode were crucial. Though the finger of guilt has often been pointed at Goebbels, whose radical anti-Semitism has often been offered as a reason for this act of retribution, the systematic night of terror could not have taken place without the technological equipment of the police state. And within this police state the Schutzstaffeln of Himmler and Heydrich played a predominant role.

8

THE SS AS A
BUSINESS CORPORATION

If you consign thousands of people to concentration camps, they become a charge on the public purse.

Their presence in the camps might result from your paranoid feeling that, left to roam freely within German society, they are likely to undermine the purposes of the State. But this is a suspect economic policy since it means your victims become a burden on the resources of the economy.

The only solution is to make certain that the inmates of the camps are put to work, so that they feed themselves, clothe themselves, construct the camps, build the access roads, engage in some activity as a result of which the running costs of the camps are met, and finally, pay for the housing and living costs of the guards who act as their overlords.

This would make the camps self-financing. But you could go one step further. You could make sure that the camp inmates not only cover all of their own expenses but are driven to work harder so that they actually make a profit for you. This attitude only became pronounced to the police officials within the SS after the camps had been in existence for some years because they were somewhat backward as economists.

The first concentration camps had contained workshops because it had not escaped the eyes of the SS leaders that not only was work of moral benefit to the prisoners, but somehow the costs of their detention had to be met. And from the earliest days after the Nazi seizure of power in 1933 the SS had involved itself in business operations. In December 1934 the Nordland-Verlag GmbH—Nordland Publishing House, Inc.—was founded. Its object was to publish books, pamphlets, and tracts dedicated to popularizing Himmler's theories concerning the special mission of the SS. In 1936 the factory at Allach which turned out "artistic" objects for SS men who had gone in for child-breeding in a big way, was purchased by Himmler and renamed "Porcelain Manufacture Allach-Munich Inc." Its activities were scrutinized by Himmler throughout its life, eventually being moved to Dachau in 1937. Here it operated from a large factory next to the SS exercise square outside the concentration camp compound. About half of its production was supplied to members of Himmler's personal staff, who were "allowed" to purchase items at a 40 percent discount. As a business, the Allach factory never got off the ground. It carried too high overheads, its financial dealings were never clear, its artistic styles were poor, and despite the attempts by accountants to persuade Himmler to give up or reorganize what he had come to see as his pet business, he refused to close it down.

Another early activity of the SS in business was the work undertaken by a firm known as Anton Loibl, Inc. SS-Hauptsturmführer Anton Loibl had had a long association with the Nazi movement. He was decorated with the "Blood Order" and the Golden Party Badge. He invented a kind of illuminated disc which, when applied to the pedals of a bicycle, had the effect of making the rider visible to traffic in the dark. This interested Himmler, who as chief of the German police, thought its universal application might reduce the number of road accidents. From June 1939 the illuminated pedal discs invented by Loibl must by law be part of every bicycle sold in the Reich. This prescription was to make Loibl a rich man, since he owned the patent on his invention. But in a tit-for-tat arrangement with Himmler, Loibl undertook to pay 50 percent of his annual profits into the coffers of the SS. Himmler, it must be stressed, on no occasion ever made personal use of these moneys. They were directed to the Ahnenerbe-Stiftung (an institute for research into Germanic ancestry) or Lebensborn (the SS institute for pairing SS men with suitable partners for breeding children).

A special SS savings organization called Spargemeinschaft-SS was founded in late 1935. It made it compulsory for each SS man to contribute one mark each month toward a common fund. This fund was designed to be used to liquidate any debts incurred by members of the SS which they were unable comfortably to meet out of income. This was to take the form of interest-free loans. By the summer of 1939 not one SS man ever received any of these loans and the capital was used to finance other nascent economic undertakings of the SS.

Himmler's preoccupation with the German past induced him to found a company in 1936 called "Society for the Protection and Maintenance of German Cultural Monuments." This organization consumed large sums of money since it was responsible for financing the reconstruction of the castle at Wewelsberg. The labor force needed to put Himmler's plans into effect came from the concentration camps, and at one time no less than one thousand workers from the camps were installed in the temporary work camps near Wewelsberg.

The above were the initial economic overtures of the SS and were colored by Himmler's predilection for research into history. It was clear, however, that with its far-reaching ramifications the SS was in an ideal position to enter the German economy on a much wider basis. But Himmler was no economist, and it was not until a man named Oswald Pohl joined his staff that the SS made its first entrance into big business. Indeed, the economic activities of the SS bear the stamp of Oswald Pohl.

Pohl was born in Duisburg in 1892 and on completion of his education entered the German Navy, where he had set his sights on obtaining a high position in naval administration. In April 1918 he was awarded the rank of naval paymaster and by the end of the First World War was a naval lieutenant. He studied law at Kiel and then reentered the reconstituted German Navy. Like countless others who ended up in the SS, he did service with the Freikorps. In 1920 he entered the Freikorps Loewenfeld and participated in their activities in Upper Silesia and the Ruhr. He joined the Nazi party and the SA in 1926 and from 1929 to 1931 was the local Nazi agent and SA leader in Swinemünde. In these capacities he founded the naval division of the SA in Kiel. He also entered the Kiel City Council and became active in the local Hitler Youth organization. By 1933 he enjoyed the rank in the SA of Sturmbannführer, or major.

Himmler first met Pohl in May 1933. As Reichsführer-SS he was inspecting the German fleet at Kiel in the company of other leading Nazis. Himmler was intrigued: Pohl had considerable administrative experience and, what was even more exciting, appeared to know something of that dark science known as economics, about which to the end of his days Himmler was totally confused. There could be no doubt of Pohl's ideological soundness. Himmler quickly realized that Pohl was just the man he had been looking for to assist him in setting up a suitable administrative apparatus for the expansion plans he had been diligently laying for his SS. He offered Pohl the position of Leader of the SS Administration Office with the rank of Standartenführer (colonel), and, after some hesitation, Pohl accepted.

Pohl excelled in his new position. On June 1, 1935, he was made Reichskassenverwalter or Chief Financial Officer of the SS. This made him responsible only to Himmler and gave him entry into the German Treasury itself. On January 30, 1937, Pohl became Gruppenführer (Major-General) and on April 30, 1939, he headed a new organization called Wirtschaft- und Verwaltungshauptamt (Main Office for Economics and Administration). In this capacity he was in control of huge sums of money. The entire police forces of the Reich, the SS-Verfügungstruppen out of which the Armed-SS grew, the administration of the concentration camps, the activities of the Gestapo and SD, all came within his administrative and financial competence. On April 20, 1939, his official status was that of "Ministerial Director," immediately under Himmler in the Ministry of the Interior, and Leader of the Main Office for Economics and Construction. Pohl was not as well versed in economics as Himmler had supposed and encountered severe problems he was unable to resolve.

Deutsche Erd- und Steinwerke (DEST) was by far the most adventurous of the businesses in which the SS became engaged. It was founded in April 1938 with the ridiculously small capital of $2,500. It was intended to meet the enormous demands for building materials which Hitler's ambitious plans for the reconstruction of several German cities necessitated. To a large extent the type of stone and bricks needed to implement these plans was determined by Albert Speer, Hitler's architect, to whom had been entrusted the historic task of putting Hitler's wishes into effect. It was a limited liability company and like all such associations was compelled by law to contain in its articles of association an "objects" clause which would list the purposes of its activity. Among those offered by DEST were: (1) the exploitation of quarries and the obtaining of natural stones, (2) the production of bricks, and (3) the undertaking of road construction. Labor was critical in all these pursuits. A captive labor force existed in the concentration camps. In fact, the selection of sites for the later camps was often determined by their proximity to appropriate quarries. Speer and Himmler agreed to obtain the needed building materials by exploiting the inmates of the camps. The overall economic aspects of this arrangement were to be supervised by Oswald Pohl.

So far it seems as if the pundits of the SS and the Nazi party had arrived at a highly successful arrangement from their point of view. They had a captive labor market. They would not be impeded on any irritating union problems. The number of working hours could be fixed by one criterion only, and that was how long their labor force could stand up to the harsh rigors of this heavy work with a totally inadequate diet.

But they had forgotten one important factor. The SS guards of the Death's Head Units spent their time beating up the prisoners. This they had been urged to do tacitly or openly by their superiors. They had therefore taken up brutality as a way of life, and this proved habit-forming.

You could not beat a man senseless and then tell him to get up and work in a quarry. Neither could you give him a diet of two hundred calories a day and get him to work an eleven-hour shift. You could not, in short, have it both ways.

The activities of DEST fell within two main categories. First was the work of quarrying for appropriate stone and granite. The first quarry was located at Flossenburg, and work started in 1938. The establishment of the concentration camp at Flossenburg followed soon after. By May 1942 no less than 1,700 inmates of the camp were involved in the heavy work of obtaining granite suitable for building purposes. Because of the urgency with which Hitler's and Speer's work was to be undertaken, Flossenburg was eventually equipped with a variety of mechanical aids to maximize output. Other camps were sited near appropriate digging areas, especially those of Mauthausen, Natzweiler, and Gross-Rosen. After the Anschluss (annexation) with Austria, both Pohl and Himmler repaired to Mauthausen to determine whether it offered the correct proximity to the nearby stone quarries. The demanding and dangerous work at Mauthausen resulted in a high casualty rate. At its peak the number of prisoners engaged in this work varied between 2,000 and 4,000.

The selection of Natzweiler can be attributed to Speer. He was particularly eager to obtain the special reddish granite which existed in abundance in this area of Alsace. After the occupation of France thousands of prisoners were put to work to establish the camp at Natzweiler which they would then use as base.

The second activity of DEST was the manufacture of bricks and clinker for building. One week after the founding of the company, Pohl announced that the SS leadership intended to start work immediately in the neighborhood of Weimar, which of course meant that the labor force at the camp at nearby Buchenwald would be exploited. The camps at Oranienburg, Berlstedt, Neuengamme, Stutthof, Auschwitz, and Treblinka were also involved in the second activity.

The volume of production in 1939 of DEST—its first full year of operation—reached only $400,000, but by 1943 it had a turnover of $3 million.

A further important economic enterprise founded by the SS was the Deutsche Ausrüstungswerke GmbH, an attempt by Pohl to centralize the work which took place in the different camps at the workshop level. The products of carpenters, electricians, and locksmiths were first collected in the summer of 1940 from the camps at Sach-

Young Nazis burn books and pamphlets considered *ungerman*. *(Imperial War Museum)*

Naval Captain Ehrhardt (bearded), leader of the notorious Ehrhardt Brigade. Taken during the Kapp Putsch, 1920. *(Bundesarchiv)*

Hitler and Ernst Roehm at the Nuremberg Party Rally in September, 1933. *(Robert Hunt)*

Himmler (*left*) and Ernst Kaltenbrunner (*right*) on a visit to the concentration camp at Mauthausen. *(Robert Hunt)*

Himmler visits Dachau in May, 1936. *(Bundesarchiv)*

Mr. and Mrs. Heinri
Himmler. *(Bundesc
chiv)*

From an official Nazi document in which Himmler testifies to his Aryan background. *(Bundesarchiv)*

Himmler and Hitler on Hitler's birthday, April 20, 1939, viewing a march-past of the Leibstandarte-SS Adolf Hitler. *(Bundesarchiv)*

1942: Reinhard and Lina Heydrich attend a concert in Prague a few days before the successful attempt on Heydrich's life. *(Bundesarchiv)*

Reinhard Heydrich. *(Bundesarchiv)*

(Left), in the Warsaw Ghetto, units of the SS round up Jewish victims for extermination. *(Robert Hunt)*

Ernst Kaltenbrunner, Heydrich's successor at the Reichssicherheitshauptamt. *(Robert Hunt)*

Adolf Eichmann. *(Robert Hunt)*

Oskar Dirlewanger, commander of a Waffen-SS brigade—part of an Einsatzgruppe—which comprised poachers, professional criminals and men under court-martial. *(Robert Hunt)*

Some of the SS women who assisted in the administration of the concentration camps. *(Imperial War Museum)*

Himmler inspects the Mauthausen concentration camp in the company of Kaltenbrunner and the camp commandant. *(Robert Hunt)*

senhausen and Buchenwald. The object was a form of economic rationalization, and the Deutsche Ausrüstungswerke ended up servicing the output of a large number of camps. National needs as interpreted by the economic leadership of the SS were to replace the individual inclinations of the camp commandants in determining both the type of work to be undertaken and the eventual distribution of the products. By the end of the war, the company had the proportions of a giant industrial undertaking. In 1943 it "employed" no fewer than 15,000 concentration camp inmates. It also concluded a deal whereby it would purchase from Messerschmidt (chiefly known as aircraft manufacturers) a supply of tools, equipment, and the technical know-how of its engineers in exchange for having Messerschmidt personnel supervise the work of the camp inmates. After 1942 the main activity of Deutsche Ausrüstungswerke was directed to the war effort, and some 90 percent of its work consisted in the manufacture of munitions containers, bullet casings, guns, and other army equipment.

Within the general war economy of Germany, all these activities appeared to have a rational purpose. But the economists of Pohl's office had not reckoned with the cranky preoccupations of their leader, Himmler. He had been absorbed in the study of herbs and their uses for many years and was determined to use his new resources to follow this hobby. To this end, the Deutsche Versuchsanstalt für Ernährung und Verpflegung (German Experimental Institute for Nutrition and Provisioning) was founded in January 1939. As a result practically every concentration camp was provided with special gardens in which herbs were cultivated and their medicinal uses studied. While beyond the garden wall the ghastly process of mass murder was taking place, within the cultivation areas scientists were busily applying themselves to the study of Himmler's pet theories. The Commandant of Auschwitz, Rudolf Hoess, was as besotted with this subject as Himmler was and claimed, "The purpose is to remove all alien plants and artificial medicines from the German people and to bring them back to the use of benign, tasty German products and natural herbs."

The Gesellschaft für Textil- und Lederverwertung (Textiles and Leather Society) founded by the SS in June 1940 was principally occupied in providing the Armed-SS with uniforms and was designed to keep female inmates of the camp at Ravensbruck busy. It also produced uniforms for prisoners and perfected certain processes whereby shoes and boots could be made out of packed straw for troops stationed in Norway and Russia. Furriers were also used to provide fur-lined greatcoats for the SS, fur anoraks, and fur hats and gloves. In the autumn of 1942 some 5,000 women prisoners were engaged in these activities and by 1943 the total volume of production reached $2 million.

Originally the concentration camps were meant to be centers in which potential political and social opponents of the Nazi regime could be brutalized. The development of the SS as a big-business corporation suggested far different uses for the inmates. They were now a labor force. As a result of this difference in purpose, between the brutal acts of the policeman and the orientation of the businessman, the SS found itself subject to a form of schizophrenia. What were the economists of the SS to do about the tradition of barbaric cruelty their police associates in the camps had established? They had no moral quarrel with them. It was simply that beating up prisoners was bad for business. The economic exploitation of prisoners came within the sphere of Pohl's Office D-11 of the Wirtschaft- und Verwaltungshauptamt. The daily treatment of prisoners was a police matter which depended on the individual inclinations of the camp commandant and his underlings, who had become professional sadists. How could the gap be bridged?

The position was aggravated further because in order to fulfill the economic targets of Pohl and his associates, work parties from the camps often had to make sorties to neighboring sites outside the camp compounds. This they did under strict surveillance, but it made great demands on SS security arrangements. The interests of the police and the economists within the SS therefore ran along totally different lines, which were continuously at variance with each other.

Pohl wondered what he should do. Finally he devised a remarkably simple solution. The camp commandants should be made responsible for the economic output of their camps. Some form of financial incentive should be offered them to ensure their active collaboration with his office. So there was to be industrial incentives within the chaotic system which obtained in the concentration camps.

What should these incentives be? Pohl pondered for some time. He decided they should vary from camp to camp. If you were a commandant at Dachau or Ravensbruck, you received a supplement of about $45 per *month,* while if you were at Natzweiler you could earn $15 on top of your salary. As financial incentives these are so small that they must assuredly reflect the pettifogging influence of Himmler. They also point to the small-time business mind of Pohl who, had he had greater experience in industry in a free economy, might have been tempted to offer more meaningful sums.

To coordinate his thinking on these difficult issues, Pohl issued a memorandum on April 30, 1942, which was distributed to all concentration camp commandants and contained the following directive:

> The leadership of a concentration camp and all the economic activities undertaken by the SS within its sphere lay firmly in the hands of the camp commandant. He alone is responsible for the viability of the various enterprises. The SS labor leader within the camp is responsible to the camp commandant for carrying out the economic tasks assigned to the camp. He thereby carries joint responsibility with the commandant for any failures. The camp commandant is alone responsible for the full use of the available work force. In order to maximize output, the work force must be exploited literally to the point of exhaustion. . . . Carrying out this order will clearly place substantially greater demands on the commandant than has hitherto been the case. Since conditions vary from camp to camp it is impossible to set down some common approach which will apply universally. Therefore the entire initiative rests on the individual camp commandant. He must combine specialized knowledge in military and economic affairs with astute and wise leadership of groups of people in such a way as to realize highest potential of performance.

These words might have satisfied Pohl's doubts but had very little effect other than to endorse the view each camp commandant had that he was master in his own house. Police officials do not necessarily make good businessmen, but they readily recognize an increase of individual power, and since their lives within the camps had consisted of abusing this power at the expense of their captives, the effect of Pohl's directive was to make for further conflict within the camps. The commandants understood little of the economic process. If Pohl wanted more production, this meant to these police officials simply wielding the whip more fiercely. Not surprisingly, this did not increase production.

In the background, Himmler attempted to keep himself informed on the vast potential of labor within the camps. He was entranced with the idea that if one trained these captives, once the war was over, the SS would have at its bidding the expertise of thousands of masons and builders to implement the reconstruction plans of Hitler and Speer. In December 1941 he wrote an enthusiastic memorandum to all camp commandants, with copies to Pohl and Heydrich, in which he stated:

> I have ordered SS-Gruppenführer Pohl by the end of the war to provide at least 5,000 stonemasons and 10,000 bricklayers from the ranks of concentration camp prisoners. . . . If it is realized that before the war in Germany we only had about 4,000 qualified stonemasons, it is easy to see the extent of this training plan. . . . To fulfil this program each camp commandant must pay special attention to the following:
>
> 1. To increase the ability of selected prisoners by sensible measures, if need be by additional food and clothing.
> 2. The camp commandants . . . bear the responsibility for the success of what up to now has for many been totally impossible. Years ago many SS specialists maintained that you could not make skilled workers out of prisoners. These gentlemen have in the meantime been forced to persuade themselves of the opposite. . . . I therefore expect everyone involved in this activity to work together in fullest cooperation. . . .

The administrators of the Deutsche Erd- und Steinwerke made literally hundreds of applications to camp commandants to release certain prisoners who appeared suitable for training as masons or bricklayers. But permission first had to be granted by the Reichssicherheitshauptamt (Reich Main Security Office), which alone had the authority to decide on the question of release of prisoners. In all the years the economists pressed to implement Himmler's order, only thirty-five prisoners were eventually taken out of the camps for training.

Furthermore, at the lower level of SS guards there was little interest in the economic activities of the prisoners. They were there to be beaten. They were *staatsfeindlich,* enemies of the State. If they collapsed while they worked an eleven- or twelve-hour day carrying rocks, that was perfectly in order. Gruppenführer Gluecks therefore wrote a circular to camp commandants in December 1943 in which he said: "I understand that mainly in the smaller working parties very little or no work at all is being achieved. The NCO and his assistants simply stand around and take no notice of the prisoners. One corporal with whom I recently spoke actually told me that he and his troop were expressly forbidden to urge the prisoners to work. This is of course absolute nonsense. Every NCO and private must see to it that the prisoners under his control are put to work. I do not need to stress that under no circumstances should the prisoners be beaten or kicked. . . . They must be urged to work verbally. . . . I would ask you to arrange a weekly lecture to the leaders of your working parties to instruct them on this obvious duty of the guards. . . ."

As the demands of total war increased, particularly during its latter stages, Pohl was determined to get more and more production out of the camps. The enlightened measures Himmler had elaborated in 1941 can be compared with Pohl's directive of November 1943: "I must insist that a working day of at least eleven hours even during the winter months be prescribed for prisoners. The only exceptions are those who are working outdoors where the hours of daylight are a limiting factor. However, those prisoners occupied in the factories or workshops must do an eleven-hour day Monday to Saturday inclusive and if need be they must work Sunday mornings too."

Pohl was not a very judicious economist. The daily output of work of concentration camp inmates varied between 5 percent and 10 percent of that which obtained in similar occupations outside the camps. Simply put, it meant that you had to use many hundreds more prisoners within the camp system to perform jobs than you would if you employed ordinary "outside" labor. And these hundreds had to be housed (however primitively), fed (however inadequately), and supervised by more and more guards. Therefore the *real* economic costs of using concentration camp labor were immeasurably higher than was appreciated by the administration of the SS.

How were the SS companies financed and from whom did they receive their working capital?

They were initially registered as private limited liability companies with transparently small capital in relation to their ambitious schemes. Shareholders were usually Pohl himself and Himmler. Gigantic bank loans had to be negotiated. Here the conniving Himmler paid off handsomely. No fewer than three of the directors of the Dresdner Bank were members of that exclusive circle, the Friends of the Reichsführer-SS. They were Professor Emil Meyer, Dr. Karl Rasche, and Fritz Kranefuss. What is more, each of these gentlemen carried SS rank. Over the years the Dresdner Bank loaned the Economic Office of the SS no less than $7 million, all apparently on the sole guarantee of Heinrich Himmler. However, the Dresdner Bank was a commercial undertaking and levied prevailing rates of interest.

Accordingly by 1939 the SS began to cast about for cheaper sources of money. They claimed that they were after all involved in a program of public works and made overtures to the Reichsbank itself for large loans at preferential interest rates. Their initiative was rewarded, for in October 1939 the Reichsbank authorized an advance to the SS Company DEST of $2 million at the absurdly low interest rate of 3 percent. This was eventually dropped to 2.5 percent, which was of course way below prevailing market rates. A further method of raising working capital devised by the SS economic leadership was to issue promissory notes based on the provision of future quantities of bricks. This device was approved by Speer, who himself authorized interest-free loans of $2.5 million. Pohl also managed to get his hands on the assets of the German Red Cross from whom he obtained funds amounting to $2 million.

Finally, the SS economic leadership had at its disposal the assets of the inmates of the camps, particularly of the Jews they had murdered. They planted SS-Gruppenführer Frank in the Reichsbank itself and through his good offices managed to obtain some $7.5 million at the absurdly low interest rate of 2 percent, totally unsecured.

Since labor costs were negligible and since borrowing money cost them little or nothing at all, it might have been expected that the SS ran a very successful business. The legal status of SS enterprises as limited liability companies compelled them to produce annual balance sheets and profit-and-loss accounts. Until about 1940 many of their activities showed only minor profits and their larger undertakings produced substantial losses. As the war progressed and as all economic enterprises were coordinated, subsequent profits were used to offset earlier losses and what was left was generally used to pay taxes or was ploughed back. But at no time were profits ever distributed to the "shareholders." The shares were considered to be the general property of the SS as a whole, as were the overall assets of the various companies. This in turn led to a series of discussions among the legal and economic experts of the SS as to what in fact the SS really constituted. Technically it was a division of the Party. But there is no doubt it resented any such interpretation of its status. As the years went by, the SS increased its sphere of operations for one purpose only, and that was to emerge as a self-perpetuating totally independent organization, untrammeled by the Party, unanswerable to the various Reich ministries, and totally dedicated to bringing a New Order to Europe and the world. Since Oswald Pohl was the central figure of these various enterprises, as Head of the SS Economics and Administration Office, he began to worry about who might succeed him should he die. Somebody had to carry out the true purpose of the SS. There should be no room for some aspiring tax consultant or legal expert to undo his good work. Accordingly on October 27, 1943, in the presence of a notary public he signed a transfer document which on his death assigned to Himmler all the assets of which he was both titular and real administrator. It was then up to Himmler to determine the best course of action in harmony with the true spirit of the SS. In a report issued as early as June 1939, SS Colonel Dr. Salpeter noted that despite the divergent legal origins of the SS enterprises, despite the various sources of capital which had been raised to finance them, "Nothing alters the basic legal fact that behind it all stands the SS as a political association with special functions."

The nature of the legal niceties with which the different SS bureaucrats, lawyers, and economists concerned themselves cannot screen the real purpose of the exercise. This was to release the SS from any form of control by Party or State and to make it a totally independent organization, as some have claimed, a state within a state. Although the establishment of legal liability companies shows that the radicalism of the SS did not lead them to invent some new form of economic enterprise, we have the word of Oswald Pohl himself in a memo to his associates dated July 11, 1944: "I repeat here what I emphasize at every opportunity; the purpose of our economic undertakings is not the pursuit of profit, but the establishment of things which are of concern to us in the spirit of the SS, thus in accordance with the pronouncements of the Reichsführer-SS."

9

THE SS ABROAD
BEFORE THE WAR

The SS magazine *Das Schwarze Korps* on January 28, 1937, contained an editorial which vilified that most august institution, the German publishing house of Degener, known all over the world as the publishers of the German *Who's Who*.

Who's Who for 1937 contained a series of names which incurred the wrath of editor Günter d'Alquen and his colleagues. In its pages were "Jews, literary emigrants, political swindlers, former Socialist party hacks, pacifists . . . and of course the entire intellectual backwash of the Palestinian colony in Vienna."

The SS could not wait to get its hands on this disgusting assembly of renegade Germans who had fled from Germany to Austria to escape the consequences of Nazi persecution. Furthermore, it was their avowed intention to cleanse Austria, their German sister-nation, of these antisocial elements which were still at large and which must be removed once the Anschluss had taken place. In fact they had to wait until March 1938 to put their plans into effect. Immediately after the Anschluss a shuttle service was established in which trains full of undesirable deportees made their way regularly from the Austrian capital to the concentration camp at Dachau.

The SS had already demonstrated singular ineptitude as early as July 1934 in its attempt to incorporate Austria within the Reich. At the time Austria was governed by a right-wing administration headed by Chancellor Engelbert Dollfuss. Threatened by Austrian Nazis on the Right and extremists on the Left, Dollfuss was in constant touch with Mussolini in Italy for advice on how to run the country. At the time, Mussolini was far from being the devoted ally of Hitler he was to become; in fact he looked with suspicion at Hitler's obvious intentions to extend German influence into the Balkans, which Mussolini considered to be part of Italy's natural operational area. He was at great pains to persuade Dollfuss to establish a fascist state in Austria. He urged Dollfuss to deal firmly with both Social Democratic and

Nazi functions to achieve this. In February 1934 a threat was made by the Social Democrats to undermine the economy by a general strike. Dollfuss exploited this threat to justify the use of artillery against workers' quarters in Vienna. He banned the Austrian Nazi party and founded Anhaltelager, detainment camps, in which he imprisoned his extremist opponents. Hitler was thereby placed in a quandary. He wanted Austria, but he did not want to alienate Mussolini. Therefore a situation had to be arranged whereby it looked as if Austria had turned to the Nazi cause through its own spontaneous activities. Germany could pretend to observe these events as a disinterested outsider. Hitler issued a proclamation in which he stated that Austria's independence should in no way be tampered with. At the same time he gave Theodor Habicht, the leading Austrian Nazi, a directive to pursue the real interests of Germany by initiating acts of terror and sabotage to bring about the collapse of the Dollfuss government.

Groups of the banned Nazi party in Austria began to engage in acts of terror. Whenever there was the slightest chance of their being apprehended by the Austrian police, they would simply disappear over the German frontier. They laid bombs at railway junctions and in areas where tourism flourished, thereby hoping to undermine the Austrian economy. Several thousand armed men called the "Austrian Legion" were positioned just across the German frontier to wait for their marching orders, orders which would permit them to invade Austria once the "provocation" of their Austrian brother Nazis became intolerable. It was clear to Dollfuss that their presence must have been sanctioned by Hitler. Despite this, he hung on steadily.

The takeover was obviously not proceeding with the speed the Nazi government in Germany considered necessary. Accordingly a putsch was devised in which the men of SS-Standarte 89 were to be employed.

On the morning of July 25, 1934, Dollfuss was presiding over a Cabinet meeting. Immediately after he intended to pay a visit to Mussolini; indeed his wife and children had already been sent to Italy ahead of him. News of an impending attack on his life leaked through to him, but he had had such threats before and refused to believe it, despite the fact that a certain Austrian member of parliament called Fey insisted that this time the Nazis meant business. Dollfuss did not know what to do. He was anxious to finish the business of the day so that he might begin his journey to Italy. Finally he dismissed the Cabinet and asked his ministers to return to their respective offices and await further developments. He himself remained in the Chancellory together with Fey and a man named Karl Karwinsky who was Minister of State Security.

The men of SS-Standarte 89 had clothed themselves in the uniforms of a famous Austrian regiment and made their way at the appointed hour in trucks to the Chancellory building. The few soldiers guarding the entrance to the forecourt gave the trucks permission to drive on through. There was no reason not to. Once inside the courtyard the disguised SS men jumped out of the trucks, rapidly disarmed the few policemen there, and stormed the building. The old palace of the famous Austrian statesman Metternich was like a rabbit warren, but the SS-Standarte 89 had exact plans and rapidly occupied all key positions. All the government officials and servants were assembled under guard in the courtyard, while the exterior of the building was policed by additional SS troops still in Austrian army uniform.

All of this caused a considerable amount of noise. Minister of Security Karwinsky urged Dollfuss to leave the building by some inconspicuous route before he was apprehended. But all exits had been cordoned off and Dollfuss and his accomplices decided to return to the Cabinet room. En route they encountered a group of SS men among whose number was a certain Otto Planetta. Planetta withdrew his pistol and shot Dollfuss from a distance of two feet. His aim was faulty and the bullet entered Dollfuss's armpit, which caused him to reel about. Planetta aimed for a second time and the bullet entered the Austrian Chancellor's throat. At this point Dollfuss lost consciousness.

Two of the SS assassins picked up the Chancellor and stretched him out on a nearby sofa. They threw a sheet over him and waited for some message to reach them from their comrades whose mission was to occupy the radio building.

Meanwhile, an additional SS troop had indeed made its way into the radio building. Technicians who were supervising the transmission of a lunchtime concert were instructed to interrupt the program and announce: "The government of Dollfuss has retired. Dr. Rintelen has taken over the business of government." Dr. Rintelen was the Nazi appointee who at the time was in the Hotel Imperial in Vienna, awaiting the news of the success of the putsch before forming a Nazi government.

But the SS men in the exercise had made one very costly error. In all of their precise planning they had omitted to occupy the radio transmission center at Bisamberg. Here, the technicians who were loyal to Dollfuss, on hearing the above announcement, simply turned off the entire network. Hundreds of Nazi groups through Austria who had been waiting impatiently for instructions over the radio were therefore without the guidance they needed before they could act.

Dollfuss's ministers had assembled at the War Ministry. They telephoned President Miklas, who immediately ordered Education Minister Schuschnigg to carry on the affairs of government and invested him with full powers to quell the putsch. Austrian Army and police units rapidly disarmed the SS troops who had occupied the Vienna radio station. A certain amount of ineffectual shooting took place in various parts of the country, but this was short-lived and it soon became clear that the putsch had failed.

Meanwhile Dollfuss, Fey, and Karwinsky were still prisoners of the SS-Standarte 89 in the Chancellory. Austrian police had surrounded the building but were rendered immobile lest they endanger the life of Dollfuss.

Equally indecisive were the SS captors themselves. They even asked Fey what course of action he felt would be most appropriate. So much for the value of SS leadership courses initiated by Heinrich Himmler. Schuschnigg issued an ultimatum to the SS men that if they did not voluntarily surrender, government troops would storm the building.

They behaved in a traditional manner. The dying man was refused both a doctor and a priest. One of them placed a piece of dampened cotton wool on his forehead, but that was all they were prepared to do for him. At 3:45 P.M. Dollfuss died.

The SS captors still sat on in the Chancellory, incapable of further action. They had a dead chancellor on their hands and they had an Austrian minister and an Austrian member of parliament as prisoners. They were in a building surrounded by the Austrian gendarmerie. The German Foreign Ministry decided it was time it did something for the stranded SS men. It sent German ambassador Rieth to the Chancellory building on the Ballhausplatz.

On arrival outside the Cancellory, Rieth turned to an Austrian official and by way of conversation said: "What a strange business!" "Your Excellency," answered this official, "I find it quite remarkable that you can find no other words to describe this frightful event. The guilt for this bloody act and for what has happened here lies beyond the Austrian frontier."

Rieth then turned to a member of the Austrian Cabinet to ask for his intervention and understandably enough was coldly received. "What is going to happen now is entirely our affair," he was told,

"and incidentally I should not recommand you to attempt to intervene
by advising us to negotiate with rebels."

"Under these circumstances," said the German ambassador, "I do
not believe I have any further function here," upon which he simply
walked away.

The SS, in its first sortie abroad, had distinguished itself by its ineptitude and inefficiency. It had run the risk of alienating Mussolini,
potentially Germany's most trusty ally, and it had shown itself to be
composed of a mob of bullies adept at handing out physical punishment but incapable of politically sophisticated action.

Until the Anschluss in 1938 the SS had to content itself with a
series of gradual encroachments on the work of the Abwehr—Army
counterintelligence service—and the Foreign Office. The Abwehr was
their own entree to sealing the fate of Austria. This was largely due
to the existence within the SS of a number of disaffected members of
the SD who felt they had lost in the internal battle for power with the
Gestapo. If they could show some expertise in the field of foreign intelligence work their wounded pride would to a considerable extent
be assuaged. They had first to arrive at some kind of understanding
with the Abwehr and its chief, Admiral Canaris, a former superior of
Heydrich while he had been in the Navy. As an Army department
the Abwehr enjoyed a relatively independent role in the Nazi administration. A compromise which was called at the time the "Ten Com-
mandments" attempted to define the different roles of the Abwehr,
the Gestapo, and the SD. It did not reckon on the insistent ambitions
of the SD, which gradually infiltrated the network of foreign secret
services and behaved in a somewhat clumsy fashion. Canaris was
continuously under pressure from his own men, who asked him to
put a stop to the meddlesome interference of these brash amateurs.

The unspoken war between Canaris and Heydrich came to a head
as a result of what has been called the Tuchachevsky Affair. In 1936,
SD agents advised Heydrich that Stalin's position was threatened by
the formation of an opposition group under the leadership of Marshal
Tuchachevsky, who occupied the exalted position of Deputy
Commissar for War. Heydrich was entranced at this news. He would
use it for two purposes. He could feed it back to official Russian circles and undermine Stalin's faith in the Red Army. This would
doubtless result in a purge. He could also steal a march on the Abwehr. At one stroke he could undermine Stalin's regime and prove to
Hitler that his own SD rather than the stuffy officials in the Abwehr
had unearthed the facts.

The problem was, how was Heydrich to provide proof of the existence of dissident Soviet generals and then transmit it to Stalin? Then he had a brainstorm. Throughout the period when the German Army had been under the command of Hans von Seeckt in the 1920s, German officers had been seconded to Moscow to assist the new Soviet Republic in training its armed forces. This was no novelty in German history. For centuries the Prussian General Staff had favored a rapprochement with Russia so that it might turn its energies more profitably to containing the French "threat" to the West. Documents therefore existed in the files of the German War Ministry which bore the signature of Russian generals. They had nothing to do with a campaign against Russian civil leadership, but they could be copied. They could then be transferred to faked incriminating documents.

Heydrich summoned a man called Alfred Naujocks. Naujocks was in charge of an SS office whose function was to provide false travel permits and forged documents. The two men discussed the wording of the messages which were purported to have passed between the "conspiring" Soviet generals, and Naujocks then went back to work. So obsessed was Heydrich with his inspiration that he failed to pay any attention to the warning of one of his own men, Hauptsturmführer Jahnke. Jahnke maintained that the real source of this rumor was a Russian exile living in Paris who worked as a double agent, acting for both the SD and the Soviet Secret Police. Jahnke was upbraided by Heydrich and even placed under house arrest. The moral of this, which did not escape Jahnke, was that when Heydrich had an idea, it was safer to agree with him than to place obstacles in his path.

Once the documents had been prepared at Naujock's office, they had to reach the Soviet Union. None other than Benes, President of Czechoslovakia, was persuaded to act as intermediary. Via Prague the existence of these highly incriminating documents was made known to Stalin. He sent a representative of the Soviet Secret Service to Berlin to negotiate their release so that he could study them. The story has been recounted that Heydrich demanded the sum of three million rubles for these forged documents. This sum was paid. But the Soviets had stolen a march on the SS. The ruble notes were as forged as the documents they had purchased!

Whether the Russians ever believed in the authenticity of Heydrich's documents and whether the Red Army purge would have taken place without them is a subject of endless speculation. But on June 11, 1937, Tass News Agency announced that Marshal Tuchachevsky and seven Red Army generals had been examined by a special tribunal and condemned to death because "they had maintained treasonable relationships with leading military circles of a foreign power which was pursuing a policy hostile to the Soviet Union."

No doubts existed in Heydrich's mind. It was he and his SD which had created this fracas. What was even more exhilarating for him were the further developments in Russia. For the Tuchachevsky trial was followed by a systematic purge, and within a year half of the Soviet officer corps was eliminated. The Soviet Army would need years to replace these experts. As a fighting force its effectiveness had been placed in jeopardy in the foreseeable future.

Old hands like Canaris and the Russian experts in the German War Ministry were aware that Stalin had decided to rid himself of Tuchachevsky and clean out the Russian Army stable long before Heydrich had his inspiration. But at the time Heydrich went around jubilantly announcing that he and his SD had emasculated the entire Soviet Army. This filip to the SD was sorely needed; they could now hold their heads high and Heydrich could demonstrate that his new intelligence methods were far more effective than those practices by the so-called experts of the Abwehr. Although outwardly Canaris would behave cordially toward Heydrich, he was repelled by his sordid tactics and detested the swagger of the man. The Tuchachevsky Affair crystallized the enmity between SD and Abwehr and meant for Canaris the start of that schizoid existence in which his overwhelming patriotism as an old-fashioned German conservative was always placed in the balance by the repulsive behavior of his opposite numbers in the SS and SD.

The most significant warning of the role to be played by the SS outside of German national frontiers came immediately after the Anschluss with Austria in March 1938.

They now found themselves with a new area in which they could determine who was and who was not *staatsfeindlich*. Himmler himself landed at Vienna airport at three in the morning of March 12, 1938. In his party were Gottlob Berger, Karl Wolff and many other high-ranking SS officials. He was received by the chief of the Austrian SS, Ernst Kaltenbrunner, and Odilo Globocnik, both of whom were to be engaged in mass murder during the course of the war. Himmler's first duty was to arrange a reception for his Führer at Linz and set the stage for Hitler's triumphant entry into his favorite Austrian city. Once he had satisfied himself that security arrangements were tight and that the streets had been suitably bedecked, he repaired to Vienna where he set up his headquarters in the Imperial Hotel. That very night, the first mass arrests took place.

The main target of SS activity in Austria was the Jews, but there were several specific groups which were dealt with beforehand. Catholic priests, Communists, Freemasons, monarchists, and even boy scouts were rounded up, and three weeks after the Anschluss a special train carried no fewer than 165 former Austrian civil servants to Dachau. Many died there; the rest had to endure seven years of captivity. The survivors were to play an important role in the postwar Austrian government. Among them was Dr. Figl, who became Vice-Chancellor, and Dr. Geroe, who was appointed Minister of Justice. By the end of 1938 the enemies of the State did not need to be transported to Germany. Himmler and Pohl had already selected Mauthausen as a suitable site for a concentration camp, and this lay within Austrian frontiers.

It was to the Jews that the officials of the SS and Gestapo addressed themselves with the utmost dispatch. This in part must have resulted from the Führer's early exposure to Viennese anti-Semitism while a teenager in a Viennese rooming house. In Vienna Heydrich founded the "Office of Jewish Emigration," whose function was to secure large sums of money from those Jews who had the wherewithal to purchase exit visas. The alternative was death or unendurable persecution in the concentration camps, so any Jew who was able to get his hands on the money exacted by Heydrich's office considered himself privileged. As a money earner for the SS, the Office of Jewish Emigration was in an unparalleled position. This office was eventually to take over the question of Jewish "emigration" from all quarters of the greatly extended Reich and was placed under the leadership of Adolf Eichmann. Before the war many Jewish children were able to purchase their freedom from bondage under the Nazis by joining one of the several Jewish Youth "transports" to Holland (where they were eventually to learn that their liquidation had only been postponed) and to England.

Within months of the Anschluss, Austria had the trappings of a police state. It became an SS state in which *Schutzhaft* (protective custody) was the key word, it had concentration camps, and the entire apparatus of Nazi institutions was brought to bear on its captive population. It must not be forgotten that to a considerable extent the Nazi ideology had persuaded many Austrians that a union with Germany was in their better interests. The newsreel pictures showing huge crowds lining the route the German troops took into Austria, often hysterical with delight, bear testimony to this. There are a variety of reasons for these emotions. Jews had played a prominent part in Austrian cultural life, and anti-Semitism had been more rife in Austria than in Germany since the end of the nineteenth century.

Prominent Austrian politicians, among them Fritz Luger, had even made anti-Semitism the mainstay of their political platforms. In addition, the collapse of the Hapsburg Empire at the end of World War I had placed a once gigantic state in the position of a secondary power, so that union with Germany appeared to have distinct political and economic advantages. By 1938 Germany was an expanding, confident nation and for many Austrians union was definitely attractive. Finally, any Austrian patriot who considered Mussolini the safeguard of Austrian independence was to be bitterly disappointed. In contrast with the displeasure the Italian dictator had expressed at the bungled Putsch of 1934, when the Anschluss took place in 1938 he offered Hitler his approbation. Indeed, Hitler was so anxious about Mussolini's attitude to what was obviously a form of annexation that he telephoned him immediately after the *fait accompli* to gain assurance that he still enjoyed the support of his Italian ally. On receiving Mussolini's blessing, Hitler repeated seven times in a voice combining jubilation with gratitude: "I shall never forget you, never, never, never!" Hitler was true to his word. Despite the poor military showing of Italy during the war, despite the fact that he was surrounded by men who repeatedly told him that all Mussolini had done was climb on the German bandwagon, Hitler remained loyal to the end. The most prominent daredevil of the SS, Otto Skorzeny was sent with a special SS squad to rescue Mussolini from a mountain prison in Italy after his regime had been overthrown.

One of the effects of SS activity in both promoting and cementing the Anschluss was to cause Foreign Minister Ribbentrop to indulge in some soul searching. The activities of the SS abroad were encroaching on areas which he considered his own. He could hardly challenge Himmler and Heydrich. What he could do was make certain that he joined in their heightened status. Accordingly, very shortly after the Anschluss he enquired of Himmler whether his State Secretary and Undersecretary of State (Weizsaecker and Woermann) could be given an SS rank. Himmler immediately agreed. Rivalry between the SS and the Foreign Office undoubtedly existed but could be contained if some of the prominent officials in the Foreign Office were given SS status. It would also give Himmler reasonable ground for extending his police work to the activities of the Foreign Office. Ribbentrop realized that he had received the worse side of this bargain. While he entertained fears that his activities in foreign affairs were under the surveillance of the SS, he felt impelled to accept his own promotion within the SS hierarchy to the elevated position of General of the SS, after the fall of France. Within Ribbentrop's own bureau, an official called Martin Luther was soon to become a devoted member of the SS, and during the war came to work closely with Eichmann's Office of Jewish Emigration.

Once the nazification of Austria had shown itself to be proceeding to their satisfaction, Himmler and Heydrich addressed themselves to the question of Czechoslovakia. Hitler had made no secret of his intention to annex the Sudetenland, where the Nazi press was informing the world that German minorities were being cruelly abused by their Czech neighbors. As early as June 1938 an order was issued by the SD to recruit "Action Commandos." These were to follow German Army units into the annexed territories to "secure political life and the national economy." In effect this meant the murder of anyone suspected of being an opponent of the new regime. These Action Commandos were the kernel of what were later to become the Einsatzgruppen of the war, which took on the task of the physical annihilation of large sections of the population.

In Czechoslovakia the Action Commandos were robbed of their steam for two reasons. In the first place the annexation of the Sudetenland proceeded without difficulty, and in the second place the German Army resisted any attempt by Himmler to get his SS and SD into what was considered by the Army to be its exclusive domain. When the Munich crisis occurred, the Commander in Chief of the Army, von Brauchitsch, and his Chief of Staff, Halder, were obstinate in their decision not to allow the riffraff of the SS and SD to involve themselves in what were purely military matters. It was only as the war progressed, and Hitler became more and more disenchanted with the vacillating and often recalcitrant moods of his generals, that the SS and SD were to be given a free hand in and behind the Army lines. As the generals fell out of favor with their Führer, the ambitions of Himmler gained his wider approval.

It was not until August 1939 that the SS was given a further opportunity to try its hand in foreign affairs again.

Hitler had determined to invade Poland. He was irritated by the guarantees given by England and France to protect Poland's frontiers against an attack by a foreign power, but he was not to be diverted from his avowed course of action. In any event, the Western democracies had shown during the Anschluss and during the Munich debacle when they had abandoned Czechoslovakia that they were not to be taken seriously. Nonetheless, the press of the world had to be persuaded that if Germany invaded Poland, it was as a result of extreme provocation by the Poles.

Heydrich had a plan to meet just such a requirement. During the night before the German attack, frontier incidents must be staged which would prove to foreign journalists that the Poles themselves had started the war. Heydrich's sinister idea was that detachments of his SD should clothe themselves in Polish army uniforms and "occupy" the German radio station at Gleiwitz near the German-Polish border. Having done so, they were to bellow various anti-German slogans into the microphone, while brother SS detachments, also dressed in Polish uniforms, were to conduct an assault on German customs posts and the German Forestry Institute at Pitschen. During the course of August 1939 military attachés from the various foreign embassies in Berlin sent dispatches back to their governments indicating the presence of large formations of German troops along the Polish frontier.

If the Germans and Poles were to be engaged in battle, it was clear to Heydrich that some bloodshed must appear to have taken place. There must be some corpses around. In Heydrich's words, "Actual proof of Polish attack is essential both for the foreign press and for German propaganda."

Heydrich had to secure some bodies: the casualties of the "war." He instructed his Gestapo to secure what he termed "canned goods" from the concentration camps. This meant giving a lethal injection to certain inmates of the camps, clothing them in appropriate uniforms, and then leaving the corpses in persuasive array on the "battlefield." He discussed his idea with Himmler and found that it met with his approval. They then jointly submitted it to the Führer, who considered Heydrich's stratagem to be inspired.

From the SD office in Berlin teleprinters were quickly engaged in transmitting instructions to SS-Standarten 23 and 45 stationed in the area of Upper Silesia to deliver about one hundred of their number who were familiar with the Polish language and who were suitable for carrying out a special mission. Naujocks, who had distinguished himself in the Tuchachevsky Affair, was ordered to supervise the attack on the Gleiwitz radio station. "For the sake of appearances," Heydrich informed him, "the responsibility for the acts which are to follow must be placed on other shoulders." Naujocks was instructed to proceed to Gleiwitz with five of his best men, reconnoiter the Gleiwitz area, lie low, and wait for the receipt of the message "Granny dead." Heydrich told him, "You must not have any contact with any German authority in Gleiwitz about this affair. None of your men must carry any SS or SD identity papers or any other documents indicating their German nationality."

To set the stage further, Heydrich ordered Brigadeführer Jost to supply the necessary Polish army uniforms, advised SS-Oberführer Rasch that he was to arrange the attack on the Forestry Institute at Pitschen, and told SS-Oberführer Mehlhorn to get the Wehrmacht to clear the Hochlinden area. For Hochlinden was to be the site at which the "Battle" was to occur. The "attackers" in Polish uniform were to assault Hochlinden from the Polish area to the south and move against the "defenders," the German frontier police under the command of SS-Standartenführer Trummler.

The "canned goods," corpses from the concentration camps, were to be provided by the head of the Gestapo, Mueller. The Abwehr under Admiral Canaris obligingly provided 250 Polish uniforms, Polish weapons, and Polish Army paybooks. These were all assembled at SS-Standarten 23 and 45 in Upper Silesia, where men during those August days practiced drill under an officer who shouted commands in Polish. Other units, which were designated to perform the role of guerillas, were issued civilian caps and ordinary jackets and trousers. Rehearsals took place satisfactorily and by the end of the third week of August all was ready. The various SS units were sent to their assembly areas. All that was now needed was word from Hitler. But the Führer was hampered by developments on the diplomatic front.

After giving the order to proceed on August 25, Hitler promptly withdrew it. Apart from the fact that England had concluded a pact of mutual assistance with Poland, Mussolini was getting cold feet. The Duce did not feel, so he instructed his ambassador to inform Hitler, that he could participate in what was so demonstrably an act of aggression. The Wehrmacht paused, but Heydrich was in a difficult position. The "Polish" contingent under Obersturmbannführer Hellwig was already on the march. It was impossible for Heydrich to stop them. They opened fire on the German customs post at Hochlinden on August 25, fire which was immediately returned from the German side. The confusion was only brought to an end after the intervention of a furious Gestapo-Mueller.

The second order to proceed came from the Führer on August 31. The show was to be staged at 4:45 A.M. the following day. On the afternoon of August 31, Naujocks was informed by telephone that Granny was dead. That evening he assembled his men and made for the radio transmitter at Gleiwitz.

Mueller, who was stationed at nearby Oppeln with trucks loaded with corpses from the concentration camps, started to get busy. One corpse had to be offloaded at Gleiwitz to lend authenticity to the attack.

At about 8:00 P.M. Naujocks and his men stormed the radio station at Gleiwitz. "We fired off our pistols in the broadcasting room," he was later to declare, "and we loosed off a couple of warning shots into the ceiling to make a row and scare people."

Once again the SS showed it had not done its homework thoroughly enough. They knew how to storm a building, but they did not know how to interrupt a broadcast already in progress, and this was an essential ingredient in the affair. Anti-German slogans had to be shouted in the Polish language for the whole enterprise to hang together. To anyone listening to the broadcast at the time, all that could be heard was a confused series of shouts, none of which was particularly intelligible. Finally one of the SS men discovered an instrument called a storm microphone which was normally used to override transmissions in the event of a storm to explain the existence of static. By use of this microphone it was possible to make a series of mysterious statements in Polish, interspersed with pistol shots. After four minutes of this charade, Naujocks, obviously convinced that he had played his role in the Gleiwitz affair, instructed his men to withdraw. He was pleased to note, on his departure, that one of Mueller's corpses lay at the entrance to the radio station.

At the Hochlinden customs house, a certain Josef Grzimek reported that as he left the ruined building he found himself stumbling over various objects in the dark. "I bent down," he later testified, "and saw several men lying motionless on the ground. They were wearing Polish uniforms . . . and their heads were shaved. . . . When I tried to pick one of them up I found he was totally rigid."

The Wehrmacht had already started its assault on Poland; the tanks were already on the move. But to Germans at home, the activities of the SS and SD on the Polish frontier provided the necessary smokescreen to justify "German retaliation." What happened at Gleiwitz, so the *Völkischer Beobachter* reported on September 1, 1939, "was clearly the signal for a general attack on German territory by Polish guerillas."

10

THE LAST DAYS
OF REINHARD HEYDRICH

By September 1941, Reinhard Heydrich was far from being a satisfied man, despite the fact that his restless energy had resulted in his gradual accumulation of more and more appointments.

In the first place, the administrative machine of the SS which he had helped to create was becoming unwieldy. Together with Himmler he had extended the empire of the SS, but this had involved the setting up of countless offices and a huge bureaucracy. The more tasks the SS assigned to itself, the more difficult it became to supervise the entire machine. The nominal coordination of all the activities of the SS within the Reichssicherheitshauptamt did not conceal from Heydrich that the left hand often did not know what the right was doing.

In the second place, even though everybody in Germany would have readily admitted that next to Himmler, Heydrich was the most powerful man in the Reich, Heydrich was irritated by the gap which existed between real and titular authority. He could see that Oswald Pohl was firmly established as economist-in-chief of the SS, and while Heydrich did not care a fig about economics, his policeman's mind looked with mistrust at what he did not understand.

In many ways, the Third Reich of Hitler had catered only too auspiciously to the sadistic drives of Heydrich. His high-pitched staccato voice issued orders to all and sundry, his overwhelming love of intrigue had enabled him to set up the notorious "Kitty salon," a night club in Berlin to which high-ranking foreign dignitaries were continuously invited and in which all rooms were bugged and two-way windows proliferated.

At the end of July 1941 Goering, as head of the Four Year Plan, had given Heydrich the authority to supervise and oversee the "Final Solution of the Jewish Problem." This Heydrich took to mean the liquidation of all Jews within the occupied areas. But there were many other departments involved and he rarely saw eye to eye with them. Particular obstructions emanated from the office of the Four Year

Plan itself. These men had economic targets to meet, targets which were essential, so they claimed, for the successful completion of the war. Jews should be murdered, but not until they had done their bit for the greater good of Germany, as munitions workers and slave laborers. In August 1941 Hitler had promised Goebbels that the deportation of the Jews of Berlin could proceed forthwith. But because of the objections of the economists of the Four Year Plan, who claimed the Jews were engaged in necessary war work within the Reich, their eventual deportation was deferred until 1943.

In May of 1941, when Hess made his abortive flight to Scotland to negotiate a separate peace with England, Heydrich very probably considered himself to be Hess's most suitable replacement. But he was outdistanced by Martin Bormann, who immediately stepped into Hess's shoes and who, like Himmler and Heydrich, was assiduously cultivating his own areas of control, eventually to become the *éminence grise* of the Third Reich.

When the Russian campaign started, in June 1941, Heydrich arranged a six-week secondment for himself to the Luftwaffe as a pilot. For a man who held so many high positions in the administration of the Reich, this was a serious step and can only really be understood in terms of Heydrich's own psyche, ever restlessly looking for new avenues of activity.

After his stint with the Luftwaffe, Heydrich was offered a new post, that of Reich Protector for Bohemia and Moravia. It was a position previously occupied by a former Foreign Office official called Constantin von Neurath. Neurath's policies, so determined Hitler, were far too liberal. He had even permitted student demonstrations to occur there. One man, obviously, could be relied upon to retrieve the situation: Reinhard Heydrich.

Since April 1939 the Czechs of Bohemia and Moravia had had their own parliament. The "Reich Protector," was there to make certain that German interests were properly supervised.

Heydrich accepted the position, naturally without giving up his various appointments in Berlin. He must also have been aware that to absent himself from SS headquarters in Berlin was a really dangerous step for it would remove him from the scene of real power. Despite these reservations, he quickly established himself in Prague. Within weeks of his arrival, the Gestapo had arrested all opposition and destroyed the Czech resistance movement. Lest any further doubts existed as to the radicalism with which he proposed to quell Czech resistance to German rule, he arranged a bogus trial in which the Czech Premier, Alois Elias, was condemned to death. Within weeks of his accession, Heydrich had earned for himself the nickname "Butcher of Prague."

And then the most surprising thing happened. The wave of terror, which had entirely subjugated the Czech populace, was suddenly replaced by a series of benevolent measures. These were largely aimed at the Czech working class, for Heydrich quickly realized that resistance would come, in the main, from the middle-class intelligentsia. He requisitioned luxury hotels in fashionable holiday resorts and made them available to industrial workers. He increased the rations for two million in industry and issued 200,000 pairs of shoes, a rarity in those days, to workers in the munitions plants. He also announced that political persecution was a thing of the past.

This method of transacting deals with one's opponent was entirely in keeping with Gestapo methods. It was also totally consonant with Heydrich's image of himself as a quick-witted and devious strategist. To use the truncheon with the right hand and pacify the victim with the left is a well-worn procedure used by political police throughout the world. In Heydrich's experience, it bore substantial results. For despite the fact that the Czechoslovak form of government, devised by Masaryk after the First World War, was claimed to be one of the most democratic ever conceived, in its social provisions it was somewhat wanting. To combat these omissions, Heydrich made workers and peasants socially acceptable and enlarged the system of social welfare. At the Hradshin Palace in Prague, Heydrich and his wife, Lina, daily held court to a series of delegations of workers from Czech industry. And there is no doubt that to a considerable extent, Heydrich had taken the steam out of the Czech resistance movement by presenting himself as a public benefactor.

These events were highly satisfactory to Hitler, who felt that his confidence in Heydrich had been amply endorsed. But in England, they were viewed with alarm. In London, Benes, leader of the exiled Czech government, was extremely worried. He and his compatriots could hardly expect to retain the sympathy and unconditional support of the British while reports of a passive population in Bohemia and Moravia filtered through intelligence channels. Benes had his eyes on the future. The population of Czechoslovakia must be shown to have been a continuous thorn in the side of the occupying Germans if the free Czechs were to exact maximum benefits at the postwar conference tables.

There seemed only one sensible thing to do. "Benefactor" Heydrich must be killed. This was agreed to in December 1941 by the exiled Czech cabinet in London. From their knowledge of German behavior, it was clear to Benes and his associates that the murder of Heydrich would be followed by the most severe acts of retribution, and these would undoubtedly strengthen the weakened resolve of the domestic Czech resistance movement.

The plan for Heydrich's assassination was worked out in London. Two men, Jan Kubis and Josef Gabcik, were chosen and trained for a parachute drop in occupied Czechoslovakia. Once landed, they were to make contact with known Czech resistance circles and select the appropriate time and place for the murder of Heydrich.

So keen was Benes on the speedy implementation of this plan that he insisted on condensing the very concentrated course of training for these two Czech NCOs. They attended special intelligence units in Manchester, received training in sabotage at Cambusdurroch in Scotland, and were given their final sessions in a house near Dorking in Surrey.

Contact was made with reliable resistance circles in Czechoslovakia. Flares were lit at an agreed point, and the two men were dropped from a British aircraft by parachute. They then went into hiding to apprise themselves of Heydrich's movements.

Despite his training in security methods, Heydrich liked to consider himself as something of a daredevil. Instead of driving around with a heavily guarded escort, he used an open Mercedes car, almost as if inviting somebody to take him on. For Heydrich, life was a fencing match, and at fencing, Heydrich considered himself a master.

He lived in a villa at Panenske-Breschen, close enough to Prague to enable him to commute easily to his quarters in the Hradshin Palace. Kubis and Gabcik, aided by two additional recruits from Czech resistance circles, conducted a yard-by-yard survey of the route which Heydrich's Mercedes took in its daily journey. In the outer suburb of Prague known as Holesovice, they took careful note of the fact that the road entered a hairpin bend before it negotiated the Troja bridge. The car would be forced to reduce speed at this point, and so this seemed to offer the best spot on the route where Heydrich could be shot down.

They knew that there would be only two men in the car—Reinhard Heydrich and his driver, Klein. They also knew that the Mercedes normally reached the hairpin bend at nine-thirty in the morning. Accordingly, once all plans had been rehearsed, the four men stationed themselves at intervals on either side of the bend on the morning of May 27, 1942.

On this particular morning Heydrich was one hour later than usual, and the would-be assassins were becoming anxious. But suddenly the signal was given. Gabcik withdrew his sten gun from his coat and jumped into the roadway in the path of the oncoming car. He took careful aim; he could see the faces of Heydrich and his driver quite clearly. But when he pressed the trigger nothing happened. The trigger was locked. Behind him Kubis acted with dispatch. As the Mercedes pulled up, Kubis threw a hand grenade into it, and the car was wrecked.

But Heydrich appeared unharmed. A tall man, he jumped out of the convertible, shouted something at Klein, his driver, withdrew his revolver from his holster, and charged up the road in hot pursuit of Kubis and Gabcik. It looked as if he might actually catch up with Kubis—indeed, as he ran, he fired successive rounds from his revolver at him. Fortunately for Kubis, a tram at that moment obstructed Heydrich's line of fire and Kubis was able to make his getaway on a bicycle he found outside a nearby house.

Gabcik acted more slowly. It was as if he could not believe that the mechanism of his sten gun had let him down at the vital moment. But after a few seconds delay, he threw it away and took a revolver out of his pocket, running in zigzag fashion away from his pursuer, dropping for cover every now and again, and firing at Heydrich as he went. He suddenly saw Heydrich throw his revolver to the ground and assumed that the Protector's ammunition had run out. Then Heydrich clutched at his right hip and began to stagger. Gabcik escaped.

When Heydrich was transferred to a Prague hospital it was discovered that Kubis's grenade had in fact done its work. Heydrich's stomach and ribs had been penetrated by parts of the car's springs and upholstery, and some of the horsehair, with which the seating was stuffed, had entered his spleen. It is astonishing evidence of Heydrich's pertinacity that he had managed to run at all, having sustained such wounds. Despite all the efforts of the doctors, his life could not be saved. He hung on for nine days, but eventually died on June 4, 1942.

A massive state funeral was arranged for Heydrich in Berlin, at which his Führer described him as a "man of iron." In accordance with SS ritual a death mask of Heydrich was made: a testament to one of the most ruthless perpetrators of terror produced by the Third Reich. According to a police official called Wehner, who was summoned to Prague to investigate the circumstances of Heydrich's murder, the mask showed "deceptive features of uncanny spirituality and entirely perverted beauty, like a cardinal from the Renaissance."

There was now nobody in Germany to challenge Himmler's leadership of the SS. From that day on, the history of the SS became the history of Heinrich Himmler.

In Czechoslovakia, events proceeded in a way which surpassed even the expectations of the leader of the Czech government in exile, Benes and associates. There were no fewer than ten thousand arrests. A village called Lidice, near Prague, which was supposed to have harbored Heydrich's assassins, was razed to the ground and all its male inhabitants shot. In all, a conservative estimate of the reprisals instituted by the SS and Gestapo was that 1,300 people were put to death for the murder of Reinhard Heydrich.

11
THE OCCUPATION OF EUROPE

The expansionist plans of Hitler were aimed primarily at the east. Vast tracts of Poland, the Baltic states, and Russia were to be added to the Reich to create the necessary living space to which he claimed the Germans were entitled.

From a strictly military point of view all of Hitler's operations in Western Europe were undertaken to protect the rear while dealing with the eastern question. The Nazi-Soviet pact was designed to arrange a temporary understanding with Russia while Hitler could eliminate the threat of intervention from the west. Once Germany's western frontiers had been secured, he could do what he had always intended: create a gigantic area in the east in which Germans could settle. In his view England would give up the struggle once faced with the *fait accompli* of a German-occupied Western Europe.

The function of the SS in this plan was to eliminate all possible sources of opposition to the New Order, to liquidate the Jews, and to supervise the resettlement of Germans on farming lands made available to the Reich by its acquisition of new territories.

Before Germany invaded Poland, Hitler told his assembled generals, "I have ordered my Death's Head Units to the east with the order to kill without pity or mercy all men, women, and children of Polish race or language." The German General Staff therefore knew that unparalleled atrocities would take place in Poland. But these, so they rationalized, would be committed by the SS and should throw no cloud over the noble profession of bearing arms. If they dedicated themselves to strategy, they could not themselves be held responsible for the vagaries of the SS. The German generals were making a pact with the devil which was to have disastrous consequences for them.

The diary entry of General Halder for October 18, 1939, summarizes a conversation he had had that day with General Wagner, the Quartermaster-General, who had come fresh from a meeting with the Führer. "We have no intention of rebuilding Poland," Hitler told Wagner. "Polish intelligentsia must be prevented from establishing itself as a governing class. A low standard of living must be preserved; cheap slaves. . . . We must create total disorganization. . . ."

The same generals attended a conference with Hitler at the Obersalzburg on August 22, only nine days before the armies rolled into Poland. This nature of Hitler's remarks can scarcely have left them in any doubt as to his intentions. "Things will happen which will not be to the taste of German generals," he told them, "but you should not interfere in such matters; simply restrict yourselves to your military duties."

This question of interference or noninterference by the German Army officers in events taking place within their own operational areas was soon to be raised. On September 10, 1939, some members of an SS artillery brigade employed fifty Jews on a bridge-repairing project. As soon as their work was finished, all the Jews were assembled in a nearby synagogue and shot. The SS men appeared before a court-martial and were each sentenced to one year in prison. The Commander of the German Third Army, General von Kuechler, refused to confirm the sentence on the grounds that it was too lenient. At this point Himmler himself intervened and released the accused SS men, saying that a "general amnesty" absolved them from being subject to court-martial procedure. The happy division of labor between the Army generals and the SS which the former had thought would release them from moral responsibility was untenable from the start. Atrocities proliferated in Poland. When Canaris, head of the Abwehrdienst, attempted to take a firm stand with Keitel, he was told, "If the Army wants no part in these occurrences it will have to accept the SS and Gestapo as rivals." Canaris was quick to realize that this meant the attachment of SS liaison officers to each Army command. "I pointed out to Keitel," he wrote in his diary, "that I knew extensive executions were planned in Poland and that particularly the clergy and nobility were to be exterminated. Eventually the world would hold the Wehrmacht responsible for these deeds."

The consequences of supping with the devil were speedily being made known to the generals. Heydrich was dispatched to Army High Command by Himmler on September 19, 1939, and gave General Wagner a picture of what the SS proposed to do in their housecleaning in Poland. Housecleaning meant the elimination of "Polish Jews, intelligentsia, clergy, and nobility." Wagner's response was to urge Heydrich to postpone the action. He told Halder that he had impressed on Heydrich that "housecleaning be deferred until the Army was withdrawn and the country turned over to the civil administration in early December."

Lest the Army High Command entertain any further doubts as to what the SS intended to do in Poland, Heydrich issued them a copy of his plans on September 21. The first stage was to be the rounding up of Jews and their confinement in city ghettos. This would be step one on the road to mass slaughter.

When Russia had annexed that section of Poland to which its understanding with Germany entitled it, and when Germany had incorporated within the Reich those frontier areas it had been demanding since Hitler's accession, what was left of Poland was designated as an area of "General Government." This was placed under a Governor-General named Hans Frank. On the day after his appointment, this erstwhile president of the Academy of Law and the German Bar Association, announced that "the Poles will be the slaves of the German Reich." Frank's brief from Hitler contained the following directive: "The men capable of leadership in Poland must be liquidated and those who follow them must be liquidated in their turn. There is no need to burden the Reich with this; no need to send these elements to Reich concentration camps." Clearly the cost of a bullet was far less than that involved in transporting them to Germany and having them become a further drain on the German public purse.

On October 6, 1939, Hitler made a long and somewhat disjointed speech to the Reichstag in Berlin. The term *population exchanges* featured prominently in it. On the following day he published a decree announcing the formation of a "Reich Commissariat for the Strengthening of German Nationhood." Its chief was to be Heinrich Himmler, and as far as could be determined it was to deport Poles and Jews from the newly annexed territories and arrange their replacement by *Volksdeutsche,* or ethnic Germans. These were Germans who had been "forced" to live outside the Fatherland because of Germany's overpopulation. A curious statistical ratio was to be maintained between the deportees and the new immigrants. For every two persons "exported," one German was to enter the new territories. There he might farm and pursue the biological directives of the SS.

All deportees were to be moved to the General Government area under Hans Frank, east of the River Vistula. On October 9, 1939, Himmler ordained that 550,000 Jews and all Poles not suitable for "assimilation" (by which he likely meant to foment trouble for the German occupying forces) were to be transported to the General Government.

In this welter of strange bureaucratic monoliths, the Reich Commissariat (RKFDV) was to act as a coordinating agency for two other SS departments. One was the Volksdeutsche Mittelstelle, which before the war had been concerned with the welfare of Germans domiciled abroad. The other was the Rasse- und Siedlungshauptamt (RUSHA), which was the brainchild of Walter Darré; its mission was to study racial ancestry and biological selection.

During the winter of 1939/40 the first "resettlements" took place. "In weather forty degrees below zero," Himmler was to recount to his men, "we had to drag away thousands, tens of thousands, hundreds of thousands; we had to have the toughness—you must listen to this and then forget it immediately—to shoot thousands of leading Poles . . . otherwise revenge would have been taken on us later. . . . In many cases it is much easier to go into battle with a company of infantry than it is to suppress an obstructive population of low cultural level or to carry out executions or to haul people away or evict crying and hysterical women."

Getting rid of the Jews and Poles and slaughtering them en route to the General Government of Hans Frank proved easier than the second task of the SS: providing the recently arrived "ethnic" Germans with farms and housing. These Germans had been uprooted from various areas in the Ukraine, Poland, and Russia where they had lived for centuries in small communities. The object of the plan was to incorporate them into the geographical area of the Greater German Reich, which by now had extended its frontiers many hundreds of miles eastward. The Reich, not totally geared to a war economy, could do little for these ethnic Germans, who found themselves on alien soil. They lived rather like displaced persons, moving from one makeshift camp to another. As late as August 1943 there were still 100,000 ethnic Germans without occupation in the annexed territories and 22,000 still living in camps. Hans Frank grumbled that to introduce around one and a half million people into his own area, which already had a population of twelve million, must result in considerable overcrowding.

Aside from the moral horror of the project, its administrative impossibility caused problems to the Party purists at the SS Main Office. Walter Darré had kept meticulous records of all the Polish farms which would come under the control of the Reich on the successful annexation of that country. The large rural estates were to be broken up and handed over to ethnic Germans. But the exigencies of war and the incompetence of SS administrators precluded the successful completion of his plans, and Darré remained a very disappointed man until the end of the war. Furthermore, officials from Alfred Rosenberg's Racial Political Office poked their noses into this cauldron.

By December 1939, according to Reitlinger in his *SS: Alibi of a Nation,* "the whole machinery of spoliation and eviction was in full swing." Jews and Poles were pouring eastward into the newly created General Government, while racial Germans from Volhynia were heading westward toward the Reich. Apart from these two cross-currents there was in the General Government itself a huge upheaval of Jewish life which involved nearly two million people. The Jews were concentrated into a number of large towns as a prelude to the creation of ghettos and also into a rural area south of Lublin. The directors of this movement, Himmler's higher SS police leaders and Heydrich's commanders of the Security Police and SD were in many respects independent of Hans Frank's civil administration and absolutely independent of General Blaskowitz, the military governor. The result was a weird bureaucratic chaos which explains why Hans Frank found forty thousand German civil servants insufficient to run a country "half the size of Italy."

Blaskowitz was well aware of the activities of the SS units. His hands were legally tied, since his only authority over the SS was to step in in cases of "mutiny or revolt." This did not prevent him from drawing up an extensive memorandum in December 1939 bitterly criticizing the higher SS and police officials in Poland.

Having written the memorandum, Blaskowitz seemed uncertain what to do with it. There was little point in submitting it to the SS Main Office; local SS administrators were obviously acting with the blessing of their superiors in Berlin. He toyed with the idea of presenting it to Hitler, but he knew, from his discussions with other high-ranking Army officers, that the only likely result would be to provoke the Führer into one of his now quite familiar splenetic outbursts. Blaskowitz finally decided to hand his memorandum to Brauchitsch, Commander in Chief of the Army. It stayed in Brauchitsch's pending tray. Blaskowitz resigned his post in protest, which for a while endeared him to a circle of officers and civilians who had been trying to create suitable circumstances for a coup d'état. But he was soon to take up his military career again, serving on various fronts throughout the war and finally surrendering Holland to the British. He maintained his dislike of the SS throughout the campaigns, was nonetheless arraigned at Nuremberg after the war, and finally committed suicide there in 1947. Many of his fellow detainees at Nuremberg believed he had been murdered there by SS prisoners, but this notion was without foundation.

The pattern of SS activities proceeded along well-worn lines throughout the war. The Wehrmacht would advance, closely followed by Himmler's officials. Once territory had been secured, the SS would arrange the mass murder of huge numbers of the local population and the incarceration of the rest in concentration camps.

But the Waffen- or Armed-SS was often engaged in front-line fighting with the Wehrmacht. Here they were hampered by an almost total lack of understanding of strategy. "I once spent an hour and a half," said Wilhelm Bittrich, "trying to explain a situation with Sepp Dietrich [commander of the Leibstandarte Adolf Hitler] with the aid of a map. It was quite useless. He understood nothing." Bereft of real skill at senior officer level, the Waffen-SS, although a totally dedicated group of men, had not been exposed to proper training in tactics and strategy. Its various units were laws unto themselves. As early as 1936, when Himmler had appointed Paul Hausser as head of the SS-Verfügungstruppen—out of which the Waffen-SS grew—he incurred the wrath of Sepp Dietrich. And Dietrich enjoyed a special place in the Führer's esteem. Himmler was most concerned not to alienate him. He wrote: "My dear Sepp, your officers are good enough to recognize me personally. Otherwise the Leibstandarte is a complete law unto itself. It does and allows anything it likes without taking the slightest notice of orders from above." This was quite accurate. Dietrich's men indulged in undignified scraps with Wehrmacht soldiers and he embarked on his own recruitment campaign in competition with the General Staff.

Sepp Dietrich needed a reprimand. Even the vacillating Himmler was compelled to speak sharply to him. "For the last time," he wrote, "I ask you to stop these things. I can no more admit to the Wehrmacht that I am unable to get the Leibstandarte to conform to the orders and instructions of the entire Verfügungstruppen than I can tolerate the continuance of these extravagances on the part of the Leibstandarte." As early as 1938 General von Fritsch was heard to remark, "All sources agree that the attitude of the SS-Verfügungstruppen toward the Army is frigid if not hostile. One cannot avoid the impression that this hostile attitude is deliberately cultivated."

The social composition of the Waffen-SS shows that its men came from different backgrounds than those of the regular army. In the Army some 50 percent of all officers were from military families; in the Waffen-SS barely 5 percent. Peasant stock only provided 2 percent of Army officers, while in the Waffen-SS 90 percent came from the land. The number of conscripts into the Waffen-SS from cities was negligible.

The battle between Army and SS was eventually resolved in favor of the SS once Fritsch and Blomberg, guardians of the honor of the

German officer caste, had been deposed: This occurred after the successful maneuvers of the Gestapo to discredit them on trumped-up charges. In January 1939 Brigadeführer Petri of the SS Main Office made the following triumphant comment in a speech: "The Wehrmacht has been forced to recognize that the pertinacity of Heinrich Himmler in pursuit of his aims is stronger than its own resistance to the innovations of the Third Reich."

The Waffen-SS went to war with the Wehrmacht on the invasion of Poland. They were not trained for modern warfare. They lost more men, through foolhardiness, than did regular Army units. Their commanders seemed incapable of conducting operations which were in any way complicated. Their annoyance with the "old boys" in the General Staff deepened. But their fortunes took a turn for the better when a new recruit appeared on the scene.

His name was Gottlob Berger. Like Himmler, he wanted to build the Waffen-SS into an army which would be independent of the Wehrmacht generals. He was a particularly astute and Machiavellian operator. There was one source of supply of men over which the Wehrmacht had no control. This was the Death's Head Unit (Totenkopfverbände) which had policed the concentration camps. It released immediately some 50,000 men for an enlarged SS army. The Death's Head Units were under the command of the notorious Theodor Eicke who had handed Röhm a loaded pistol and invited him to commit suicide in 1934.

It was in May 1940 that the Death's Head Division of the SS received its baptism of fire, in the French campaign. Its men, reared in the brutal traditions of the camps, were soon to show the methods they brought to the front. Eicke found units of the British Expeditionary Force defending La Bassée canal in front of Bailleul with considerable stubbornness. He decided to force the canal, regardless of the cost to his men.

Among his company commanders was a Lieutenant Fritz Knoechlein, who lost his head as the battle raged. After sustained attack by a numerically superior force, the British ran up the white flag to surrender. Knoechlein ordered his men to mow them down. As the British soldiers walked out to what they believed was honorable captivity, the SS units massacred them all. In a farm known as Le Paradis the dead and wounded were left in a heap against a barn wall. General Hoepner, who commanded the army of which the Totenkopf division formed part, railed at Eicke and told him he was not a soldier, but a butcher.

Yet if you were not a military theorist, the Waffen-SS might earn your grudging respect. Imbued with National Socialist ideology and with a supreme disregard for the decimation of their numbers as they engaged the enemy, they gained considerable success. Their thirst for battle outweighed their sense of reasonable military calculation. When the Russian campaign was under way and Waffen-SS units were used to reinforce German lines, many a Wehrmacht commander felt bound to extend admiration to them for their fighting spirit. The Waffen-SS grew dramatically as the war progressed:

    1940: 100,000 men
    1941: 220,000 men
    1942: 330,000 men
    1943: 540,000 men
    1944: 910,000 men

In view of the heavy losses it sustained in a series of last-ditch stands and its disregard for human life, including its own, it is surprising that it grew so radically. Two sources, however, were made available to it. Within Germany it competed with the Wehrmacht for recruitment. Height requirements were reduced to five feet five inches. The quality of the men it absorbed was the antithesis of the exacting requirements Himmler had laid down before the war. A second source of supply was from ethnic Germans. At its peak, these accounted for over 200,000 members. Nazi purists had already determined that men from "Nordic" countries like Denmark, Norway, and Holland qualified racially. Sympathizers from Belgium under the fascist leader Degrelle provided a source of recruitment. And in the east, in the Ukraine and the Baltic provinces of Estonia and Latvia, a fertile source was discovered. These non-German recruits were not animated by the idea of establishing the Nazi Superman in Europe. They were violently anti-Communist and believed they were joining in an anti-Bolshevik campaign. Furthermore, they were extremely anti-Semitic. The Einsatzkommandos, or extermination squads, used for mowing down Jews contained many units from eastern Europe. So much for the theory that only Germans could have perpetrated the crimes committed in the name of Germany against other races.

If the general tone and bearing of a typical Waffen-SS unit in 1943 is compared with its equivalent of 1940, there are very substantial differences. In 1943 the volunteers from Rumania and Croatia were a disappointment to "idealists" like Gottlob Berger and Theodor Eicke. Eicke himself wrote, "A large number of the racial Germans can only be described as intellectually substandard. They do not understand the words of command and are inclined to insubordination and malingering. . . ."

This is not difficult to understand. The officers in charge of the training of the new recruits had survived Hausser's cadet schools and had been indoctrinated by Gottlob Berger, who among other things was a fanatical gymnast. Young men from Flanders, Holland, and Norway, who had been assured that they were joining a multinational force which would usher in a new era in European history, were subjected to the brutal training methods of their German overlords. In Norway, having joined the Viking Division of the Waffen-SS, having sworn the SS oath, many recruits simply deserted. They collected together to protect themselves against Berger's recruiting officers.

By early 1943 applications to leave the Waffen-SS were received daily from Danes, Dutchmen, and Belgians. Himmler was furious and railed at the "iniquitous and psychologically mistaken treatment" his German SS training officers had meted out, for this was having the effect of drying up his sources of supply.

One further effect was that such loyalty as existed was restricted to that between the divisional commander and his men. Lip service might be paid to Himmler, but there was no doubt that the Waffen-SS units were becoming more like the old Freikorps as the months went by. This had to spell danger to Himmler. His nose quickly detected the scent of possible rivalry. Had he created a new SA? The signs were apparent to him in March 1942 when he said, "I see here a major danger; that the Waffen-SS will start to lead its own life, pleading exigency of war. . . ." Crank and pedant as he was, Himmler was quick to detect possibly divisive elements within his own organization. It was quality which had enabled him to build up his empire within the rival satrapies of the Nazi state. Felix Steiner, who had contributed so much to Waffen-SS ideology, even went so far as to describe Himmler, with considerable justification, as a "sleazy romantic." So uncertain was Himmler of his ground that he simply countered by informing Steiner that he was his "most insubordinate general," instead of having him dismissed and consigned to a concentration camp.

The coordination of mass murder was not, however, the function of the Waffen-SS. This was the work of the department of the SS known as the Sicherheitsdienst, or SD, and the concentration camps, assisted by German industry and a huge German bureaucracy. The machine of mass extermination did not achieve the proportions for which it is notorious until the Russian campaign was under way. It was at the postwar Nuremberg Trials that the activities of the Einsatzgruppen, or extermination squads, were described under cross-examination by the men who had led them. Although their work was supposedly aimed at the elimination of "partisans," this was very loosely interpreted by the men involved. The following exchange between the American prosecuting attorney John Arlan Amen and Otto Ohlendorf will provide a clear appraisal of their activities (Ohlendorf was Head of Amt III of the Reich Main Security Office, and himself commanded an Einsatzgruppe in the east).

Amen: How many Einsatzgruppen were there?

Ohlendorf: There were four: A, B, C, and D. Gruppe D was not attached to any Army group but was assigned to the German Eleventh Army.

Amen: Who was Commander in Chief of the Eleventh Army?

Ohlendorf: At first Ritter von Schober, and later von Manstein.

Amen: Did you at any time have a conference with Himmler?

Ohlendorf: Certainly. Himmler was in Nikolaev in the late summer of 1941. He summoned the leaders and men of the Einsatzkommandos and repeated to them the order for liquidation and stressed that leaders and men who were concerned in these measures did not carry any personal responsibility for carrying them out. He alone, and the Führer, bore this responsibility.

Amen: Do you know how many people were liquidated by Einsatzgruppe D while under your leadership?

Ohlendorf: Between June 1941 and June 1942 about 90,000 were reported to have been liquidated.

Amen: Does this figure include, men, women, and children?

Ohlendorf: Yes.

Amen: On what are your figures based?

Ohlendorf: On reports submitted by the Einsatzkommandos to the central Einsatzgruppe.

Amen: Were these reports placed before you? Did you personally see and read them?

Ohlendorf: Yes.

Amen: Did you personally supervise any mass murders?

Ohlendorf: I attended two mass murders as an inspector.

Amen: Will you explain to the Court the procedures used.

Ohlendorf: The site generally chosen was at a deep trench or extensive dugout.

Amen: In which position were the victims shot?

Ohlendorf: Either standing or on their knees.

Amen: What happened to the corpses once they had been shot?

Ohlendorf: They were buried.

Amen: What measures were taken to ensure that the victims were actually dead?

Ohlendorf: The unit commanders were ordered to attend to this and if necessary to finish off those who were still alive.

Amen: Were all these victims, women, men, and children, murdered in the same manner?

Ohlendorf: Until the Spring of 1942, yes. Then we received an order from Himmler that in future women and children should be killed in the gas wagons.

Otto Ohlendorf, a man of middle-class background, with the benefits of a university education, appeared in no way moved by the disgusting scenes to which he had been witness and which he had helped to administer.

Why did Himmler, in the spring of 1942, decide to use different methods to murder women and children? The answer can be found in the testimony of another high-ranking SS officer, Erich von dem Bach Zewelski. "In August 1941 Himmler ordered Arthur Nebe, leader of an Einsatzgruppe in Minsk, to murder one hundred people in his presence, among them numerous women. I stood at the side of Himmler and observed him. When the first shots were heard and the victims collapsed, Himmler began to feel ill. He reeled, almost fell to the ground, and then pulled himself together. Then he hurled abuse at the firing squad because of their poor marksmanship. Some of the women were still alive, for the bullets had simply wounded them." Shortly after this, Ohlendorf received the order to discontinue shooting women and children and to use the gas wagons instead.

Amen: Can you describe to the Court the construction of these gas wagons and their appearance?

Ohlendorf: They were basically sealed trucks. They were built so that once the motor was running, gas was introduced into them which led to the death of the occupants within ten to fifteen minutes.

Amen: Which organization was responsible for staffing the officers of the Einsatzgruppen?

Ohlendorf: Leaders were provided by the State Police, the Criminal Police, and to a certain extent from the SD.

At this point defense counsel for the SS and SD asked Ohlendorf whether the individual officer could refuse to execute his orders "with any chance of a successful outcome." Ohlendorf replied that this was out of the question because anybody refusing to obey would be court-martialed and this would produce "the appropriate sentence."

These mass murders could not be kept from German Army formations. They caused dismay and horror among many regular German Army officers. A report has survived written by a certain Major Roesler attached to the 528th Infantry Regiment, who was so affected by what he saw that he wrote to his commanding officer, the Commander in Chief of the Ninth Army, General Schierwind, on January 3, 1942:

> At the end of July 1941 the 528th Infantry Regiment was in transit from the West to Zhitomir where it was to occupy new quarters. On the afternoon of the day we arrived there I moved into my Staff HQ. From here we could quite clearly hear a large number of salvos followed by pistol shots which we decided must have been taking place nearby. I went to have a look, accompanied by the Adjutant and the Ordnance Officer. We got the impression that some cruel drama must be taking place. After a while we saw numerous soldiers and civilians streaming across a railway embankment, behind which, so we were told, firing squads were engaged in hectic activity. The whole time we could not see over the other side of the embankment, but every now and again we could hear shrill whistles which were followed by continuous machine-gunning. Some time later there were isolated pistol shots. When we had finally climbed up the embankment we saw a picture which, unexpected as it was, gave an impression of horror and barbarism. A grave had been dug into the soil, about seven to eight meters long and four meters wide. A pile of earth which had been dug to form the grave was at the side. This pile and the walls of the grave were absolutely sodden with streams of blood. The grave itself was filled with innumerable human corpses of all types and both sexes, so that one could not even guess at its depth. Behind the wall was a police unit commanded by a police officer. Their uniforms were spotted with blood. Round about, in a large circle, stood groups of soldiers who were already stationed there, some of them in bathing trunks; also numerous civilians with women and children. As I approached the grave I witnessed a scene which until this day I cannot forget. Among the corpses in the grave lay an old man with a

white beard who still carried a walking stick over his left arm. He gave evidence of still being alive; he appeared occasionally to be trying to breathe. I asked one of the police officials to put an end to this man's life. The officer smiled at me and said: "I've already plugged him seven times in the stomach. Don't worry, he won't last much longer." The victims in the grave were not placed there in orderly fashion, they were simply left to lie where they had fallen. . . . During my service in the First World War, in the French and Russian campaigns of this war, I have never witnessed anything which had a more devastating effect on my spirit. I saw much unpleasantness when a member of a Freikorps in 1919, but I have never seen anything to compare with what I have just described.

This report, as Major Roesler maintained, was submitted to his commanding officer, General Schierwind. One wonders what the General did with it. Did he, like so many German serving officers, try to console himself with the knowledge that this was not the Army's business, and that these acts were perpetrated by thugs acting under orders from the SS? If so, he was in for a nasty surprise, because after the notorious "Commissar Order," the SS had the right to enlist German Army personnel to assist them in the execution of its mission. Nominally the Commissar Order was a directive issued by Hitler to shoot on sight the special Communist officials Stalin had attached to all Soviet Army Units. But to the SS, anybody was a commissar. Ulrich von Hassell, one of the most prominent members of the German resistance circle against Hitler, wrote in his diary on August 18, 1941: "The whole War in the east horrifying—general demoralization. A young officer, now in Munich, receives an order to shoot 350 civilians (supposedly partisans) herded together in a large barn, many women and children among them. The officer refuses and is told what the consequences of disobedience are (death), asks for ten minutes to think it over, and finally carries out the order with a machine gun. So overwhelmed by the experience that later, slightly wounded, decides never again to return to the front."

It may be asked whether the men who constituted the rank and file of the Einsatzgruppen belonged to those sadistic elements of society which exist everywhere and at every time. To a certain extent this is so. One of the most notorious of the Einsatzkommandos was led by Oskar Dirlewanger, whose brigade consisted in the main of professional criminals, often serving sentence under the civil courts for murder. According to von dem Bach Zewelski at Nuremberg, "In my opinion there is a clear connection between the speech given by Heinrich Himmler early in 1941, before the attack on Russia, in which he maintained that the purpose of the Russian campaign was the decimation of the Slav population by thirty million people, and the intention to put this into effect by using troops of lower caliber."

But the middle-class intellectuals, the products of German university training, the economists, lawyers, and statisticians who manned the offices of the SS and SD could hardly be claimed to have belonged to the professional criminal elements in German society. There is of course a difference, not moral but psychological, in consigning millions of people to death on paper, and actually crowding them into mass graves and sullying your hands with blood. It was this difference which caused Himmler to seek the advice of the technologists on how best to construct gas wagons. It was these considerations which impelled Himmler to inform his men that they needed to steel themselves against any feeling of remorse in the execution of their "historic mission."

It is probable that if Himmler had not made that journey to Minsk in August 1941 he would not have altered the methods of mass killing. For only after it did he so diligently court the technicians of German industry with a view to streamlining the process of genocide by the use of modern technology.

But what the Reichsführer-SS had seen at Minsk, and what he was determined never to witness again, convinced him that if thirty million Jews and Slavs must be done away with, it must be performed "cleanly" and "efficiently." His stomach could not take the old methods. His demands on the attentions of the masseur Felix Kersten became more numerous, for only in Kersten's hands would his stomach give him any peace.

If technology were to be used for mass murder, it must be put into effect at carefully chosen sites. These were the concentration camps.

Typical of these were the ones at Auschwitz, Treblinka, and Bergen-Belsen. For a description of the techniques employed, the testimony of the commandant of Auschwitz, Rudolf Hoess, at Nuremberg, gives a most revealing picture. Under cross-examination by Dr. Kurt Kauffmann, defense counsel for Obergruppenführer Kaltenbrunner, Hoess testified as follows:

Kauffmann: Is it true that from 1940 to 1943 you were camp commandant at Auschwitz?

Hoess: Yes.

Kauffmann: And during this period hundreds of thousands of humans were sent to their deaths. Is this correct?

Hoess: Yes.

Kauffmann: Is it further true that Eichmann told you that at Auschwitz a total of more than two million Jews were murdered?

Hoess: Yes.

Kauffmann: Men, women, and children?

Hoess: Yes. . . . In the summer of 1941 I was personally summoned to Berlin by the Reichsführer-SS, Himmler. He gave me to understand—I cannot remember the exact words—that the Führer had ordered the final solution of the Jewish question and it was the function of the SS to execute this order. If this did not take place now, the Jewish people would destroy the Germans. He had chosen Auschwitz because it was suitable as a center of rail communications and offered a large enough area for enclosure. I was in command of Auschwitz until 1 December 1943 and estimate that at least 2,500,000 victims were liquidated there by gassing and cremation. At least a further half million died by starvation and illness, which gives a final total of approximately three million deaths. This figure represents some 70 to 80 percent of all persons who were sent to Auschwitz. The rest were selected for slave labor in the camp. Of the total number of victims there were some 100,000 German Jews and a large number of mainly Jewish citizens from Holland, France, Belgium, Poland, Hungary, Czechoslovakia, Greece, and other countries. About 400,000 Jews from Hungary alone were liquidated in the summer of 1944. The commandant of Treblinka told me that during the course of half a year he had liquidated 80,000. His duty was mainly the liquidation of all Jews from the Warsaw ghetto. He used monoxide gas, and I considered his methods not particularly effective. When therefore I established the liquidation chambers in Auschwitz I decided to use Zyklon-B, a crystallized prussic acid, which we injected into the death chambers through a small aperture. Depending on climatic conditions the people in the chambers generally died within three to fifteen minutes. We knew when the occupants had died because their shouting stopped. We normally waited about half an hour before we opened the doors and removed the corpses. After they had been dragged out, our special commandos took the rings off the corpses and pulled out any gold teeth they might have. A further improvement we introduced on methods used at Treblinka was that we built gas chambers which could take 2,000

people at once, while the ten chambers at Treblinka only had a
capacity of 200 each. The method we used to select our victims
was as follows: Two SS doctors were on duty at Auschwitz to
examine the new arrivals, who came in large transports. The
prisoners had to pass in front of one of the doctors who immediately made the decision about them. Those capable of work
were sent into the camp. The others were immediately transferred to the liquidation centers. Very young children were always killed, since because of their youth they were unable to
work. In many cases women tried to hide their children under
their skirts, but when we discovered them they were of course
sent to their death. We were supposed to carry out this liquidation in secret, but the disgusting and nauseating stench which
resulted from the continuous burning of bodies, permeated the
entire area. . . .

The problem of the disposal of the corpses created scenes of horror at all camps. One eyewitness from Bergen-Belsen, Dr. Charles
Bendel, gave the following description at Nuremberg: "Now the true
hell began. The special commandos made every effort to perform
their work as speedily as possible. They seized the corpses by the
wrists, they looked like devils. Men who had previously had human
countenances could no longer be recognized. A lawyer from Thessa-
lonika, an engineer from Budapest, they were no longer human
beings, for even as they work they are impelled on by the truncheons
and sticks of the guards. And during the whole time, people are shot
by the mass graves, people who could not get into the gas chambers
because these were already overloaded. After about one and a half
hours the process is concluded and a new 'transport' from crema-
torium number four has been dealt with."

Sometimes small-gauge electric railways were used to transfer the
corpses from the gas ovens into the crematoria. Under the administration of Oswald Pohl, chief economist of the SS, what remained of
the bones was ground into a fine powder. Pohl's function was to
translate the "assets" of the victims into money deposited in the SS
bank accounts. Accordingly, gold fillings, jewels, cigarette cases,
watches, clothing, spectacles, and human hair were carefully sorted
out and stored for conversion into liquid assets for the SS Main
Office. On August 6, 1942, Pohl wrote a memorandum to the commandants of sixteen extermination camps, saying, "In all camps
human hair must be collected. Women's hair can be used in the manufacture of socks for U-Boat personnel and for employees of the

State Railways. It is ordered that the hair of female prisoners must be carefully kept, after disinfection. As to men's hair, it is only of use to us if it has a length of at least twenty millimeters."

Himmler's high-ranking amanuensis, Odilo Globocnik, had no misgivings about the necessity of the work taking place in the concentration camps. He had a meeting with Hitler and an official from the Ministry of the Interior, Dr. Herbert Linden, in 1942, and the following exchange took place:

Dr. Linden: Herr Globocnik, do you really think it is a good idea simply to bury the corpses instead of cremating them? We could, after all, be succeeded by a generation which does not understand our work. . . .

Globocnik: Gentlemen, if we are succeeded by a generation which is so mealy-mouthed and soft that it does not appreciate our gigantic task, the entire National Socialist movement will have been in vain. On the contrary, in my opinion we should place in each grave a bronze plaque which bears the inscription that we had the courage to pursue this great and necessary enterprise.

Hitler: Exactly, Globocnik! That is entirely my view!

The SS attracted a number of doctors and scientists who, ostensibly in the interests of science, conducted experiments on the inmates of the camps under the most ghastly conditions. Experiments involving sterilization (naturally without anesthetic), injection of bacteria, typhus, cholera, yellow fever, diphtheria, which all resulted in the death of their human guinea pigs, were undertaken in a large number of camps. Himmler showed special interest in the experiments conducted by SS Dr. Sigmund Rascher, who worked in the field of human resistance to extremes of cold and heat. At Ravensbruck, a women's camp, SS-Brigadeführer Professor Hans Clauberg boasted that it lay within his capacities to sterilize up to one thousand women daily.

It is obvious that a very sizable number of men employed in German industry, without even a nominal membership in the SS, were involved in the mass slaughter. The equipment used at the death camps had to be manufactured somewhere, the poison gases used, the vast bureaucracy to coordinate the statistics, all added up to one thing: that thousands of ordinary Germans were employed indirectly in perpetuating the machinery of the SS state as exemplified by the concentration camps. In addition, as the demands of total war became more and more pressing, the supply of labor within the Reich had to be augmented. It was to the SS that the Reich economists turned to implement a program of importing foreign labor into Germany. By the autumn of 1944 no fewer than 7.5 million foreign laborers were working in Germany, almost without exception seized in the occupied territories by SS units, often aided by the Wehrmacht. The available work force was supplemented by two million prisoners of war, about a quarter of whom were compelled to work in the munitions industries.

SS units used a simple device. Anywhere in occupied Europe an entire town quarter was sealed off. As you were going about your business you were seized, separated from your family, and sent off to a German factory. No questions were asked, and to offer resistance was foolhardy. The SS administration readily acceded to a request from the famous German armaments firm of Krupp for additional "labor." Six hundred Jewish women from Buchenwald were sent to the Ruhr. The enormous use of slave labor in the Krupp enterprises necessitated the employment of at least one doctor; a standard health must be maintained commensurate with achieving expected production figures. At one of Krupp's work camps, a Dr. Jaeger reported: "Its inhabitants were kept for nearly half a year in dog kennels, urinals, and old bakeries. The kennels were three feet high, nine feet long, six feet wide. Five men slept in each of them. Prisoners had to crawl on all fours. . . . There was no water in the camp."

The war between economic needs and genocide assumed renewed vigor in 1944. Speer, as Minister for War Production, wanted the foreign workers to work. Himmler was bent on the pursuit of cruelty and persecution. The two aims were not easily reconciled. If a foreign worker, miserably underfed, ill-treated, and exploited, offended any of the rules laid down by the SS he was likely to be shot out of hand, or imprisoned. In the first half of 1944 no fewer than 300,000 arrests were made for minor "crimes." The inroads these actions of the SS made into Speer's labor supply will be readily appreciated. Speer spoke of his problems to Hitler and advised him that Himmler was robbing him of anything from 30,000 to 40,000 workers each month. Presumably under pressure from Hitler, Himmler undertook to release convicted prisoners after a shorter sentence.

The giant German industrial undertakings showed little understanding of the relationship between effort and reward. They did not appear to appreciate that a certain minimum diet was required to ensure reasonable work rates from their slaves. I. G. Farben, a huge corporation, found it feasible to hand out prisoners a bowl of soup at lunchtime, but the famous firm of Krupp, which employed a large number of Jewish women from Hungary, made them work in appalling circumstances. They were both possibly guided by the belief that there was a never-ending source of supply; certainly moral considerations played no part at all.

As the fortunes of the Reich deteriorated in the later stages of the war, the higher SS leadership was at pains to destroy the evidence of what had taken place in the extermination camps, for fear of the retribution which the undoubtedly victorious Allies would exact.

This led to two courses of action. The pace of extermination was speeded up. On the other hand, those whom the capacities of the gas ovens could not absorb, must be evacuated.

Accordingly, when Soviet troops penetrated the German Army Group Center in June 1944, a desperate attempt was made by the SS leadership to evacuate the remaining inmates of the camps westward. The problem was compounded because of Allied advances on the western front. In the east, there were still 85,000 prisoners in Auschwitz when Russian gunfire could be heard. There was no time to kill them in the gas chambers and they were eventually returned to the Reich, bringing with them typhus. In the west, Natzweiler in Alsace had to be hastily evacuated. According to Eugon Kogon, a previous inmate of Buchenwald, prisoners at the camp in Lublin actually formed a committee and despite the efforts of SS personnel, refused to be evacuated. On July 24, 1944, they overcame their SS guards and handed them over to Red Army units.

12

RESISTANCE IN THE
WARSAW GHETTO

The defense mounted by the occupants of the Warsaw Ghetto in 1943 was the only occasion during the history of the SS in which it found itself faced by an enemy as tenacious and dedicated as it was itself.

As the German armies rolled across Russia, SS and police units followed closely on the heels of the troops and set up their headquarters in the occupied towns and cities. In many cases they relied on the ignorance of the local Jewish population. In Kiev, for example, Einsatzgruppe C simply placed posters at appropriate points throughout the city. "The Jewish population," they reported to SS headquarters in Berlin, "was invited by poster to present themselves for resettlement. Although initially we had only counted on 5,000 to 6,000 Jews reporting, more than 30,000 appeared. By a remarkably efficient piece of organization, they were led to believe in the resettlement story until shortly before their execution."

It may be asked why the Jews reported. There is one clear answer to this. Nobody untrained in the barbaric formulae of National Socialism could possibly imagine that entire communities were to be put to death. "Resettlement," that ghastly euphemism, might mean unparalleled hardship, loss of home, separation from family, and transfer to work camps, but it was not within the imagination of the Jews that it could signify death. What was certain was that if you did not report, you would be seized by an SS police unit as you slunk about the town, and then shot for not having reported. The idea of extermination camps was as alien to the Jews of Europe as it was to the millions of people of the world who were horrified in the later stages of the war by the pictures of unbelievable barbarism circulated in the newsreels.

Heydrich, as will be recalled from his comments at the meeting of leading German bureaucrats after Kristallnacht, was originally against the sealing off of Jews in ghettos, because he believed this would create technical problems for his police forces. But when Hans Frank became overlord of the General Government of Poland, he conceived the idea of compelling all Jews to wear a distinguishing sign. By the end of 1939, the Gestapo decided that it would after all be better, for technical police reasons, to have all Jews grouped together in distinctive city quarters, or ghettos. Heydrich himself issued a memorandum in which he stated: "It must be the first aim for the implementation of German measures against the Jews to separate them from the rest of the population. They must be transferred into ghettos, with separate quarters for men and women. These can be administered by a Jewish Council. The supervision of the boundaries between the ghettos and the outside world is the job of the police." This was achieved with considerable thoroughness. Millions of Jews found themselves shut off from the world by high walls, barbed wire, and other defenses carefully watched over by SS and police units. In the words of William Walsh, American prosecutor at Nuremberg, "By the end of 1942 the Jews within the General Government of Poland were herded together in fifty-five ghettos." To attempt to leave these ghettos inevitably meant a death sentence.

Having assembled the Jews in ghettos, the next problem to be faced by the SS was how best to dispose of them. Himmler conceived the idea of simply letting them starve to death. To an extent, this worked. The German Ministry of Food and Agriculture proclaimed on September 18, 1942: "For the forthcoming rationing period, Jews will no longer receive meat, meat products, eggs, milk, etc. etc." Hans Frank decided that the daily bread ration permitted by the Ministry, of 143 grams, was too generous, and on his own authority reduced it to 20 grams and added that the monthly ration of jam would be 100 grams and of fat, 50 grams. In his diary he commented laconically, "During the winter months the rate of deaths will doubtless increase, but then this war will bring with it the total annihilation of the Jews." Frank was right; death from starvation was a daily occurrence in most ghettos, and a daily roundup of corpses took place.

The trouble with death through starvation, in the eyes of the SS, was that it was a lengthy process and tended to spread disease which could, if uncontrolled, extend to non-Jewish quarters and thereby create a dangerous situation behind the army lines.

Accordingly, those Jews who were capable of slave labor for the war economy should be put to work; the rest must be liquidated. In the ghetto of Warsaw, workshops were set up in which those Jews who were *arbeitsfähig,* or capable of work, were employed. Their "employers" were in the main, German entrepreneurs. One of them,

Walter Toebbens, actually "employed" no fewer than 15,000 slaves. For Toebbens the results were particularly interesting, since it transformed him into a multimillionaire within a relatively short period. He had, of course, to share his profits with the local SS officials, particularly Globocnik.

This in no way satisfied Hans Frank. Like so many "idealists" within the Nazi movement, he was not interested in economic output. He committed his thoughts to his diary once more: "I must say quite openly that we have to finish off the Jews one way or another. . . . Basically we can only extend our sympathy to the German people, not to any other people in the world. As an old National Socialist, I have to say: Should any of the Jewish tribe survive the war, our victory will only be a partial one. . . . We must eradicate the Jews whenever we find them and wherever possible."

In the ghetto of Warsaw the eradication plans were put into effect. According to a report of SS-Brigadeführer Jürgen Stroop, "the Jewish quarter in the city of Warsaw [measuring some four kilometers by two and a half] is occupied by some 400,000 Jews. It contained 27,000 apartments and, on average, each had some two and a half rooms. It was separated from the rest of the city by high walls and barricaded streets. . . ." According to William Walsh, on average the occupancy within the ghetto was six people to a room.

In 1941 Himmler's policy of death through starvation resulted in 44,630 deaths. However, a commission of Jewish doctors estimated that it would take a further five years to eliminate the entire population by starvation. This startled the SS officials on two counts. In the first place it was clear that the Jews must be receiving food from other sources. In the second, since a commission of Jewish doctors had been established, it meant that the Jews were organizing themselves to study their collective problems and attempt to find a solution to them.

The high walls surrounding the ghettos looked impenetrable, but in fact there were subterranean canals, sewers, odd holes in the structure of the walls, and occasionally a helpful Polish policeman to give aid. In the main, the children in the ghetto managed to secure rations by creeping along the wider pipes under the ground in the sewers and getting into the city.

The fact that several hundred thousand inmates of the Warsaw ghetto did not die of starvation is largely due to the activities of the Jewish children, who were small enough to leave and reenter the ghetto through the Warsaw sewage system. This they managed to achieve despite the increasing vigilance of Himmler's police units, who manned every possible escape route from the ghetto. Another source of supply to the inmates of the ghetto derived from the fact that Jewish working parties often had to make their way, under armed escort naturally, from the Jewish quarter to the workshops in which they were "employed." Although on-the-spot checks as to numbers were carried out regularly, and although the prisoners were forced to empty their pockets in front of the German police (with the threat of immediate death if food were discovered on their persons) there is no doubt that the system contained some loopholes.

Within the ghetto itself, only one tram was in operation. It was for the exclusive use of Jews and instead of bearing a number, it displayed prominently at front and rear the Star of David. However, at its narrowest point, the ghetto was crossed by a further sideline connected to the main tramway system of Warsaw. Trams using this line were ordered to travel at high speed and no stops were permitted. This did not prevent Polish children from throwing out sacks of food onto the street within the ghetto precincts, which then were immediately picked up and secreted away by the waiting Jewish children. So efficient did this means of provision become that at one time a few cows were mysteriously introduced into the ghetto and coaxed up to the third floor of an apartment building, thus providing a source of milk for the babies. To an extent, Globocnik and other officials of the Gestapo, SS, and SD were content to see the activities within the ghetto continue, for they were a constant source of personal enrichment, enhanced by a widespread system of bribery and extortion.

At enormously inflated prices, it even became possible for the Jews to purchase a sizable amount of weaponry; rifles, pistols, and hand grenades were smuggled in, obtained from various quartermasters of the German Army and also from the Italian Army of the east stationed at Lvov.

Intelligence regarding these activities eventually made its way to Berlin, to the Reichssicherheitshauptamt, and reached the ears of Heinrich Himmler himself. It was very probably due to his intervention that on July 20, 1942, the Jewish Council received the order from the SD to deliver 60,000 Jews for labor service. Groups of SS commando units made their way up and down the streets and buildings of the ghetto to round up the victims. By this time, the Jews had organized a resistance committee. One of their members, a certain Bernard Goldstein, records in his memoirs:

> We had no doubt that these transports would carry the
> people to certain death. The difficult task of obtaining

more exact information about this was assigned to Zalman Friedrych, one of the most courageous and active comrades in our movement. A Pole, who worked on the railways, and who knew the direction the trains normally took, advised Friedrych about their route. With great difficulty, Friedrych finally reached Sokolow. There he learned that the Germans had constructed a small sideline to the village of Treblinka. Every day trains laden with Jews would be shunted onto this new line. In Treblinka there was a large camp. The inhabitants of Sokolow had heard that terrible things were happening at Treblinka, but they did not know exactly what these were. In Sokolow, Friedrych accidentally came into contact with a comrade of ours called Azriel Wallach, a nephew of Maxim Litvinov [the previous Soviet Foreign Minister]. He had just managed to escape from Treblinka and was in a dreadful state: heavily burned, bleeding, his clothes in rags. Friedrych learned from Wallach that all Jews who had been transported to Treblinka were immediately massacred. They were taken out of the trains and were told to take a bath, after which they would be transferred to their working quarters. Then they were driven into hermetically sealed chambers and gassed. Wallach had escaped because he had been instructed to clean out the goods wagon and had used this opportunity to flee. Friedrych returned to Warsaw with this story. So we were in a position to give the ghetto an eyewitness report of what actually happened to our deportees.

Yet this eyewitness report found little credibility among the inmates of the Warsaw ghetto. It was simply beyond their belief, and many of them continued to obey the orders issued by the SS units to report for "deportation." Only gradually did the Jews come to believe in the authenticity of what was rumored about their final destination.

On January 18, 1943, an astonishing thing happened in the Warsaw ghetto. A crowd of Jews being herded together for deportation by an SS guard suddenly drew pistols concealed in their clothing and opened fire on the guards. They then raced back into the nearby buildings for cover.

The SS commander in Warsaw, Ferdinand von Sammern-Frankenegg, beside himself with rage, immediately ordered a full raid on the ghetto to unearth the culprits. But they had apparently disappeared from the face of the earth. Frankenegg contented himself with bombing a few Jewish houses, but nobody would reveal the identity of those who had fired on his guards.

Himmler waited until February 16, 1943, before ordering the ghetto to be razed to the ground. But he apparently could not rely on the efficiency of Frankenegg or Globocnik, for these two were far from ready to destroy the source of their new-found wealth. Accordingly, Himmler ordered his trusty SS-Brigadeführer Jürgen Stroop to take over matters in Warsaw. On April 19, Stroop entered the ghetto with three armored cars and three cannons. According to the report Stroop was later to give to Himmler, what followed his entry into the ghetto went along these lines:

Before we started our action, the boundaries of the Jewish area were cordoned off in order to prevent the Jews from breaking out. On our first attempt to penetrate the ghetto we were driven back by the Jews who fired on our armored cars. . . . On our second attempt, despite continuous fire by the Jews, we managed to comb out the entire complex of buildings. Our opponents were compelled to climb down from the rooftops . . . and retreat into the cellars and canals. In order to prevent regrouping in the canal system, we flooded it, but this was rendered ineffective by the Jews, who blew up all the outlets. . . . The main fighting force of the Jews, which contained a number of Polish partisans, withdrew to the Muranovski Square. They intended to defend this area with every means at their disposal in order to prevent our further penetration of the ghetto. The Jewish and Polish flags were raised on a building as an appeal to the inhabitants to rally to their cause. . . . After the first few days, I realized that our original plan could not be realized. The Jews had everything they needed; chemicals for the manufacture of explosives, clothing and munitions from the Wehrmacht, arms of all types, especially grenades and Molotov cocktails. The Jews had also managed to set up pockets of resistance in factories. One such pocket could only be eliminated by the second day by the use of flamethrowers and artillery fire. . . . In the course of the action, it became clear that the entire system of streets and buildings was connected to the canal system and . . . below ground level the Jews could conduct their operations without hindrance. . . . While at the start, it seemed simple to capture cowardly

Jews in large numbers, in the second half of the action it became more and more difficult. There were always fighting units of twenty to thirty people and Jewish youngsters of eighteen to twenty-five with an equivalent number of women to assist them. . . . It was no rarity to see these women firing from pistols in both hands . . . they often concealed hand grenades under their skirts to throw them at the last moment at the men of the Waffen-SS, the Police, and the Army.

On 23 April 1943 the Reichsführer-SS issued an order via the Higher SS and Police Leader in Crakow, to proceed against the ghetto more rigorously. . . . I therefore decided to undertake the total destruction of the ghetto by burning down block after block. . . . The longer resistance lasted, the more relentless were the men of the Waffen-SS, the Police, and the Army, who performed their duties tirelessly in true fraternity. . . . If you take into account that the majority of men of the Waffen-SS had only had three or four weeks training before they were called to perform this task, special mention must be made of their courage. . . .

Despite the "courage" of Stroop's newly trained Waffen-SS units, it was not until May 16, 1943, that he could report that the action in the Warsaw ghetto was concluded. Each day he sent reports to his superiors in Crakow. Here are some excerpts from his teleprinter messages:

April 23: Today we divided the ghetto into 24 districts, each of which was thoroughly combed out. Result: 600 Jews and bandits captured, some 200 Jews and bandits shot, 48 bunkers, mostly very cleverly constructed, bombed out. . . . Total deported since the start of the action, 19,450. The next train leaves Warsaw on 24.4.43.
April 24: The Jews apparently prefer death in the large fires we have started, to surrender to our troops. . . .
April 25: . . . Tonight the entire ghetto is covered by an enormous sea of flames. . . .
April 26: . . . According to the testimony of captured Jews, a large number have gone mad as a result of their exposure to the heat. . . . During today's activities we burned down entire apartment buildings. This is the only

and final method of coercing these subhumans to come to the surface. . . .

April 27: . . . The Jews continued firing until the last moment and then even jumped out of fourth-story windows onto the streets. Cursing Germany and the Führer, they leaped out of the burning windows and balconies.

May 8: . . . Each time we unearth yet another bunker, the Jews continue to defend themselves with whatever weapons they still have: light machine guns, pistols, and hand grenades. . . .

May 10: Jewish resistance continues without abatement. . . .

It was not until May 16, 1943, that Stroop could report to his superiors: "The previous Jewish quarter of Warsaw no longer exists. The total of captured and shot Jews is 56,065."

On the orders of Himmler, the entire area was razed to the ground. An architect in the employ of the SS, SS-Obergruppenführer Heinz Kammler, was entrusted with the destruction of the remaining buildings. He executed his job methodically, and the whole district of four by two and a half kilometers was systematically converted into a desert of dust and stones. Only a few surviving Jews managed to escape into Warsaw, defy the net of the SS and avoid deportation to Treblinka, and live to tell their story.

13
THE SS AFTER
JULY 20, 1944

There was only one organization within the Third Reich capable of overthrowing the Hitler regime, and with it, the police and extermination machine of the SS. That was the Army.

Until the Russian campaign in 1941, any leading generals of the Wehrmacht who might have entertained the idea of taking over the destiny of Germany were emasculated on two counts. The first was that their Führer's diplomacy had, before the war, won them inspired and costless victories. The second was that his generalship had seemed brilliant. The Rhineland had been reoccupied, the Anschluss with Austria had taken place, Czechoslovakia and Poland had been taken, and all with immediate success and considerable military élan. Veterans of the First World War looked about themselves with amazement as the German armies rolled through Belgium and France in 1940. They remembered only too well how in the 1914–1918 war they had sat in trenches for months and years to gain a few hundred yards of territory. Now their tanks rolled across the countryside in almost serene disregard of the much vaunted French Army and despite the opposition of the British Expeditionary Force.

There were a number of civilians who wanted to end the iniquitous system of destruction initiated by Adolf Hitler. There was even a retired Colonel-General called Beck who did his utmost to use his considerable standing with the General Staff to persuade them to imprison the Führer and take over the affairs of state. On one matter, all these civilians were united. They must address themselves to the commanding generals of the Wehrmacht and find some among them to prepare a coup d'état.

In this endeavor they were remarkably unsuccessful. It was only after the defeat of the Germans at Stalingrad that their pleadings began to carry any weight. And curiously enough, it was not only the surrender of Paulus at Stalingrad which mobilized the German resistance movement within the Wehrmacht; it was the Nazi party official line on the treatment of Russian defectors.

When the Germans embarked on their speedy advance into Russia in June 1941 they found, to their considerable astonishment, that large numbers of Russians, peasants, workers, and soldiers considered them to be liberators. A curious situation resulted in that the armed troops of one police state were believed by the very people whose territories they were occupying to be their liberators. By the end of 1942 no fewer than 800,000 Russian citizens had either defected from the Red Army or had announced their willingness to work for the Germans in their common aim, which they believed to be the overthrow of Stalinist oppression. The Russian soldiers wanted to fight alongside the Germans. They remembered only too well the Stalinist purges of the 1930s, and their comrades, the peasants, remembered the appalling consequences of the collectivization of the land.

A leader was found for this enormous number of Russians in the person of General Andrey Andreyevitch Vlasov, a hero of the Soviet Union, a member of the Russian Communist party, a man with a peasant background. After his stout defense of Leningrad as commander of the Second Soviet Shock Army south of that city, after his repeated requests to Stalin to permit him to withdraw from an impossible situation had been refused, Vlasov decided to surrender to the Germans.

After a great deal of inner debate Vlasov determined that the real enemy for the Russians was Stalin himself. After a few weeks as a prisoner of war, he announced his readiness to found a Russian Liberation Movement. He prepared leaflets which were scattered in thousands behind the Russian lines and had the effect of drawing more and more defecting Russian troops into his camp. He then urged his captors to give him a command. The officers in the Wehrmacht were delighted. Their Führer was bent on impossible tasks in the east. The only possible way of filling in the gap in manpower created by the surrender of Paulus at Stalingrad was to use Russian units under Vlasov. For wherever he appeared Vlasov was acknowledged by the Russian prisoners to be their most popular general.

The good news was conveyed to the Führer at his headquarters. But to the dismay of the Wehrmacht officers, Hitler seemed unmoved. On no account, so he maintained, could the Slav subhuman be allowed to fight alongside the German. The Russian's sweat and brawn could be used. He could clean out latrines, drag gun carriages, and perform a list of duties consonant with his lowly status, but to allow him to fight was totally out of the question.

A direct approach to the Führer seemed useless. The pro-Vlasov Wehrmacht officers also had to contend with the vagaries of the Nazi Propaganda Ministry, which continued to issue literature portraying the Russian as a subhuman. Once again, racial theory became an obstacle to military and economic expedience. Months went by while the fortunes of the German armies deteriorated. Endless discussions took place on such matters as whether Vlasov should be given a command and, if so, which flashes and insignia his troops should wear. Vlasov himself became disillusioned. There was only one issue on which he expressed surprise. It seemed clear from his dealings with several high-ranking German officers that they not only disagreed with the policies of their Führer, but were prepared to say so. Open criticism of Stalin in the Soviet Army, Vlasov knew, was out of the question. How much more democratic did the German way of life appear by contrast!

It is therefore no accident that when the attempt at a coup d'état by the German Army took place, it was the brainchild of staff officers who had done service on the Russian front. Stauffenberg, von Treszkow, Stieff, and many others had all been driven to desperation by Hitler's attitude and by that of the Propaganda Ministry toward the question of the Russian Liberation Movement. Even if moral considerations were discounted, Hitler's refusal to use the Russians amounted to logistic absurdity.

It took time before the plotters discovered the right man for the job of removing Hitler. They eventually found him in the person of Colonel Count Claus Schenck von Stauffenberg, a brilliant, aristocratic staff officer from Swabia. He had been heavily wounded in the African campaign and had only one eye and one hand, and on the remaining hand just two fingers and a thumb. But he had three precious qualities. He was resolute, he was brave, and even more importantly, as assistant to the Commander in Chief of the Reserve Army, he had access to the Führer.

On July 20, 1944, Stauffenberg planted his bomb under a table just a few feet away from Hitler at the headquarters in Rastenburg. Hitler survived the explosion and then the SS entered the picture.

As guardians of the personal safety of the Führer, they could be accused of incompetence bordering on stupidity. Hitler considered that providence had saved him for his sacred work. But this was small consolation for Heinrich Himmler. He felt a deep sense of personal responsibility. Hitler dispatched him to Berlin, where he might unearth the traitors. Clearly the prime suspect was Stauffenberg, who had unobtrusively left the Führer's bunker once the bomb had been activated. Before leaving for Berlin, Himmler telephoned SS-Oberführer Piffraeder of the Gestapo and instructed him to proceed immediately to the War Office in the Bendlerstrasse and arrest Stauffenberg.

Piffraeder did not think it necessary to turn up at the Bendlerstrasse with an armed guard. He made his way there, asked somebody where he might find Colonel Count Stauffenberg, followed directions, and suddenly, to the astonishment of the conspirators, announced to Stauffenberg that he was under arrest. Stauffenberg immediately informed Piffraeder that the reverse was true and Piffraeder meekly walked away under armed guard.

Himmler's police had been aware that various resistance circles in Germany had been toying with the idea of organizing a putsch. But Himmler was so far off target that he had actually supported a proposal to make Stauffenberg Hitler's Chief of Staff. Once it became clear to Hitler that the leadership of the Reserve Army had been plotting his assassination, his paranoid mind came up with only one possible successor, and that was Heinrich Himmler.

Therefore, to his existing titles as Reichsführer-SS and Chief of the German Police, Himmler, on July 20, 1944, added yet another: Commander in Chief of the Reserve Army. It was a strange appointment, since Himmler had next to no military knowledge. It reflected Hitler's increasing paranoia: Better an insipid ignorant commander he could trust than a highly trained one who might kill him.

While Hitler was at his headquarters at Rastenburg, Himmler stationed himself in a special train of fourteen coaches. This was in a siding twenty-five miles from Rastenburg. There was a villa nearby, but Himmler did most of his work in the train, for it had one inestimable advantage over the villa: it was mobile. In the event of an air raid, the train could be shunted into a nearby tunnel. On July 20, 1944, Himmler's masseur, Felix Kersten, was in attendance at the villa. There he saw his patient in a state of great anxiety preparing to descend on Berlin, "to root out the reactionary brood." In fact, Himmler did not hurry to Berlin. He first went to Rastenburg to offer his congratulations to Hitler on having survived the attempt on his life. The bomb had exploded at 12:42 P.M., but it was not until 5:00 P.M. that Himmler was seen at Rastenburg taking leave of Hitler with the words, "My Führer, you can leave it to me."

Leaving it to Heinrich Himmler meant major surgery for the German body politic. Investigations proliferated. Under the doctrine of

Sippenhaft, which meant the arrest of all relatives of anybody implicated in the plot, wives and children were dispersed. The greatest roundup of "enemies of the State" took place in Germany since the Night of the Long Knives.

The investigations took place under the supervision of Heydrich's successor at the Reichssicherheitshauptamt, an ex-lawyer from Linz named Ernst Kaltenbrunner. In a radio address to the German people during the night of July 20–21 Hitler claimed: "The circle of these conspirators is very small and has nothing in common with the spirit of the German Wehrmacht and, above all, none with the German people. I therefore give orders now that no military commander and no private soldier is to obey any orders emanating from this group of usurpers. I also order that it is everybody's duty to arrest, or if they resist, to shoot on sight anyone issuing or handling such orders. I am convinced that with the uncovering of this tiny clique of traitors and saboteurs there has at long last been created in the rear that atmosphere which the fighting front needs. . . . This time we shall get even with them in the way to which we National Socialists are accustomed."

While Hitler claimed that only a tiny clique was responsible, the investigations conducted by Kaltenbrunner resulted in some 5,000 executions, and in addition thousands of others were sent to concentration camps. Reports of the interrogations were sent almost daily by Kaltenbrunner to Martin Bormann, head of the Party Chancellory, who was continuously at Hitler's side. This police work continued until the very end of the war, and the notorious People's Court which tried the accused under the Nazi judge Roland Freisler sat for months. The first of the trials, which took place on August 7, condemned to death Field Marshal von Witzleben, generals Stieff, Hase, and Hoeppner, and many other officers. They suffered an agonizing death—suspended from butcher's hooks on piano wire. All of this was filmed and shown to Hitler the same evening in the Reich Chancellory. The perspicacity of Admiral Canaris did not save him from imprisonment and eventual death. For, wise old intelligence officer that he was, when Stauffenberg telephoned him on July 20 to advise him that Hitler had been assassinated, Canaris, in full knowledge that his telephone was being tapped, replied: "Really? Who did it? The Russians?"

For some fanatics, the attempt on Hitler's life was parallel with the circumstances in which Germany was defeated in the First World War. Thousands of members of the Freikorps in 1919 and 1920 believed that had it not been for the activities of left-wing saboteurs in the *Etappe,* or rear, Germany would not have lost the war. These saboteurs had stabbed the Fatherland in the back in its hour of need. Now it seemed as if history was to repeat itself, for once again German leadership had been stabbed in the back. The difference was that this time those to blame were members of the military caste instead of left-wing radicals. This was a theory which gained a certain currency in Germany in the immediate postwar years and was propounded by Otto Ernst Remer, who played a decisive role in unearthing the conspirators in Berlin.

The failure of July 20, 1944, represented the final erosion of the status of the German officer caste. The fate of Germany was now firmly and irrevocably placed in the hands of the fanatical SS; Himmler's appointment as Commander in Chief of the Reserve Army confirmed this. If Hitler had been able to pursue his plans without the officers of the Wehrmacht, he would cheerfully have executed all its members. But he could not proceed without them. His SS units had shown that as tacticians they were useless.

After July 20, 1944, Himmler was in control of the Police and Secret Service. He was in charge of the Reich Ministry of the Interior. No fewer than thirty-eight Waffen-SS divisions were under his command, and as Commander in Chief of the Reserve or Home Army he was now overlord of all armed forces in the Reich. Hitler ordered him to create fifteen new divisions. Himmler was compelled to scrape the barrel of German manhood and the "Volksgrenadier" divisions were hastily put together. "What we are waging now," proclaimed Himmler in August 1944, "is a sacred war of the people."

The new recruits in the Volksgrenadier divisions were those too young or too old to have seen previous service. They were unprepared and untrained for their tasks. Himmler assembled their officers and tried to inspire them with compelling oratory: "I give you the authority," he ranted, "to seize every man who turns back; if necessary to tie him up and throw him in a supply wagon . . . put the best, the most energetic, and most brutal officers of the Division in charge. They will soon round up the rabble. Anyone who answers back will be put up against a wall." In emulation of the citizens of Leningrad who had fought to the last man, woman, and child against the Germans, Himmler called his new force the "National Socialist People's Army." He got his recruits from the factories and from schools, and his officers were, almost to a man, totally untrained.

Himmler planted his SD and Gestapo spies in each military unit. It was not long before these agents sent their reports to the Reichsführer-SS. "From Obergruppenführer Hofmann, Higher Police

Leader Southwest: Lt.-Colonel Graf is politically unreliable, must request his urgent dismissal. Also Lt.-Colonel von Hornstein should be dismissed; said to have a Jewish grandmother." A saner use of manpower would have recommended the sending of SD informers to the front, but Himmler was so entrenched in the pursuit of racial defectives that he encouraged his army of informers and considered their employment a precondition of success for his Volksgrenadiers. He managed to assemble additional forces numbering half a million men by the end of October 1944. They were dispatched to the front after the most cursory training. Once this had been achieved he addressed himself to the question of maintaining a last-ditch stand within the Reich's frontiers. The Werewolf scheme was created. It demanded that the most dedicated Nazi partisans would be distributed throughout Germany to impede the progress of the enemy from rooftops, trees, bunkers, and ditches. He dreamed of securing a fortress in the Bavarian Alps to which the Nazi elite might retire for the final battle. Summary courts were established that had the right to try and condemn any deserter, and lest there were any doubt as to the fate which a deserter might meet in their hands, he distributed posters throughout the country bearing the slogan "Every deserter will find his just punishment. His infamous behavior will entail the direst consequences for his family." Here was evidence of a return to the notorious Vehmgerichte, the summary courts established by the Freikorps in 1919 and 1920, which chose and tried its victims in secret and then murdered them. On trees around Germany, hanging figures could be seen carrying the placard: "I am hanging here because I left my unit without permission."

When the leader of the Polish insurgents, General Bor-Komorowski, with his 35,000 partisans, embarked on an attack in Warsaw against the German occupying forces, it was to Himmler that Hitler turned, rather than the Wehrmacht. Himmler sent the most brutal men in his SS to deal with the Poles: von dem Bach Zewelski and Oskar Dirlewanger, who had done service with the Einsatzgruppen, perpetrated such crimes on the Poles that even Guderian, the last Commander in Chief of the Wehrmacht, protested to Hitler.

In the months between July and November 1944 Himmler had shown considerable resourcefulness as an organizer. A grateful Führer extended to him the distinction of taking his place at the celebration of the Munich Beer-Hall Putsch. On November 9 Himmler, entranced at this singular honor, made the commemorative speech in Hitler's place. Himmler was totally transported by his recent achievements. He indulged more and more in a fantasy world. Guderian told him that at the next Russian offensive there just would not be any German troops available to offer resistance. This evoked from Himmler the reply, "You know, Colonel-General, I don't really believe the Russians will attack at all. It's all an enormous bluff."

There were others in the Third Reich who still had their feet on the ground and were still jockeying for position within its hierarchy. Among them was Martin Bormann. He was by no means pleased to see Himmler's star on the ascendant. On the other hand, there seemed no way of stopping him. Then one day he decided that if Himmler could be removed from Berlin, his influence must wane. Why not give him command of an army in the field? That would keep him quiet for a while. It was well known that Himmler had frequently spoken of his wish to be a soldier at the front. Why not grant him this wish? Bormann presented the idea to Hitler.

The command eventually assigned to Himmler was that of Commander in Chief Upper Rhine. An army group had to be placed between Karlsruhe and the Swiss Frontier to meet the threat of a breach of the Rhine by the British and Americans in Alsace. Himmler formed his new army with great élan. Once he had done so he appeared to be quite content to remain hidden in his quarters in the Black Forest to study reports. He dismissed people he did not trust, accusing them of inefficiency. In his absence certain SS dignitaries felt that their interests might be better served by pandering to Martin Bormann, who always had the ear of the Führer. Kaltenbrunner cultivated Bormann, and Gruppenführer Fegelein, who was Himmler's personal representative at the Führer's headquarters, defected to the Bormann camp.

Those still loyal to Himmler, who far outnumbered the defectors, attempted to warn him of what was happening in Berlin. Gottlob Berger, in a somewhat cynical phrase, wrote to Himmler urging him to give up his army appointment and return to SS headquarters in Berlin, "because I sense that when the Reichsführer-SS is not in the headquarters, our political work suffers badly." In his new role, Himmler chose to disregard these rumors. He was now a soldier; he had realized the ambition of his life and continued to sit in the Black Forest. When the German counteroffensive began under his leadership, it looked as if it might gain an initial success, but within a short time the allies had repelled the German advance. He was given a second chance at generalship in January 1945 when, despite the entreaties of Guderian, he was given command of an army in Pomerania in an attempt to contain the enormous Russian offensive. Here again, Himmler failed, as Guderian had predicted.

While Himmler continued to pay lip service to Adolf Hitler, "the greatest genius of all times," he could see the writing on the wall. The sad fate of German troops on all fronts could not escape his eyes. It was clear that Germany would be defeated; it was only a matter of time. The much vaunted secret weapons to which Goebbels referred could not hide this fact. After July 20, 1944, Himmler was the second most powerful man in the Reich, and it occasionally occurred to him that he would exercise that power in the better interests of Germany. Was it possible, he asked himself, by clever maneuvering to negotiate a separate peace and salvage what he could for the Thousand Year Reich? It never dawned on him that the enemy would find the idea of sitting at a negotiating table with Himmler ludicrous. He began to conceive of himself as the possible savior of Germany, and with it, that Nordic race whose fortunes had so obsessed him.

Overtures were made to the Western powers. As emissary he used his trusted Walter Schellenberg, Head of the Foreign Section of the SD. Astonishing scenes took place. Toward the end of February 1945 a Swedish representative of the Red Cross named Folke Bernadotte drove into Germany in a car bearing white stripes. The Luftwaffe had been told that this car must be unmolested, and its stripes could readily be seen from a height of a few hundred feet. Bernadotte was on his way to meet Heinrich Himmler. As far as he knew, his mission was to persuade Himmler to release Danish and Norwegian prisoners from various concentration camps and give them free passage to the Swedish frontier.

The two men met on February 19, 1945, in a clinic at Hohenlychen near Berlin. At this stage the heavy responsibility of his various offices were telling on Himmler. He spent more and more time in the hands of his masseur. His stomach gave him little peace. He delegated work to underlings. The meeting with Bernadotte took place in the quarters of the chief doctor, Karl Gebhardt. Bernadotte recalled in his memoirs: "When Himmler suddenly appeared before me, with his horn-rimmed glasses, in the green uniform of the Waffen-SS, without any decoration, he looked like some insignificant official. If I had met him on the street I should have paid no attention to him at all. He had small, delicate, sensitive hands and I noticed they were well manicured. I certainly saw nothing diabolical in him and noticed nothing of the famed coldness of his eyes."

Bernadotte told him why he had come. "If I accede to your request," said Himmler, "the Swedish newspapers will declare in massive headlines that the war criminal Himmler is attempting to evade his responsibilities at the last minute and to clear himself before the world, because he fears the consequences of his actions."

Himmler, always in difficulty when asked to take decisive action, could not bring himself to disclose the real nature of his invitation to Bernadotte. So the meeting broke up. But in April he invited Bernadotte again. On this occasion he said, "I am prepared to do anything in my power for the German people, but I have to continue the battle. I have sworn loyalty to the Führer and am bound by this oath."

Bernadotte decided the time had come for frankness. "Do you not see," he asked, "that Germany has in fact lost the war? A man in your situation has no right to obey his superior blindly. He must have the courage to take measures which will be of service to his people." At this point Himmler was summoned to the telephone. On the advice of Schellenberg he now asked Bernadotte to go to General Eisenhower and offer the capitulation of all German forces on the western front. Bernadotte was bewildered. He considered the proposal for a while and said he would follow Himmler's suggestion once two conditions were met: (1) Himmler must publicly declare that he had succeeded Hitler because Hitler was no longer able to perform his functions owing to illness. (2) Himmler must dissolve the Nazi party and immediately replace all Party officials.

In Bernadotte's view these conditions would be unacceptable to Himmler, but to his surprise, Himmler acceded. Bernadotte did not know, naturally, of the various other overtures Himmler had been making to the outside world. As early as 1943 he had used the connections of the German industrialist Arnold Rechberg to make contact with the Western powers and discuss the possibility of a separate peace with the West. At the time Bormann and Ribbentrop had scented out Himmler's initiative, which was then quickly abandoned. Now, however, Himmler was only too ready to undertake any action which might save his skin. While issuing orders for the immediate hanging of any deserters, he entered into correspondence with Dr. Hillel Storch, the representative of the World Jewish Congress. An emissary of Storch, Dr. Norbert Masur, was permitted to fly from Stockholm to Berlin, his safety personally guaranteed by Himmler. The purpose of the meeting was to discuss with Masur the possibility of the release of Jewish inmates from the concentration camps. At the same time, Himmler negotiated with a former president of Switzerland, Musy, over the possibility of sending Jews from the camp at Belsen to Switzerland. Again, via Schellenberg, who had contacted the Swedish banker Wallenberg, he attempted to renew his overtures to Eisenhower to obtain a separate peace with the West. In other words, Himmler, consistent with his vacillating nature, was doing everything to redress the situation. What he had failed to understand was that the terms of unconditional surrender were quite unambiguous. Germany must surrender on all fronts. The happy dream entertained by many Germans that they could drive a wedge between the Soviets and the Western powers was never to be realized.

Himmler accepted Bernadotte's conditions and promised the early release of internees from Denmark and Norway. But he was still haunted by the fear of a reprisal from Hitler, should the Führer learn anything of his negotiations. He therefore sought a rationalization which would at one time salve his conscience and enable him to present the Allies with his sudden volte-face from mass murderer to peace negotiator.

Himmler decided to make Hitler's state of health the fulcrum of his activities. He talked about it at length with Schellenberg. He referred repeatedly to the bent stature of the Führer, to his deteriorated demeanor, and to the fact that his hands had begun to tremble. He even consulted Professor Max de Crinis, chief of the psychological department of the Charité Hospital in Berlin, and the Reich Health Minister, Dr. Leonardo Conti. These doctors voiced their suspicion that Hitler had Parkinson's disease.

Himmler went on long walks with Schellenberg, inviting him to endorse his views. On one occasion, in a deep forest, away from all ears, he said to Schellenberg, "I don't think we can work any longer with the Führer. He is no longer able to fulfill his duties. Do you think de Crinis is right?"

"Yes," replied Schellenberg.

"But what should I do?" asked Himmler anxiously. "I can't simply have him murdered, or poisoned, or have him arrested at the Reich Chancellory. . . ."

"There is only one possibility," said Schellenberg. "You must go to the Führer, tell him the facts, and compel him to resign."

"That is out of the question!" replied Himmler, terrified. "The Führer will go into a rage and have me shot on the spot!"

"Well, you can take measures against that possibility," urged Schellenberg reasonably. "After all, you are the superior of a great number of higher SS leaders who could readily arrange his arrest. And even if that didn't work, you could use the doctors. . . ."

It was not as easy as that for the indecisive Himmler. He walked about the woods for an hour and a half with Schellenberg, wondering what might happen if he were Hitler's successor. "The Party would have to be dissolved immediately," he confided. "we'd have to found a new party. What do you think would be a suitable name?"

"What about 'Party of the National Assembly'?" suggested Schellenberg, who by this time must have been puzzled at the strange tangents in which his superior's mind appeared to wander.

While these conversations were taking place, the death machines in the camps continued to function and the Soviet Armies approached the gates of Berlin. But Himmler remained indecisive until the last. During the night of April 20–21 he had yet another conference with Bernadotte at Hohenlychen. "He looked," reported Bernadotte, "as if he could not sit still in one place. He kept tapping on his teeth with his fingernails." Himmler repeated continuously, "The military situation is grave, very grave," which was of course a considerable understatement. He urged Bernadotte yet again to try to persuade Eisenhower to allow him to negotiate a separate peace with the West. Later Bernadotte told Schellenberg, "I am extremely doubtful that the Allies would accept a capitulation on the western front alone. . . . And anyway, there is not the slightest chance of Himmler's playing any role in a future Germany."

The final meeting between Himmler and Bernadotte took place on the night of April 24, 1945. They had to repair to an air-raid shelter because of the heavy bombing. The electrical system failed, and they had their discussion by candlelight. Himmler said, "Hitler is probably already dead. If not, he will die in the next few days. Until now I have been bound by my oath. But now the situation has changed. I admit that Germany has been conquered. What should happen now?" Himmler was quite convinced that he had been nominated Hitler's successor. "In the present situation I can act freely. I am prepared to capitulate on the western front and give these troops clear passage to the east. However, I am not prepared to capitulate in the east." He renewed his efforts to persuade Bernadotte to arrange a meeting for himself with Eisenhower. To Schellenberg he said, "When I meet Eisenhower, should I simply bow, or offer him my hand?"

But the meeting was not arranged. This did not prevent Himmler from indulging in fantasies at his last meeting with Bernadotte. "I should say the following to Eisenhower: 'I declare that the Western powers have defeated the German Wehrmacht. I am ready to capitulate unconditionally on the western front.' "

"And what will you do if your offer is rejected?"

"In that case I should take over command of a battalion on the eastern front and shall fall in battle."

When he took leave of Bernadotte, Himmler climbed into the

driver's seat of his car and told him, "I am now leaving for the eastern front." And then, with a slight smile, "After all, it is not very far."

Some twenty-three years earlier Himmler had written in his diary: "Oh, if only there were war again . . . departing troops!"

As if to complete this absurd comedy, he ran his car into the barbed wire surrounding the building in which he had met Bernadotte.

It took some time before SS men could disentangle it.

14
ADOLF EICHMANN:
THE NCO AS VISIONARY

Adolf Eichmann deserves special study in any history of the SS on two counts. In the first place, as Hannah Arendt has declared in her book *Eichmann in Jerusalem;* "The trouble with Eichmann was precisely that so many were like him, and that the many were neither perverted nor sadistic, that they were, and still are, terribly and terrifyingly normal."

In the second place, the odyssey of Adolf Eichmann shows more sharply than any other source the administrative chaos in which the SS worked; its multiplicity of offices, all in a state of constant competition with one another, and the spread of its incompetence through all the various ministries of the Third Reich. For while in the final weeks of the war the SS dignitaries were busily engaged in burning files and destroying the very evidence which they knew was bound to incriminate them, their work was totally in vain. And this was not due to the fact that some of their victims survived. It was because their opposite numbers in the Ministry of the Interior and the Foreign Office did not so happily abandon themselves to the same pyromania; and in these ministries thousands upon thousands of memoranda existed, which proved the guilt of the SS in perpetrating crimes against humanity.

Otto Adolf Eichmann was born on March 19, 1906, in Solingen in the Rhineland. He was the eldest of five children, and his father was an accountant employed by a Tramways and Electricity Company. The family moved in 1913 to Linz, in Austria, where Eichmann senior continued to work for the same corporation. Unlike his four brothers and sisters, young Adolf did poorly at school. The others managed to finish their high school education, but Adolf showed little promise, and although he was later to describe himself as an engineer, he did not complete the course to which he was assigned at the local vocational school. His father determined to go into business for himself. He purchased a small mining company and gave his eldest son employment in it as an ordinary laborer. Adolf did not seem fitted for anything which required any superior talent. Through his father's influence, he obtained a job as a salesman in the Austrian Elektrobau Company. Here he stayed for two years, but at the age of twenty-two, therefore by 1928, his future looked far from promising. On a form he was later to fill out when applying for promotion within the SS he stated: "I worked between 1925 and 1927 as a salesman for the Austrian Elektrobau Company. I left this position of my own free will, as the Vacuum Oil Co. of Vienna offered me the representation for Upper Austria." In fact, no such "offer" was made to him. He obtained this position as a result of the initiative of a friend, who happened to have access to the president of the Vacuum Oil Company, a Jew named Weiss. He persuaded Mr. Weiss to employ Eichmann as a traveling salesman.

They were not good times in which to sell. The Austrian economy, like that of all other countries, was suffering from the Depression. Furthermore, it is difficult to determine whether Eichmann would have made a good salesman, even if the economic climate had been more auspicious. In any event, and as Eichmann was later to protest time and time again at his trial in Jerusalem, he was far from lucky and at all times, fate seemed to intervene against him, just when life began to look promising.

Eichmann spent five and a half years with the Vacuum Oil Company, from which Hannah Arendt has deduced that "he made a good living during a time of severe unemployment." He did testify that toward the end of 1932 he was transferred from Linz to Salzburg and that this was contrary to his wishes. "I lost all joy in my work, I no longer liked to sell, to call on customers." Finally, he was dismissed from his job—presumably because of the poor state of the economy as well as Eichmann's deficiencies as a salesman.

If it was a hard-luck story, it was one which Eichmann shared with millions of others all over the world in the Depression era. In April 1932, he joined the Austrian Nazi party, probably because it offered a brighter economic future. Soon thereafter, at the advice of an acquaintance, he entered the SS. The acquaintance was none other than Ernst Kaltenbrunner, a young lawyer from Linz who was later to replace Heydrich as Chief of the Reich Main Security Office. It is difficult to ascertain why Kaltenbrunner should have been so free with his advice. It seems that Eichmann was treated somewhat as a social inferior by him, despite the fact that both men came from what can loosely be described as the middle class. Both Kaltenbrunner and his father were lawyers, while Eichmann had little to show for his years in commerce, his father's enterprise had not prospered; if any snobbery prevailed in Kaltenbrunner's attitude toward Eichmann, it probably derived from the difference in status between a professional man and an unsuccessful businessman.

Another feature of the Austrian Nazi party was that it offered both a sanctuary and a promise to the young Adolf Eichmann. His poor showing at school, lack of formal education, and his indifferent performance in the worlds of commerce might be reversed. Certainly, jobless as he was, he had nothing to lose. Neither did he bother to read the turgid pages of *Mein Kampf,* to study the Party program, or to indulge in any similar intellectual exercises, for this would have been alien to his nature.

Once again, it seemed as if life was conspiring to produce further obstacles to the rise of Adolf Eichmann. No sooner had he joined the Party, than Chancellor Dollfuss declared it illegal and set up his detainment camps in which his radical enemies, both of the Right and the Left, were imprisoned. It seemed best to return to the Germany he had left in 1913; moreover, the SS in Austria did not offer a livelihood, and those who had joined it had to retain their usual jobs, without which they would have starved. He entered Germany at Passau, having retained his passport. He reported to the local Nazi party office and once asked one of its functionaries whether he had any connections with the Bavarian division of the Vacuum Oil Company, the very company which had dismissed him in 1932. When advised by the Passau SS unit that some military training might be useful to him, he said, "All right with me—why not become a soldier?"

The obvious place in which to put Eichmann was the Austrian Legion, stationed along the German-Austrian border and ready at all times to provide harassment to Dollfuss, a weapon Hitler was to use to coerce stubborn Austrian chancellors like Dollfuss and Schuschnigg into smoothing the path toward a German-Austrian union. Accordingly, Eichmann received training in Lechfeld and Dachau, together with other SS units stationed there. From August 1933 to September 1934 he spent his time in this fashion, eventually emerging with the rank of SS-Scharführer, which is equivalent to corporal in the regular army—not exactly promising. Of course, Eichmann could have resigned himself to permanent service within a regular SS unit. One day he might make officer. But "the humdrum of military service, that was something I could not bear: day after day always the same, over and over again the same."

So Eichmann kept his nose to the ground. He was twenty-eight, and he had gotten precisely nowhere. As he was repeatedly to maintain, he was dogged by hard luck, and here he was, a simple corporal. Then he discovered that a new section of the SS called the Sicherheitsdienst (Security or Intelligence Service) had need of recruits. Somebody called Reinhard Heydrich was in charge of the SD. Why not apply? Army life in the SS was boring. Maybe intelligence work would be an improvement.

Eichmann thought that a job with Intelligence meant working for the national Intelligence Service. "I had mistaken," he was later to report, "the Security Service of the Reichsführer-SS for the Reich Security Service . . . and nobody corrected this impression and nobody told me anything." Actually, despite the fact that Eichmann was somewhat dense, it is not so surprising that he was confused. The tremendous variety of the different SS organizations has led to confusion within the ranks of competent historians and journalists, and so perhaps it is too much to expect of Eichmann that he should have penetrated the cloud of titles and functions with which Himmler and Heydrich were surrounding themselves.

After being accepted by the SD, of whose functions Eichmann claims to have understood little, he was in for a further shock. Apart from the fact that as a new recruit he had to start at the bottom again, the job his superiors created for him, in their curiously incompetent fashion, was to conduct research within the Information Department of the SD on anything which shed light on the history and activities of the Freemasons.

It would be difficult to think of a person less suited for this task than Eichmann. He abhorred books and in fact hardly ever read anything. He knew nothing about his subject and did not even know where to start. His superiors, who had persuaded themselves, because of their familiarity with *The Protocols of the Elders of Zion,* that Freemasonry, like the churches and Bolshevism, was part of the international Jewish conspiracy, now wanted documentary evidence to support their strange ideology. Their overlord, Himmler, was entranced with the subject; he loved Masonic ritual and was eventually to set up a special museum in which Masonic regalia were collected and to which students of National Socialism might repair properly to inform themselves on this intriguing subject.

But Eichmann was totally at sea. Fortunately for him, his activities in unearthing the secrets of Freemasonry only lasted for a few months, during which, no doubt, his work must have produced the same incomprehension as algebra had at school. He was rescued from this boring activity in 1935 when he was placed in an SD department which was concerned with the "Jewish question." Among the first tasks Eichmann was given by his superiors was to read a book by the acknowledged founder of modern Zionism, Theodor Herzl, called *Der Judenstaat* (The Jewish State). To this task, Eichmann applied himself diligently. It was one of the few books he ever read in his life. Once he had digested it, he claimed it made him a Zionist for ever. At no time, so he was later to claim, did he ever envisage the physical annihilation of the Jews. The fact that the Jews existed meant that there was a Jewish "problem." This "problem" could only be solved by their removal from the areas in Europe in which they had settled, to some remote place where they might till their own soil. In 1939 he even protested the desecration of Herzl's grave in Vienna by anti-Semitic extremists. He also arranged talks with his colleagues in the SS, and distributed pamphlets to illustrate the benefits of Zionism. Since nobody wanted the Jews, he argued, what was wrong with putting them somewhere where they could cease to be a "problem"?

Eichmann warmed to his studies. He even mastered the Hebrew alphabet. This enabled him to make his way painstakingly through the various Yiddish newspapers, since Yiddish is a Germanic dialect written in Hebrew letters. At some stage he even went so far as to digest yet another book: *History of Zionism* by Adolf Boehm. He followed the activities of the various Zionist organizations, noted their different political attitudes, and was used by his superiors as a sort of spy who had access to Zionist offices and who could report on their meetings. In Germany before the war, he would be made welcome by keen Jewish Zionists, because to a considerable extent he appeared to have agreed with their purposes. Like them, he abhorred those Jews who propounded the doctrine of assimilation, the idea that with intermarriage and the gradual erosion of distinctively Jewish precepts, the Jewish "problem" would disappear. Also, like a great many of them, he had no time for religious orthodoxy, which clearly was out of step with both political expediency and modern thinking. The Zionists, whom Eichmann admired, were idealists, and since he considered himself to be an idealist, he had much in common with them.

It did not take long before the SD began to consider Eichmann as its Jewish expert. What better man, therefore, than he, to take over the operation of the Jewish Emigration Office in Vienna, which was set up immediately after the Anschluss? He now carried the rank of Second Lieutenant. He went to Vienna in 1938 in order to coordinate the expulsion of the Jews from that city and from Austria. The fact that many of them did not want to go in no way deterred him, for it was consistent with his "idealism" that if some wayward people needed to be shown how to toe the line in order to fulfill a noble idea, it was simply part of the job. "Emigration" must be forced. It was in the better interests of the Jews that it should happen in this way. Let them get out of Europe and plough their own furrow somewhere else. After all, was not this precisely the aim which had been announced loudly and firmly by Zionists throughout the 1930s? And did not his new position give Eichmann the wherewithal to execute this purpose efficiently? The cause of Zionism had therefore found in Eichmann its most effective sponsor. In Hannah Arendt's words, "Eichmann singled out his year in Vienna as head of the Center for Emigration of Austrian Jews as his happiest and most successful period."

During this year no less than 60 percent of Austrian Jews were removed from Austria. For Eichmann this was cause for jubilation. At last he had found a niche for himself, and in a good cause too, the cause of "idealistic" Zionism. It does not seem to have occurred to him that only a very few of these emigrants actually ended up in Palestine. Many of them found their way to German-based concentration camps and many were killed; the rest wandered over Western Europe or, if they had money, went to the United States, Canada, or South America.

Eichmann's colleagues in the Austrian SS had made the mistake of imprisoning enormous numbers of Jews. This, in Eichmann's eyes, was nonsense. A Jew in captivity was still a Jew in Austria. This did not solve any problems. He had a directive from Heydrich to extort enormous sums from Jews to permit them to obtain exit visas. The interests of Germany and the Jews would be better served, Eichmann thought, if the financial arrangements were smoothed. This involved streamlining the bureaucratic process. Large numbers of official papers had to be filled out, all of which involved the payment of money. According to his testimony, he tried to set up "an assembly line, at whose beginnings the first document is put, and then the other papers, and at its end the passport would have to come out as the end product." Although Eichmann had been unable to satisfy the academic requirements of an engineering course, he began to show certain gifts as an organizer and a certain talent for mass production. He became, in fact, the Henry Ford of compulsory mass emigration. It was thus, he felt, incumbent on him to show the "clients" how the system worked. So he invited prominent members of Berlin's Jewish organizations to Vienna to show them the system he had put together. These "clients" were far from happy. As one person put it, "This is like an automated factory; like a flour mill connected with some bakery. At one end you put in a Jew who still has some property, a factory or a shop, or a bank account, and he goes through the building from counter to counter, from office to office, and comes out at the other end without any money, without any rights, with only a passport on which it says: 'You must leave the country within a fortnight. Otherwise you will go to a concentration camp.' "

Eichmann could see nothing wrong with this; it was exactly what he had attempted to achieve. The problem was only that for the "clients," bereft of money, there was no country which would stamp an entry visa on these papers.

It was a problem, and one which Eichmann was compelled to tackle. He then determined that what one had to do was negotiate with Jewish organizations in foreign countries and get *them* to grant so much per emigrant, so that the expelled Austrian Jews would not be penniless and therefore would get the precious entry visas from the appropriate foreign countries. End of problem.

Once again, Eichmann considered that he and the Jews were working toward a common end. There was a Jewish "problem," and he was doing his damnedest to solve it. He considered that his time in Vienna had demonstrated his considerable skills as a negotiator and ought to have made him, Adolf Eichmann, one of the most lauded proponents of Zionism in the twentieth century. It seems never to have occurred to him that those with whom he was "negotiating" were acting under extreme duress, their backs to the wall—or that he had in no way assisted the Jews in getting into Palestine. Germany and Austria had to be *judenrein*—cleared of Jews—and all that was needed was good sense and understanding on both sides. At no time during the months of his trial in Israel would he budge from this view of himself. He had acted as intermediary and had listened sympathetically to all their problems. What he had *not* done was to examine the system as a whole nor to subject the orders he received from above to scrutiny. The fact that they were orders was sufficient for Eichmann, and within the limits set by the SS he had acted both humanely and efficiently.

"I regarded the Jews," he said at his trial, "with respect, to whom a mutually acceptable, a mutually fair solution had to be found. . . . That solution I envisaged as putting firm soil under their feet so that they would have a place of their own. And I worked in the direction of that solution joyfully. I cooperated in reaching such a solution gladly and joyfully because it was also the kind of solution that was approved by movements among the Jewish people themselves, and I regarded this as the most appropriate solution to this matter."

Eichmann's diligence in Vienna earned him promotions. When

Hitler set up a German protectorate over Bohemia and Moravia in March 1939, Eichmann was called to Prague to set up yet another Emigration Office to dispose of the Jewish community of Prague. "In the beginning I was not too happy to leave Vienna," he said, "for if you have installed such an office and if you see everything running smoothly and in good order, you don't like to give it up." In fact, Eichmann's machine was running into difficulties. It still depended on the good offices of the "receiver nations." Behind the Czech Jews there were the millions of Poland and countries of the east who would, undoubtedly, be subjected to "emigration." Even to Eichmann's stunted mind the danger signs must have become apparent. For, regardless of the Nazi attitude toward the Jews, it was abundantly clear that neither Poland nor Rumania wanted Jews. When Hitler invaded Poland, Eichmann was summoned to Berlin to occupy the post of head of the Reich Center for Jewish Emigration. The Reich had acquired, by its conquest of Poland, some additional two and a half million Jews. How could you arrange to "emigrate" them? Once again, Eichmann found himself the victim of bad luck. His streamlined apparatus in Vienna, which had been built so diligently, seemed to be relegated to the history books. So he found himself in Berlin. "There we were," he said, "sitting in a great and mighty building, amid a yawning emptiness."

But another "yawning emptiness" suggested itself to him. This was a large area in eastern Poland in the district of Radom, which he and another SS official named Stahlecker visited to determine the feasibility of settling Jews there. It was theorized that they could set up some autonomous form of government, naturally under German supervision. It was called the "Nisko" project. The Poles who lived there could be removed, or "resettled," and then the space could be made available to the Jews. Eichmann and Stahlecker were delighted on their return to Berlin to learn that their plan met with the approval of Heydrich. They did not know, Eichmann asserted, that their suggestion fitted in quite well with Heydrich's overall plan to congregate the Jews in certain areas as a precursor to their liquidation.

But to Eichmann's annoyance, they were continuously being sabotaged by other SS agencies and other Reich ministries. For instance, Hans Frank, whom Hitler had appointed as Governor General of the area, "did not want to receive any more Jews in his area. Those who had arrived should disappear immediately." The plan foundered because of the competing and interfering nature of the other Reich appointees for affairs in the east.

So Eichmann had to look elsewhere. He was helped by a memorandum that reached him in the summer of 1940 from the Foreign
Office, which asked him to work out a plan to arrange the evacuation of four million Jews to Madagascar. This came to naught. As
curiously as it had appeared, the Madagascar project was dropped.
And all Eichmann's efforts to find the Jews some place to live "failed
because of the lack of understanding of the minds concerned," so
he maintained, "because of rivalries . . . everybody vied for su-
premacy."

At the beginning of August 1941 Eichmann's belief in the solution
of the Jewish problem by emigration was to be given its final blow.
Even if we give him the benefit of the doubt and assume that until
this time he was sufficiently dense enough not to have understood
that the liquidation of European Jewry was a definite policy of the
Nazis, rather than their emigration to some distant land, by August
1941 he learned the true meaning of "final solution." For at this time
he was summoned to appear before Heydrich, who bluntly stated,
"The Führer has ordered the physical extermination of the Jews."

Eichmann's reaction to this, according to his testimony, was: "In
the first moment I was unable to grasp the significance of what he
said because he was so careful in choosing his words, and then I understood and didn't say anything, because there was nothing to say
anymore. I had never thought of such a thing, such a solution
through violence. I now lost everything, all joy in my work, all initiative, all interest. . . ."

From August 1941 therefore Eichmann knew that his supposed
espousal of the cause of Zionism had been a cover for genocide. He
had to make the decision whether to continue working within the SD
or not. The time had come for even that naive and superficial character to examine the quicksands of his conscience—to make a moral decision. The decision at which he arrived was to continue with his
work, despite his loss of "joy."

Heydrich instructed Eichmann to proceed to Lublin, to meet Odilo
Globocnik, and to familiarize himself with the methods of destruction
the SS was using there. He found that the engine of a Russian subma-
rine was being used to introduce gas into sets of buildings in which
the inmates would then be suffocated to death. "I became physically
weak," said Eichmann, "as though I had lived through some great ag-
itation." Not even this experience induced Eichmann to desert his
post. For he was then sent to Chelmno, where he witnessed the use of
mobile gas vans. Once again, Eichmann experienced nausea and revulsion. To round off his education in mass extermination, he was

sent to Minsk, where they still used machine pistols. On his return to Berlin Eichmann passed through Lvov, where he claims to have said to the local SS commander, "What is being done around here is horrible. Young people are being turned into sadists. How can one do that? Simply bang away at women and children? That is impossible. Our people will go mad."

By the late autumn of 1941 Eichmann had served his apprenticeship. It was now time to give him a function within the system of mass murder. This took the form of a sort of travel coordinator. He had to organize mass transports, arrange special trains, and collect the victims and have them dispatched to the death camps. Since Hitler had advised Himmler that the Reich must be clear of Jews immediately, the first of Eichmann's transports was concerned with the dispatch of German Jews to the east, and here he encountered certain moral problems. He had seen the gassing and shooting which had taken place in Eastern Europe and he could not reconcile it with his conscience to have German Jews suffering the same fate. In other words, despicable as it might be to liquidate Eastern European Jews in this fashion, you surely could not subject German Jews to the same fate, since they were at a superior cultural level. Accordingly Eichmann sent them to the ghetto at Lodz. This would only have the effect of postponing their execution; but that at least was something.

As noted earlier, Eichmann had come to be considered as something of a Jewish expert by the leadership of the SD. Therefore there was a reason for someone of his relatively lowly status to be invited to what is called the Wannsee Conference in January 1942. The purpose of this conference was to assemble the leading lights of the various ministries which would be involved in implementing the extermination of the Jews so that a coherent interdepartmental plan could be evolved. Eichmann found himself in the company of such distinguished civil servants as Dr. Wilhelm Stuckert, Undersecretary in the Ministry of the Interior, Undersecretary Josef Buehler, Frank's assistant in the General Government of Poland, and various representatives of Ribbentrop's Foreign Office. They all came at the invitation of Heydrich to a villa in Wannsee. Eichmann found himself therefore in very elevated company.

The situation was very flattering to him. As he listened to these educated men he gained the impression that what was happening was not really a debate, but the promulgation of a political platform. This was necessary so that the representatives of different ministries could produce their various programs. Having made their speeches, the functionaries had lunch and drinks, doubtless while Eichmann listened with some admiration to the pronouncements of these educated gentlemen who outranked him socially. He kept minutes of the meeting and, after the visitors had left, enjoyed the special privilege of remaining with Heydrich and Gestapo-Mueller for further informal chats.

The effect of the Wannsee Conference was to rob Eichmann of any feeling about his own responsibilities in the matter of genocide. He was like a freshman who had secreted his way into a senior seminar. If these powerful, learned men had spoken so freely about methods of extermination, who was Eichmann to disagree with them? Thenceforth he would do what he was told and save himself the embarrassment of self-doubt.

Eichmann entered his new role with enthusiasm. Previously he had had success as the exponent of forced emigration; now he became the technocrat of forced evacuation. He collected documents. Some came via the Foreign Office and were concerned with the denationalization of Jews in the occupied territories. Some came from the Ministry of Justice, which assisted in the "legal" expropriation of Jewish property. And finally, for transports of the size with which Eichmann was concerned, he had to work closely with officials of the German railways. Within the ghettos set up by the Nazis in Eastern Europe, Jewish Councils were formed whose function was to supply the SS units with facts and figures. They would be told how many people must report at such and such a time and such and such a place for transport to the liquidation centers. The Jewish Elders were ordered to fill in countless forms in quintuplicate so that the machine could run with bureaucratic efficiency. This process repeated itself throughout occupied Europe.

Since he had demonstrated his expertise as negotiator with the Jews, Eichmann was sent to Hungary for talks with a certain Dr. Kastner. Himmler had toyed with the idea of releasing one million Jews in exchange for ten thousand trucks which the Wehrmacht needed urgently. Kastner told Eichmann that the trucks would be delivered if the killing at Auschwitz were halted, but was told that this was outside Eichmann's competence. Since he had arrived at the conclusion that better brains than his had conceived the plan of extermination, this reply to Kastner should not come as a surprise. In fact, as the months rolled by, Eichmann ceased to ask himself any questions; he simply "did his duty" and "carried out orders."

Toward the end of the war, when Himmler, in a last-minute bid to restore his status with the enemy, attempted to halt the process of extermination, he found his most arch opponent in the person of Adolf Eichmann. For once Eichmann had been given an order, it must be carried out. There was no room for maneuver and no possibility of reinterpretation of the Führer's wishes to annihilate the Jews. Himmler's intercessions therefore became, in Eichmann's view, criminal. In these final days, Eichmann found himself in Berlin surrounded by men who were engaged in arranging forged papers to expedite their departure from a defeated Germany and from the consequences of war crimes trials. Eichmann was indignant with these defectors. It was not until the Führer himself was dead that he felt himself released from the obligation to follow Hitler's orders. So he, too, like so many other SS notables, made his way to South America under a false name, with false papers. He lived there until his apprehension by an Israeli intelligence unit and his subsequent trial in Jerusalem.

It is clear that in a different historical age and under a different set of social conditions Adolf Eichmann would have lived his life as a salesman or minor bureaucrat. If he was an anti-Semite, he was not more so than countless others of his generation. There was a logic and an order about life which was self-determined and self-perpetuating. Now and again you could see evidence of a good-luck story—like that of Adolf Hitler, who had succeeded in making it from lance corporal to Chancellor of the Reich, or possibly that of Abraham Lincoln, from log cabin to the White House. But those men had special talents and their use in no way reflected on the system. The greatest height Eichmann achieved was to be promoted to the rank of Lieutenant Colonel. This in itself was the end of the line for him, but was not really so bad if one considers that in his view he had consistently been plagued by bad luck. The world exists and we have to find our place within it. Greater brains than that of Eichmann determine human destiny. Of course, in reflection, under police interrogation in Jerusalem, he could see and would readily admit that the whole practice of genocide was wrong. For this reason he was quite prepared to go to his death as a warning to others, so he said.

What kind of a warning, one wonders? What in fact had Eichmann learned, if anything? That facile succession of catch phrases and empty platitudes which comprised his testimonies and which absorbed reams and reams of paper is devoid of the real subject matter of moral debate. Given a repetition of the circumstances, there can be no doubt that people like Adolf Eichmann would rise again. They might occasionally be nagged by self-doubt but apparently nothing would induce them to stand aside from the system as a whole and view it objectively. This is most probably the reason for which Hannah Arendt has given, as a subtitle of her book *Eichmann in Jerusalem,* the phrase: "A Report on the Banality of Evil."

15

HEINRICH HIMMLER—
THE END OF THE ROAD

At the end of chapter 13, we left Heinrich Himmler in an awkward predicament. It was about 3:00 A.M. in the morning of April 25, 1945, and he was waiting impatiently for an SS unit to free his car from the barbed wire in which it was entangled.

Bernadotte communicated the gist of Himmler's proposals for surrender to the American authorities. Himmler was dismayed to receive news from U.S. President Harry S Truman that there was no possibility of "partial capitulation." Truman ended his telegram with the words: "Wherever Allied troops meet resistance they will continue the attack relentlessly, until complete victory is established." Himmler's dealings therefore, with Bernadotte, had come to naught. He made his way to the headquarters of the Oberkommando of the Wehrmacht, at that time situated in Ploen. He had no idea at this stage that Hitler had received intelligence of Himmler's attempted negotiations with the Western Allies and that, as a consequence, he had issued the following edict: "I hereby remove, before my death, the previous Reichsführer-SS and Minister of the Interior, Heinrich Himmler, from the Party and from all his offices. Through their secret dealings with the enemy and through their attempt to assign the powers of the State to themselves Goering and Himmler . . . have demonstrated total lack of loyalty . . . and have created immeasurable damage. . . ."

Grand Admiral Doenitz had in fact taken over the reins of government in Germany, and it was to Doenitz that a somewhat puzzled Himmler repaired. Doenitz, still aware of the mighty police apparatus with which Himmler had surrounded himself, took the precaution of stationing a reliable unit of U-boat personnel around his headquarters, in the bushes and behind the trees. A few minutes after midnight on May 1, 1945, Himmler arrived. Doenitz saw him alone, but later testified that during the interview he concealed a Browning automatic under some papers on his desk. His first action was to hand Himmler a report of the radio speech in which Hitler had announced Doenitz as his successor and had condemned Himmler as a traitor. Himmler read it and grew visibly paler.

He reflected for a few moments. Then he rose and offered Doenitz his congratulations, after which he said, modestly, "Let me be the second man in the new State." This Doenitz immediately refused, arguing that he could not possibly have any "politically questionable" persons in his new government. The conversation went on for some two or three hours. Himmler seemed incapable of digesting the fact that his name was indissolubly linked with the SS machine and that, as a result, his standing with the Allied powers was nil. "Some time between two and three in the morning," said Doenitz, "he left in the full knowledge that he would not be entrusted by me with any position of leadership."

All this took place in Flensburg, a small North German town not far from the Danish frontier. Himmler retained contact with the temporary government for about a week. On May 6, 1945, having been formally dismissed from all his offices by Doenitz, he had a final conversation with Count Schwerin-Krosigk, who acted as Foreign Minister in the Doenitz government. He told the Count that he intended to go underground and await developments. Krosigk replied: "It must not happen that the former Reichsführer-SS should be picked up bearing a false name and wearing a false beard. There is no other way for you than to go to Montgomery and say: 'Here I am.' Then you have to bear the responsibility for your men." Himmler muttered something which was inaudible to Krosigk and simply disappeared.

He did in fact go underground, in the company of his two adjutants, Werner Grothmann and Heinz Macher. By this time all the intelligence forces of the British and the Americans were trying to discover the whereabouts of Heinrich Himmler.

He had shaved off his small moustache and covered his left eye with a black patch. In his pocket he carried identity papers bearing the name Heinrich Hitzinger, who was described as an official of the Secret Field Police. He had not done his homework properly, for this organization was listed by the Allies as criminal, and its members were automatically placed under arrest. Himmler, together with his two adjutants, wearing a strange variety of clothing, wandered about the countryside, attempting to lose themselves among the thousands of refugees, discharged soldiers, released prisoners of war, and foreign laborers. On May 21, 1945, they found themselves at a British control point at Meinstedt. A river flowed through this small town, and the only way to get across it and move further to the west was to use a small bridge. At this bridge a British unit exercised a very casual control over the traffic. The astounding variety of uniforms, languages, and people who were crossing defied investigation. So the British soldiers just stood there and watched, with apparent lack of interest.

Himmler and his two companions joined the line which had formed to cross the bridge. They moved nearer and nearer to the British control point. When it was their turn to cross, the former Chief of the German Police did a very curious thing. He pulled out his documents and offered them to an astonished British soldier for inspection. This was an act of unbelievable insanity. Nobody else was bothering about papers. Himmler immediately drew attention to himself because of his ingrained sense of what he thought was correct behavior. He remained a clerk to the end.

"Himmler committed the mistake," the British Second Army later reported, "of showing his papers. Most of the people who crossed the bridge did not even have any. If he had simply said that he wanted to get himself and his luggage home, there is no doubt that he would have been permitted to pass the control without . . . hindrance. The police mind of Himmler, which had taught him that only a man with papers could proceed without suspicion, was the very cause of raising our suspicions."

Naturally, at the time, in Meinstedt, nobody thought that Heinrich Hitzinger was Heinrich Himmler. He was simply a man who had a rather new-looking document which testified that he belonged to the Secret Field Police (Geheime Feldpolizei). The soldiers on duty had no option other than to arrest him. He was transferred to one camp after another, from Bremervoerde to Zeelos. In the third camp in which he was placed, at Westertimke, he found himself alone in a cell. Meanwhile, certain intelligence officers of the British Second Army began to take an interest in the case of Heinrich Hitzinger. As early as midday on May 22, 1945, there were those among them at British headquarters in Lüneburg who were toying with the idea that maybe Hitzinger was Himmler. British intelligence officers were of course desperately trying to locate him. The initials matched, the photograph roused their suspicion, and among the thousands of documents which came their way, those relating to Heinrich Hitzinger looked very promising. Sometime around nine in the evening of this day, three high-ranking officers made their way to Westertimke to interview "Hitzinger."

In the meantime, and for some reason nobody has been able to ascertain, Himmler himself asked for a conference with the camp commandant. That was a Captain Tom Sylvester. Sylvester granted permission and Himmler was led into his room.

"What do you want?" asked Sylvester.

The prisoner slowly removed his black eye patch and placed a pair of spectacles on his face.

"I am Heinrich Himmler," he said.

"Really?" said Sylvester.

"I want to speak to Field Marshal Montgomery," continued Himmler, obviously still under the impression that he had some special mission to fulfill.

"I shall advise the authorities," said Sylvester. Then he dismissed Himmler and had him returned to his cell under special guard. Shortly afterward, the three British officers from headquarters at Lüneburg arrived. They took Himmler back to Lüneburg with them. Himmler did not get to see Montgomery, and it became clear to him during the night that nobody at Lüneburg appeared interested in "negotiating" with him.

Shortly after dawn on May 23, Himmler was escorted to an apartment building in the Ulzener Strasse, which had been specially cleared for military use. There, under the surveillance of an Army doctor, Captain Wells, he was ordered to strip. He was then searched for poison. In the pocket of his jacket was a cyanide capsule, about twelve millimeters long and almost as thick as a cigarette. This, together with all his clothing, was removed, and the naked Himmler was reclothed in an English army uniform and locked in an empty room.

That evening, Colonel N. L. Murphy of Montgomery's Intelligence Staff appeared. His brief was to apprise himself of all the measures so far taken to apprehend this important prisoner and to prepare him for his first interrogation. Murphy first talked to the British officers in the building.

"Did you find any poison?" he asked.

"Yes," replied Dr. Wells, "there was a capsule in his pocket. We have it. He can't commit suicide."

"Did anybody look at his dental cavities?"

Dr. Wells shook his head. "Then you'd better do it immediately," said Murphy. "It's possible that he only had the capsule in his pocket to draw our attention away from another."

Himmler was brought in to Murphy. Dr. Wells asked him to open his mouth. Himmler's eyes narrowed and his chin began to move as if he were chewing something. Within a second, he had fallen to the floor. Wells threw himself down next to Himmler, forced his mouth open and tried to extract what was left of the capsule. Then a stomach pump was used. For twelve minutes every means available was used to restore Himmler to life. At 11:04 P.M. Dr. Wells had to admit defeat. Himmler was dead.

The corpse remained for the entire next day exactly where it had fallen, in a room in the Ulzener Strasse in Lüneburg. There it was seen by several hundred British soldiers, numerous journalists, and photographers. Nobody knew what to do with the body. Some officers on Montgomery's staff were not sure whether or not Himmler was entitled to a military burial in the presence of high-ranking German officers. Some military padres insisted that he be given a Christian burial. It is possible that the final decision rested with Montgomery. In any event, the decision was reached at British headquarters that Himmler be buried without military or spiritual ceremony at a secret place. Some staff officer made the following proposal: a wooden box should be obtained from the concentration camp at Bergen-Belsen, such as were used for some of the corpses of the inmates there. His advice was not followed.

On the morning of May 26, 1945, sergeants lifted the body of Heinrich Himmler into the back of a one-ton army truck. The driver was ordered to inform the press that his destination was unknown. An intelligence officer had selected a burial place somewhere in some woods near Lüneburg. A major, three sergeants, and the truck driver would be the only five people to know where the burial was to take place.

The three sergeants dug the grave. Himmler's corpse was placed in it. It was strangely dressed: British army trousers, a military shirt, and German army socks. One of the sergeants felt the need to say something during the interment. "Let this worm go to the worms," he intoned as he continued to shovel earth onto the corpse. A surface of grass was methodically placed over the grave, and the area was thoroughly evened out so that no sign remained.

Nuremberg was therefore denied the possibility of cross-questioning one of the Third Reich's most powerful exponents.

But there was one sequel.

Underneath a barracks near Berchtesgaden, American soldiers discovered a treasure trove which contained documents showing that its indisputable owner was Heinrich Himmler.

Among other moneys they found: £25,935, $132 in Canadian money, eight million French francs, three million Algerian and Moroccan francs, one million German Reichsmarks, one million Egyptian pounds, two Argentinian pesos, and half a Japanese yen.

They also found 7,500 Palestinian pounds!

The picture which emerges from the last months of Heinrich Himmler's life is one in which the second most powerful man in the Reich behaved in a way which alternated between indecisiveness and sheer stupidity. How, it may be asked, can this be reconciled with Himmler's previous performance in the affairs of the Thousand Year Reich? Despite his general tendency to be led, he had demonstrated considerable gifts as a politician; a man who, in the pursuit of power, had gathered to himself an impressive array of titles and whose name had caused millions throughout Europe to tremble. He could not possibly have assumed this position without possessing substantial political presence of mind.

Did he simply disintegrate as a personality? In the autumn of 1944 he was due to attend a conference of the higher Nazi authorities, but had a bad cold. He met his brother, Gebhard, beforehand. "You should take care of yourself," advised Gebhard. "Why not have the conference postponed?" Himmler looked at his brother, aghast. "Have you ever heard of Easter being postponed because the pope had a cold?" he demanded. But this interview took place when Himmler was at the height of his power. He was the principal beneficiary of the events of July 20, 1944, so possibly a dose of heady egomania was not so surprising. What is surprising is that until the end he still considered that his activities in no way precluded him from enjoying the confidence of the Allied powers. He might have a few million deaths on his conscience, but he was a historic figure, so he must have decided. So was Churchill and so was Truman. They therefore had something in common. Yet, if Himmler himself had had feelings of nausea at what he had seen in Minsk in 1942, surely he must have wondered what other prominent leaders of the world would think of his deeds. We are really asking if there were no limits to Himmler's naiveté. It was Himmler's stupidity which resulted in his apprehension by a British control unit at Meinstedt in May 1945.

His loss of touch with reality, which was certainly never a feature of his life while he was building up his personal empire, seemed to gather momentum as his leader, Hitler, deteriorated in health. There was no doubt, even to Himmler, from late 1944 onward that the Führer's medical condition would preclude him from satisfactorily concluding his mission. This was the point at which Himmler's own grasp of events deteriorated.

For he had always been led. First there were Ernst Röhm and Gregor Strasser, then "the greatest genius of all time, Adolf Hitler." And while he built his monuments to death, he had at his side a man whose nimbleness of mind and whose sadistic drives outweighed his own: Reinhard Heydrich. Heydrich was replaced by Ernst Kaltenbrunner, a relatively colorless man compared to his predecessor. This was a choice of which the power-seeking Himmler only too readily approved; there would never be a threat from Kaltenbrunner. Nonetheless, without a leader, Himmler revealed his true personality; that of a petit-bourgeois clerk in which the drive for power was always suffused with anxiety and indecision.

For the historian the strange aspect is that this vacillating character occupied the position of head of the most all-embracing system of terror the world had ever seen. It would be convenient to label him a sadistic monster, but this would be very wide of the mark. His origins in middle-class Bavaria express themselves at every stage of his career. When he had an energetic and determined leader to show him the way, he would respond with unbounded loyalty and dedicate himself to his tasks with patience and diligence. Without a leader, he returned to his true condition, that of a minor bureaucrat, bereft of any gift for public speaking, insistent on the maintenance of orderly files, watching with meanness and thrift the vast expeditures which passed through his office.

And what thoughts passed through his mind on May 22, 1945? For while senior British intelligence officers were speeding to interview him in the belief that Heinrich Hitzinger *might* be Heinrich Himmler, the victim himself revealed his true identity. Why did he not wait and see what would happen? Was it not still possible that he could deceive his captors? Why take the initiative in the way that he did? The answer must surely be that even at that late stage, he thought he could still be a grand statesman and if he gave the game away he might still find himself on the other side of the conference table.

Though his actions demonstrate total naiveté, the real question is: How did a man of Himmler's naiveté assume such power within the Third Reich? The answer has to lie somewhere in that quality of unparalleled loyalty which he demonstrated to the man who led him. This was Himmler's guarantee of office. Although that relationship between crime and punishment which is necessary to satisfy public demands for suitable connections between cause and effect is missing from the life of Heinrich Himmler, we have to reconcile ourselves with the knowledge that one of the greatest monsters the world has ever produced was pedestrian, unimaginative—in a word, ordinary.

16
THE SS AND
HUMAN BEHAVIOR

In every act of aggression, there are two participants: the aggressor and the victim. The SS was the aggressor; its victims were the human beings they dehumanized and then destroyed.

For many years after the descriptions of their activities were revealed to mankind, the SS was designated as a peculiar tribe of sadistic monsters. The moral problems involved were so enormous that it was found more convenient to say: the SS did what it did because it was manned by society's most depraved elements. This verdict, in fact, begs the question. For many of the leading personalities of the SS were relatively "normal" human beings. It is possible that given sufficient brainwashing and indoctrination, anyone might be transformed into an instrument of barbarism.

More difficult to grasp, certainly for the social psychologist, is the behavior of the SS's victims. Among these, the Jews took first place, both numerically and for the ideological reasons Himmler and the other Nazi leaders were so keen to supply. Certain facts have come to light since the first revelations of 1945 which seem to be irreconcilable with our standard view of man's instinct for self-preservation. When the Germans overran Poland and large territories of Russia, the SS enlisted the support of the Jews themselves, and made them instruments of their own destruction. This chapter in the saga of the SS is without doubt the most difficult to comprehend, for as a result of it, hundreds of thousands of people went to their death apparently in the full knowledge of what was to happen and without offering resistance.

It is only comparatively recently that this aspect of the behavior of the SS in Europe between 1941 and 1945 has been scrutinized.

In a circular issued by Heydrich in September 1941 to SS units in the occupied territories, he instructed his officials to collect the Jews in ghettos and secure their aid in arranging their own annihilation. This circular is sometimes referred to as Heydrich's *Schnellbrief,* or express letter. The Jews were to be assembled in the special area of Warsaw, Lodz, Lublin, and various other cities. This was a mammoth task. To implement it with German personnel would constitute a gigantic drain on manpower resources. Heydrich therefore conceived the plan of mobilizing the Jews themselves in this endeavor, or, as one or two commentators have cynically put it, of making the Jews honorary and temporary members of the SS.

An organization was needed for this new branch of Jewish activity. It was to be arranged under the auspices of what were to be called Judenräte, or Jewish Councils. These would be composed of the leading members of the Jewish community, those who had shown themselves, prior to the German occupation, as being ready to undertake the representation of their co-religionists.

In fact, the apparatus of the Jewish council existed for many generations prior to the German drive to the east. Within an organization called the kehillah, the Jewish Elders of a community, elected by popular vote, would meet in committee and debate such issues as Jewish social welfare, Jewish religious practices, and various other matters relating to their group. Surrounded by an alien society, it is not surprising that the kehillah should have been established and that it should have produced spokesmen, over the years, to put the case of the Jews as firmly as they could, before the various civic authorities in Poland. It was an honor to be elected in this fashion and the candidates were usually members of the liberal professions or successful businessmen.

When local SS and SD units approached the kehilloth (plural of *kehillah*) in Poland and asked them to set up Jewish Councils, they met with a variety of responses. Many members of the kehillah said that under no circumstances would they cooperate with the German occupying forces, whatever the cost, because they were only too aware of the bestial nature of German anti-Semitism. But there were others who said that it was possible, that if they themselves did not do the job of rounding up their fellow Jews and supplying the Germans with the information requested, the work would be undertaken by the Germans, and this might prove even more disastrous for the Jews.

True to their form, the SS and Gestapo units placed very considerable pressure on the Jewish Elders wherever they met with reluctance. Sometimes this took the form of shooting them out of hand. On other occasions, the Jewish representatives were informed that if they did not return with a list of "candidates" for the Judenrat by such and such a time, the entire community would be eradicated.

On the question of assembling the Jews within the ghettos, there was a considerable amount of disagreement within the various Jewish communities. Some said that the idea of a ghetto, however overcrowded and however insanitary it might become, at least had the advantage of retaining the family as a social unit. Others mocked this approach and accused its exponents of burying their heads in the sand. What was the point, they asked, of retaining the family as a social unit when the whole purpose of the exercise was to assemble the Jews merely in order to liquidate them?

Of course, the classical tradition of Judaism, to which almost the whole of Eastern European Jewry belonged, was firmly entrenched in the teachings of Hassidism, which preached nonviolence and asserted the primacy of the spirit over the body. A man's life should be dedicated to the study of the Talmud, the treasure trove of Jewish law and tradition. He should wait for the coming of the Messiah and the return of the Jews to the Promised Land, Canaan (Palestine). But if this happened, it would be the result of divine intervention, and certainly no human agency could be called upon to arrange it. To a large degree, the older and rural element of the Jews was reared in this Hassidic tradition. The younger people, particularly in the towns, had a more activist approach. They had shared in the radical inquiries into the nature of human society with their opposite numbers in the gentile camp, and many of them were ardent socialists.

Whatever their view, in the end, under the systematic coercion of the occupying police agents of the SS, Jewish Councils were set up. And members of these councils were called upon to make awful decisions, albeit under duress. They had to supply the SS with population statistics and summaries of the assets of the members of their communities. And then they had to deliver the "physical goods"—namely the human bodies—either for forced labor or for outright extermination in the gas ovens of Auschwitz and Treblinka. Furthermore, to assist the SS in this ghastly task, they had to recruit a special Jewish Police, complete with armbands bearing the Star of David, whose function was to round up recalcitrant elements who did not passively report to the collection centers within the ghettos.

It will be clear that in the vast majority of ghettos, the Jewish Police were far from popular. In fact, in certain postwar trials which took place in the displaced-persons camps in Germany, and later in Israel, survivors from the ghettos claimed that in many cases the Jewish Police behaved even worse than the Germans and, if it were possible, even more sadistically.

This particularly depressing chapter in the history of the Third

Reich has to be met squarely if we are to examine, with as much openness of mind as we can muster, the effect of the activities of the SS on human behavior.

There is really only one moral to be drawn, and that is that when an act of aggression is performed, its effect is fairly similar both on the perpetrator of the act and on his victim. Both are dehumanized; both lose those qualities which we have come to assume are endemic in the human condition. By timing, conditioning, and systematic exposure to acts of terrorism and barbarism, both aggressor and victim lost something of their humanity. For this reason, the sadistic impulses of the aggressor lose all their restraint, the passive and submissive equalities of the victim become more and more pronounced.

We are fortunate in that one of the survivors of the concentration camps of Dachau and Buchenwald was a psychiatrist named Bruno Bettelheim, who was imprisoned shortly after the Anschluss with Austria. Incredibly, Dr. Bettelheim managed to retain sufficient objectivity throughout his years of suffering to observe the behavior of the SS guards and his fellow prisoners. This testifies to his remarkable courage and has also given us a rich store of professional comment.

It is Dr. Bettelheim's contention that one major goal of the Gestapo "was to break the prisoners as individuals and to change them into a docile mass from which no individual or group act of resistance could rise. . . . In addition, the camps were a training ground for the SS. There they were taught to free themselves of their prior, more humane emotions and attitudes, and learn the most effective ways of breaking resistance in a defenseless civilian population." Dr. Bettelheim lays great emphasis on the process of initiation of prisoners into camp life. The nature of the arrest and the trauma of initial beating and investigations on arrival in the camps have produced no doubt in his mind that "the initiation was part of a coherent plan." If this is so, it presupposes that the SS guards who performed the police work and who acted as torturers did so under some type of unified guidance. In other words, they received training, possibly by men qualified in the police procedures of the Nazi State. This is difficult to reconcile with his description of the guards themselves, who were apparently drawn from very primitive social elements. If they received such "course training" it is surprising that they were of an educational level which permitted them to absorb intellectually what they were supposed to do. On the other hand, since a definite behavior pattern seems to have emerged on the part of the SS guards, it could not have taken place by mere whim or caprice. Some of their attitudes can be explained psychologically and can be related to the social mores of Germany at the time. For instance, inmates could only defecate at the start of the working day and at its end. They were thereby encouraged to despoil their clothing and to earn the humiliation from the guards which little children might have earned for similar "misdemeanors" in ordinary German society. Furthermore the words used to taunt and threaten the prisoners were full of anal references. This preoccupation with anal functions, indeed this form of treatment, can readily be shown to result from ordinary German attitudes towards toilet training and might not have been so effective in a society which was less rigid in its attitudes in this area.

But nowhere in the vast literature on SS behavior is there reference to some course to which camp guards were exposed. It is all the more surprising, therefore, that such behavior as they manifested should have been relatively uniform. When Dr. Bettelheim's spectacles broke, he asked permission from a guard to write home for a new pair. He used the words: "My glasses were broken," which infuriated the guard. As a psychiatrist he was able to interpret his persecutor's fury, and amend his words to: "I have broken my glasses." This satisfied the guard, who then gave him permission. Bettelheim's use of the passive tense outraged his persecutor. The man's wrath could only be assuaged when Bettelheim said that he himself had broken his glasses. This meant that Bettelheim had behaved like a naughty child, which was entirely in keeping with the image that the SS was apparently anxious to create and sustain.

Yet the persecutor himself needed a certain level of psychological sophistication to understand this difference, and it is extremely unlikely that if he had attended any courses on how to manipulate human beings, he would have attained the necessary expertise. Accordingly it seems more likely that the atmosphere of the camps themselves produced their own customs, rather than that, as Dr. Bettelheim maintains, the SS guards were following some pattern spelled out by Gestapo headquarters in Berlin.

Dr. Bettelheim also claims that one of the most apt methods of ensuring some degree of survival within the camps was to adopt certain behavior patterns of the SS guards. Old prisoners, for example, "modeled their way of treating fellow prisoners on examples set by the SS. . . . From copying SS verbal aggressions to copying their form of bodily aggression was one more step, but it took several years to reach that. It was not unusual, when prisoners were in charge of others, to find old prisoners behaving worse than the SS. . . . Old prisoners tended to identify with the SS not only in their goals and values, but even in appearance. . . . They felt great satisfaction if, during the twice daily counting of prisoners, they really had stood well at attention or given a snappy salute. They prided themselves on being tough, or tougher than the SS."

Although Dr. Bettelheim is at pains to stress that not all older prisoners adopted the standards of the SS, for those who did, or attempted to, there emerges one moral. It is as if the SS looked at its victims and said: "If you want to survive . . . copy us." And so, leaving aside all questions of guilt and innocence, it would seem that both victims and aggressors, having shared in the same experience, both experienced a profound dehumanization as a result.

17
THE SS IN HISTORY

The story of the SS could be considered as yet one more chapter in the unending history of man's inhumanity to man. And yet there is one aspect of the SS which distinguishes it from other planned acts of human barbarism.

There is one common theme, to which all the theoreticians of the SS constantly return.

This is the moral ascendancy of the countryside over the town.

It is this fact which places the SS firmly in the twentieth century and makes its history an inseparable part of that yearning seen on all sides today to return to a preindustrial age.

The methods of annihilation used by the SS bear the imprint of our technological age. The reasons for that annihilation belong elsewhere. Wherever and whenever the "idealists" of the SS have committed themselves to writing or speech, they have conjured up a picture of a farmer at his timeless work and they have compared this poetic vision with the perverse, iniquitous, and immoral activities which characterize town life. What they desire most earnestly is to undo the Industrial Revolution. They want to use herbs rather than "artificial" chemicals to treat human illness. They want to see artisans at work rather than masses of men on production lines. They see some romantic connection between the blood which courses through the veins of the peasant and the very earth which he ploughs.

They see the city as a Jewish device. The readiness with which men like Heinrich Himmler and Rudolf Hoess accepted the authenticity of the Rabbi's speech in the Prague cemetery is the real key to the understanding of their ideology.

Though this speech is a work of fiction, it needs careful examination because it summarizes succinctly and accurately all that the "idealists" of the SS set out to combat. The curious invention of Goedsche in his novel *Biarritz* of the meeting of the Jewish Elders in a cemetery in Prague contains a vitriolic explosion against all the evils of modern capitalism, for which the author holds the Jews responsible. Judah illustrates how he has managed to reduce the self-employed artisan to the status of a factory hand. Aaron demonstrates that by spreading the evil of freethinking, he has undermined the teachings of the Christian churches. Naphtali urges his colleagues to make certain that Jews enter the government and pay special attention to posts in the ministries of Justice and Education. Benjamin insists on the increase of Jewish entrants into the liberal professions. Menassah informs the others that the press must be firmly placed in Jewish hands.

All these statements of intention point conclusively to one fact, and that is that those who believed in this fiction most earnestly desired a return to a world in which the Industrial Revolution had not taken place.

For the vast changes that the Industrial Revolution caused, including the establishment of a gigantic urban proletariat, made it impossible for the conservative, land-oriented men who formed the ideological nucleus of the SS to come to terms with the twentieth century. The city became for them the emblem of all that was unsound and morally abhorrent. And in the city, they believed, it was the Jews who controlled life. Here is the meeting place between the conservative reaction against modern life which typifies the SS, and their anti-Semitism.

They massacred somewhere between five and six million Jews and millions of others in their avowed intention to preserve the Teutonic race. But that is not all that they did. They showed the world that society as organized in the twentieth century produces a savagery and a barbarism which is unmatched by anything which preceded them, because of their ability to mobilize modern technology in the perpetration of their crimes.

And before we dismiss them, as it has been fashionable to do, by saying that "members of the SS were savages who did not belong to the human race," we should do well to examine the direction currently being taken by similar attacks on industrial civilization. When you go to a health resort you are likely to be addressed by a genial person, who urges you to adopt a saner attitude toward modern life, so as to escape its more damaging excesses. He will speak to you of the benefits of eating organically grown foods, of the rewards of using herbs rather than "artificial" medicines when you are ill, of the dangers of life in the city both to your body and your mind. And if your mind begins to wander during his lecture, you might actually find yourself thinking you are listening to a verbatim report from the notes of Heinrich Himmler or Rudolf Hoess.

If the SS existed today it would be at the forefront of the antipollution drive, it would insist on controlling population explosion (albeit by the massacre of "surplus" population rather than by birth control), and it would contain among its number many somewhat eccentric people who dressed themselves in open-weave clothing colored with natural dyes, who led a campaign against the use of cosmetics, and who like Julius Streicher might cry: "Never become ladies! Always remain [German] girls and women!"

We must not be blinded, in our assessment of the SS, by the bestial excesses its members committed. They did most certainly belong to the human race. The path they chose to take, though littered with the corpses of innocent men, women, and children, is not an isolated one. The cause of their criminal acts is inherent in our contemporary culture and lies in the inability of the technological age to provide a suitable framework for sane human relations.

18
THE SS SINCE THE WAR

The events described in this book, especially those connected with the activities of the SS in the concentration camps and in the occupied countries, produced feelings of shock and revulsion throughout the civilized world.

They also presented problems of a moral and philosophical nature to a generation of scholars. The academic establishment of the Western world dug in its heels and settled down to the task of finding out why the SS in particular and the Germans in general had done what they did.

For some the problem was neatly sidestepped. The Germans did not belong to the human race and therefore were not subject to the same standards as the rest of us. All that was necessary was to chronicle the terrible events. Since these bestial acts were not perpetrated by humans there was no need to reconcile the behavior of the Germans with that which is normally to be considered to be human.

For others it was necessary to show that the Germans had always been beset by this tendency for cruelty, whether spontaneous or organized. Authorities on German history could draw a neat line from what Tacitus, the Roman historian, had described as the "furor teutonicus," through the barbarous activities of the crusading Teutonic Knights in Poland in the Middle Ages, on to Luther with his notorious anti-Semitism and then via the German Romantic movement and Wagner, Nietzsche, and the rejection of Reason, to Hitler himself.

For some scholars history had always demonstrated a curious schizoid quality in the Germans. On the one hand, you had poetry and philosophical speculation as exemplified in Weimar with its literary associations. On the other, you had the cruelty and Realpolitik of Prussia manifested in Potsdam. Occasionally in history one aspect of the German character would assert itself to the detriment of the other. The Nazi period, 1933–1945, was simply a reaffirmation of the worst elements in German history.

While all this was going on outside Germany, within the country itself a second type of invasion was taking place. In the years immediately following the defeat of Germany in 1945, the country was literally overrun by all kinds of fact-finders. Germany was placed under the microscope by congressional committees, Quakers, members of the Moral Re-Armament Group, by a veritable army of sociologists, journalists, and scholars. The social psychologists were disappointed to learn that nothing they could discover about the personality of Heinrich Himmler made him into a monster per se, even though what was done in his name and that of his organization, the SS, was monstrous. It would have lightened their task and made for far more satisfying reading if Himmler could have been shown to be something other than a petit-bourgeois Bavarian. Where did his blood-lust spring from? How could a man with the personality of a filing clerk, albeit an ambitious one, have built up the greatest terror machine the world had ever seen? Many a researcher returned from Germany with feelings of disgruntlement and pique at not having his prejudgments endorsed by what he had learned. For unlike Goering, Himmler did not appear to have taken drugs or indeed to have enriched himself by acquiring a huge fortune.

The Germans themselves had to remain quiet, in those years immediately following the war. For what the SS had done had been accomplished in their name. Everybody told them this and everybody reminded them that the machine of mass murder could not have been set up without their support. You could not do what the SS had done without an army of hundreds of thousands of civil servants.

The average German had other problems anyway, such as where his next meal was coming from and whether his father or uncle or brother in Russian captivity would ever be released. But if he ventured abroad, he would be unlikely to look you in the eye, because the films about the atrocities of Auschwitz and Belsen had preceded him. He was guilty by association.

However, this situation could not continue indefinitely. Once Germany had started to make its economic recovery, the odd person here and there would make an attempt to reestablish German self-repect. A voluminous literature appeared about the German resistance movement and studies were made about its leading lights, Goerderler, von Hassell, Beck, and of course Colonel Stauffenberg, the aristocrat whose bomb almost killed Hitler on July 20, 1944.

For the SS the important thing was to escape. In this its members were hampered by the vigilance of the occupying forces from the United States, Britain, and France and also by the existence, under one armpit, of a tattoo showing their blood group. Nonetheless they had friends abroad. As to who these friends were was a subject of controversy. There is, purportedly, a group called ODESSA: Organization der Ehemaligen SS-Angehörigen (Organization of Former SS Members). It has been referred to extensively by Simon Wiesenthal, a Jewish emigré living in Vienna who has been instrumental in continuing the vigilant pursuance of SS offenders. It was the subject of a best-selling novel by Frederick Forsythe and was subsequently filmed. But its existence is denied by other researchers, such as Werner Brockdorff, who says that ODESSA is a fiction and the real escape route is the so-called Roman Route, by which former SS men were and probably still are handed by one member of the Jesuit Order to another across the Brenner into Italy, where from dispersement centers in Milan, Genoa, and Rome they are transshipped to South America or the Middle East. Why the Jesuit Order should so be implicated we are not told; we are simply given the "facts." "The role of priests as assistants to the escapees has only been described in accordance with the facts," writes Brockdorff in his *Flight from Nuremberg* (Wels, 1969). "I am not in a position to establish the precise motives of papal couriers in this affair. They could be of a political, psychological or christian-charitable nature. . . ."

There is no doubt that many SS men escaped. Many were brought to trial, many were sentenced—and many were subsequently released in a short time owing to their "good behavior." In the knowledge that the rest of the world watched with great interest each time SS members were arraigned for trial, the Germans themselves demonstrated a reasonable amount of vigor in apprehending suspects. However, there is equally no doubt that with the passage of time many members of the SS found their way into prominent positions in public life, a fact greeted with occasional outbursts in the German press itself.

In the organ of the largest trade union of West Germany, *Welt der Arbeit,* the following paragraphs appeared in the issue of August 14, 1959:

Sixteen thousand participants joined the reunion of the Waffen-SS at Hameln. The police recorded the presence of no fewer than five thousand foreign cars.

The organizers seized the opportunity of inviting well-known SS members of the Third Reich. Under the pretext of attempting to discover the whereabouts of missing persons, these notorious men were made the star attraction of the meeting.

Enthusiastic applause lasting several minutes greeted the

appearance of the former commander of the Leibstandarte
Adolf Hitler, Sepp Dietrich.

A similar meeting should have taken place some months
earlier at Arolsen, where the "international register of victims of National Socialism" is maintained. But permission
to hold that meeting was withheld by the Minister of the Interior of Hesse. This time the government of Lower Saxony
saw no reason to forbid the reunion of the Waffen-SS.

We have come across Sepp Dietrich several times in these pages. It
was he who commanded the unit of the Leibstandarte Adolf Hitler
when they lay in wait to arrest and murder Ernst Röhm and the old
guard of the SA at Bad Wiessee on June 30, 1934, and it was he who
became the first Colonel-General of the Waffen-SS, even though his
understanding of tactics and strategy was somewhat suspect. Nonetheless Dietrich enjoyed the confidence of his men, for he was a
rough and ready Bavarian and immensely popular. So what, if anything, is the significance of his reappearance some years after the war
at Hameln?

It lies in two areas. The first is the attempt of the Waffen-SS to dis-
engage itself from the responsibilities of acts committed by the Totenkopfverbände, or Death's Head Units, which policed the concentration camps, or of the Einsatzgruppen, the assault squads which
operated the mass-murder machinery. All members of the postwar
Waffen-SS made one thing clear. They had nothing to do with what
went on in the camps. In the issue of the *Deutsche Soldatenzeitung* of
August 1956 Adenauer is reported to have said at an electoral meeting in Hannover: "The men of the Waffen-SS were soldiers, just like
the others. . . ." All well and good, but unfortunately for the
Waffen-SS and the former Federal Chancellor himself, the Totenkopfverbände, acting as part of the Waffen-SS, distinguished
themselves in action for the first time in the French campaign while
acting as support troops to the regular German Army so that the area
commander told the head of the SS division: "You are a butcher and
no soldier."

The second aspect of significance of the reunions of the Waffen-SS
since the war lies in the special function it has assigned to itself in
relation to a united Europe. A curious mission perhaps, but one
which they have taken particularly seriously. They regard themselves
as constituting a multinational army with a specific calling. They
most certainly are multinational. For at that meeting at Hameln were
men from Holland, Denmark, Norway, and Belgium, and certainly

some expatriate Letts and Estonians, all volunteers for the foreign legions of the SS. Their mission? To prepare the ground for a united Europe. What kind of united Europe? One which defends itself against the Bolsheviks. While economic debate was taking place by a veritable army of old dodderers, so claimed the members of the Waffen-SS, the sands of time were running out and the chances of Western Europe and the civilized world to defend themselves against the encroachments of Communism were being imperiled. The real patriots in this affair were accordingly members of the Waffen-SS.

Actually there is an interesting history to this idea. It goes back to the war years when it was assumed by Himmler and many other prominent men within the Nazi movement that once the German armies had been defeated they would join forces with the Americans and British in a joint attack on Russia. For in their view, the alliance of West with East was a pragmatic affair. At the end of hostilities surely the Americans and British would see reason and get rid of the real enemy: Russia. And certainly, Russian behavior since Yalta and Potsdam bore out their view. There were the Russians sitting in Berlin, Prague, and Warsaw. Did the West require any further evidence? And how much more time would elapse before England and the United States drew on the resources of a fanatically anti-Bolshevik army like the Waffen-SS?

These theories had a certain popularity outside of the Waffen-SS. Prominent facists in other countries assisted in the formation of what was called "Nation Europa"; if you like, an extreme right-wing version of what the rest of us considered to be a united Europe. That, at any rate, is how they saw themselves, and certainly the ex-leader of the British Union of Fascists, Sir Oswald Mosley, voiced this view. You did not have to be totally mad to accord it a grudging respect. The Russians, so the argument went, have always looked to the West. The Russian Bear under the tsars was intensely imperialistic. The fact of political change has not altered this imperialism and now Bolshevism will continue to press westward.

The steam has been taken out of the argument by various developments the Waffen-SS could not have foreseen. Russia has become far too concerned with her Chinese neighbor to engage herself further in Western Europe, and so these old men of the SS, for by now they are indeed becoming old, are giving voice to an outmoded political debate.

Probably the most significant aspect of the activities of the SS since the war is that the only section of it which has been perpetuated is the Waffen- or Armed-SS. Their members have been busily engaged in the process of dissociating their own activities from those of the General-SS. They were soldiers just like any other members of the Wehrmacht, the German Armed Forces. Why, they ask, should they be victimized for doing their duty just like everybody else? Their protestations reached a crescendo in the mid-1950s when they found that their pension rights were being challenged. And when some of them volunteered for the new Bundesheer, the German Army founded to enable Germany to fulfil its NATO commitments, many of them were turned down. They became even more furious. They founded an organization bearing the unwieldy title "Hilfsgemeinschaft der Soldaten der Ehemaligen Waffen-SS"—HIAG for short. It can loosely be translated as "Mutual-Aid Society for Former Soldiers of the Armed SS." They founded a journal in Hannover called *Der Freiwillige* (The Volunteer). In one of its early issues (June 1956) an editorial read: ". . . members of the former Armed-SS with their families and friends constitute a circle of more than one million people . . . they could have a decisive influence on policy making where voting on decisions is close. . . ."

They held, and still hold, meetings. At Karlburg in August 1957 the darling of the Waffen-SS, General Meyer (nicknamed "Panzer" Meyer because of his fame as a tank—*Panzer*—commander) addressed thousands of ex-members in the following way:

> It should not be assumed that we took any personal pleasure in participating in murderous battles or in eradicating our enemies simply because we were known to possess soldierly qualities and our bravery and expertise with weapons were universally admired. No, the fact is that we were fellows who, finding ourselves in a difficult situation, knew how to behave like men. Any other interpretation is far from the truth and is nothing other than malicious defamation. . . . Apart from the regrettable exception of one company commander at Oradour, the Armed-SS did not commit any atrocities. . . .

At Oradour sur Glane near Limoges, an SS captain was shot dead. In May 1944 the entire village of 642 inhabitants was exterminated, as a reprisal, by men of the SS Division Das Reich. The women were separated from the men and with 207 children were mown down by machine guns in the church.

An isolated action by a maverick SS Commander? So General Meyer would have us believe. But this is not true. When Fritz

Knoechlein, commanding a troop of the SS Death's Head Unit in France in 1940, as part of the Waffen-SS, ordered his men to shoot at random an entire unit of British soldiers who emerged from cover showing the white flag and with their arms above their heads, the bodies were piled up haphazardly against a nearby wall. But one of the soldiers was still alive. He told his story in a book entitled *The Vengeance of Private Pooley* and was a prosecution witness at the trial which finally condemned Knoechlein. And quite obviously the Waffen-SS was called in continuously as the execution arm of other departments of the SS. Since soldiers of the Wehrmacht were compelled to shoot civilians (see chapter 11) in barbarous fashion, does General Meyer really think we can credit his story with any truth?

This does not make all members of the Waffen-SS guilty of atrocities. It is certainly possible that a young man could have served with a Waffen-SS unit, seen action on one front or another during the war, and emerged with no knowledge whatever of mass executions. Perhaps this is why Adenauer, treading on eggshells, said somewhat grudgingly in 1956: "The men of the Waffen-SS were soldiers just like the others. . . ."

Actually this argument is not cogent. We know from the testimony of many serving members of Germany's ordinary armed forces that they were compelled to act as the executive arm of the SS; it is for this reason that I quoted Major Roesler at some length and referred to the entry of Ulrich von Hassell's diary in chapter 11. So possibly what the HIAG is saying is: "You men of the Wehrmacht have dirty hands, too. Why should you have no difficulty in collecting your pension or serving with the Bundesheer?" Unfortunately, they have a point.

Another thought-provoking aspect of Germany's attempt to come to terms with its past or to learn to live with what the SS did in those war years is the following. In 1956 Gerald Reitlinger, a distinguished British historian, published a book entitled *The SS: Alibi of a Nation*. It was in my view the best documented and researched study of the SS to have appeared at that time. The title itself and the treatment of the subject matter are all carefully marshaled to demonstrate the fact that the SS was the alibi of the German people. A German not in the SS could no longer say of the atrocities committed by the SS: "Well, every nation has its criminals. Ours were called the SS."

The book was published in Germany in 1957. Only its title had suffered a sea change. In German it was called *Die SS: Tragödie einer deutschen Epoche*—"The SS—Tragedy of a German Epoch." The two titles have very little in common; in fact, the unambiguous message of the original English was totally distorted, presumably to make it more palatable to German readers.

I have purposely minimized the activities of the SS since the war because I believe it fair to do so. The fact that Germans felt it necessary to make some efforts to reestablish their self-respect seems to me to have been unavoidable, even if, in the process, some strange reversals of the truth have been uttered. For example, Brockdorff advances the curious theory that Eichmann was a Jew. This is proved by Eichmann's familiarity with the Hebrew and Yiddish languages and also by the "fact" that he "looked Jewish." On the other hand, Heydrich was *not* one-quarter Jewish, says Brockdorff. This kind of doublethink is intriguing, but it does not exactly bring back to life those piles of bodies at Auschwitz and Belsen, or even explain how they got there, so I believe it to be an unprofitable exercise.

In what respect, therefore, does the SS live on? Not in so-called old-soldier gatherings, but in any ideological sense?

It is no accident that prominent members of the SS (Himmler, Darré, Hoess, et alia) were members of the Artamans in the period shortly after the First World War, that they saw the future in terms of an escape from the city with its perils to a more natural existence in the countryside. They dreamed of becoming yeomen farmers, each farming his own hundred acres, a rifle at the ready in the back porch to fight off any possible intruder, a little like characters in the stories of the Wild West.

Before we dismiss this as the daydreaming of cranks we should do well to look at our daily newspapers. Our cities are dying, and those left are dehumanized. We are beset with the problems of postindustrial society. We have problems of pollution, we are fouling up our environment, and many of us seem to want to return to what we believe was a more primitive but more natural environment for man. The health food shops are becoming more and more popular, and the interest in—and practice of—the occult arts, so favored by Heinrich Himmler, has not known such a boom since the Middle Ages. The flight from Science is in full swing.

Of course the SS wanted to build its new society as a master race and was committed to wiping out entire populations. We do not advocate the practice of genocide, but more and more the findings of today's quasi scientists and diagnosticians of our ills are resembling the random thoughts of Heinrich Himmler either assembled in his early diaries or voiced while in the care of his Finnish masseur, Felix Kersten.

It is this aspect of the SS, its original ideology, which places it firmly in the twentieth century.

There is another area in which the SS continues to survive. It may appear trivial at first sight, but might be more significant than we realize. A brisk trade is being done in the sale and purchase of all mementos of the SS. Mail-order catalogues exist in all parts of the world offering for sale SS daggers, SS badges, and SS uniforms. Shops proliferate selling secondhand SS equipment, and I have frequently noticed youths on motorcycles wearing the double flash of the SS on their leather jackets. It may mean nothing, of course, but perhaps it helps to illustrate how a previous generation could have been entranced by the paraphernalia of the SS, its mystic signs, its banners, and ultimately its special mission.

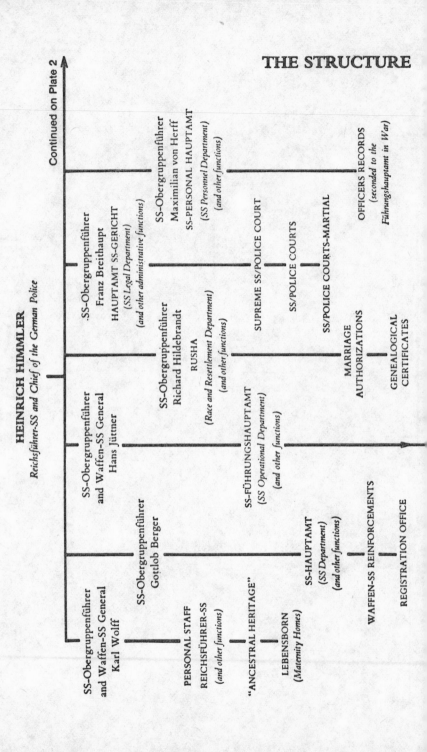

THE STRUCTURE

Continued on Plate 2

HEINRICH HIMMLER
Reichsführer-SS and Chief of the German Police

SS-Obergruppenführer
and Waffen-SS General
Karl Wolff
PERSONAL STAFF
REICHSFÜHRER-SS
(and other functions)

"ANCESTRAL HERITAGE"

LEBENSBORN
(Maternity Homes)

SS-Obergruppenführer
Gottlob Berger
SS-HAUPTAMT
(SS Department)
(and other functions)

WAFFEN-SS REINFORCEMENTS

REGISTRATION OFFICE

SS-Obergruppenführer
and Waffen-SS General
Hans Jüttner
SS-FÜHRUNGSHAUPTAMT
(SS Operational Department)
(and other functions)

SS-Obergruppenführer
Richard Hildebrandt
RUSHA
(Race and Resettlement Department)
(and other functions)

MARRIAGE
AUTHORIZATIONS

GENEALOGICAL
CERTIFICATES

SS-Obergruppenführer
Franz Breithaupt
HAUPTAMT SS-GERICHT
(SS Legal Department)
(and other administrative functions)

SUPREME SS/POLICE COURT

SS/POLICE COURTS

SS/POLICE COURTS-MARTIAL

SS-Obergruppenführer
Maximilian von Herff
SS-PERSONAL HAUPTAMT
(SS Personnel Department)
(and other functions)

OFFICERS RECORDS
*(seconded to the
Führungshauptamt in War)*

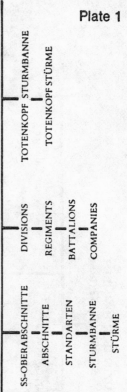

KOMMANDOAMT DER WAFFEN-SS
(*Waffen-SS HQ*)

Continued on Plate 2 →

SS-TOTENKOPF STURMBANNE

1944 strength 30,000; incorporated in the Waffen-SS 1940/41; organization under the WVHA from 1942

WAFFEN-SS

1944 strength 560,000 of which 370,000 in field units

(*the Waffen-SS was in practice under the Army*)

KOMMANDOAMT ALLGEMEINE-SS
(*Allgemeine-SS HQ*)

Peak membership (1939) 240,000

Membership at end of war 40,000

30 HÖHERE SS- UND POLIZEIFÜHRER (SENIOR SS AND POLICE COMMANDERS) —HSSPF— one to each SS administrative district (Wehrkreis in Germany proper). Directly subordinate to Himmler and in charge of all SS and Police agencies in their district.

SS-OBERABSCHNITTE	DIVISIONS	TOTENKOPF STURMBANNE
ABSCHNITTE	REGIMENTS	TOTENKOPF STÜRME
STANDARTEN	BATTALIONS	
STURMBANNE	COMPANIES	
STÜRME		

EINSATZGRUPPEN

Units formed primarily from SD, Sicherheitspolizei and Ordnungspolizei personnel; employed in the Eastern and South-eastern occupied territories to liquidate Jews and "lawbreakers." Einsatzgruppen were responsible to the RSHA. When a civil administration was installed they generally turned into static agencies of the Sicherheitspolizei and SD.

CHIEF OF THE SICHERHEITSPOLIZEI AND SD (Heydrich, later Kaltenbrunner)

EINSATZGRUPPEN

EINSATZKOMMANDOS OR SONDERKOMMANDOS

Source: Heinz Höhne, The Order of the Death's Head. London: Secker & Warburg, 1969.

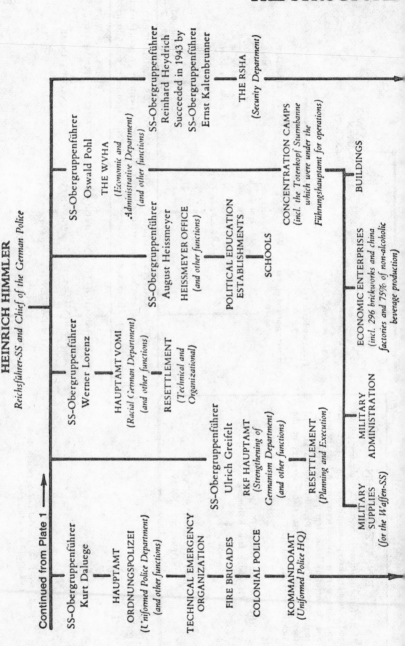

HEINRICH HIMMLER
Reichsführer-SS and Chief of the German Police

Continued from Plate 1 →

SS-Obergruppenführer
Kurt Daluege

HAUPTAMT
ORDNUNGSPOLIZEI
(*Uniformed Police Department*)
(*and other functions*)

TECHNICAL EMERGENCY
ORGANIZATION

FIRE BRIGADES

COLONIAL POLICE

KOMMANDOAMT
(*Uniformed Police HQ*)

SS-Obergruppenführer
Ulrich Greifelt

RKF HAUPTAMT
(*Strengthening of
Germanism Department*)
(*and other functions*)

RESETTLEMENT
(*Planning and Execution*)

MILITARY
SUPPLIES
(*for the Waffen-SS*)

SS-Obergruppenführer
Werner Lorenz

HAUPTAMT VOMI
(*Racial German Department*)
(*and other functions*)

RESETTLEMENT
(*Technical and
Organizational*)

SS-Obergruppenführer
August Heissmeyer

HEISSMEYER OFFICE
(*and other functions*)

POLITICAL EDUCATION
ESTABLISHMENTS

SCHOOLS

MILITARY
ADMINISTRATION

SS-Obergruppenführer
Oswald Pohl

THE WVHA
(*Economic and
Administrative Department*)
(*and other functions*)

CONCENTRATION CAMPS
(incl. the *Totenkopf Sturmbanne*
which were under the
Führungshauptamt for operations)

ECONOMIC ENTERPRISES
(incl. 296 brickworks and china
factories and 75% of non-alcoholic
beverage production)

BUILDINGS

SS-Obergruppenführer
Reinhard Heydrich
Succeeded in 1943 by
SS-Obergruppenführer
Ernst Kaltenbrunner

THE RSHA
(*Security Department*)

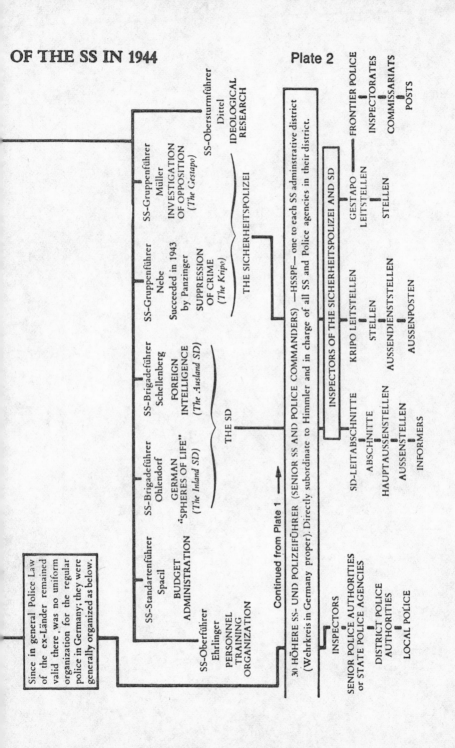

INDEX